WINDOWS OF OPPORTUNITY

WINDOWS

OF

OPPORTUNITY

HOW NATIONS CREATE WEALTH

DAVID SAINSBURY

P

PROFILE BOOKS

First published in Great Britain in 2020 by
Profile Books Ltd
29 Cloth Fair
London EC1A 7JQ
www.profilebooks.com

1 3 5 7 9 10 8 6 4 2

A CIP catalogue record for this book is available from the British Library.

ISBN: 978 1 78816 384 2
eISBN: 978 1 78283 633 9

Typeset in Times by MacGuru Ltd

Printed and bound in Great Britain by Clays Ltd, Elcograf S.p.A.

FSC
www.fsc.org
MIX
Paper from
responsible sources
FSC® C018072

To my wife Susie,
who has given me
unfailing encouragement and support
on the long intellectual journey
that has led to the writing of this book

Standard textbook economics fails to consider how differing windows of opportunity create huge variations in economic activities, and consequently also widely different opportunities for adding capital to labour in a potentially profitable way.

Erik Reinert, *How Rich Countries Got Rich . . . and Why Poor Countries Stay Poor*

Contents

Acknowledgements	xi
List of figures	xii
List of tables	xiii
Preface	1
1 The Need for a New Theory	5
2 A Dynamic Capability Theory of Economic Growth	35
3 Sectoral Systems of Innovation	59
4 City and Regional Systems of Innovation	81
5 Forging Ahead	107
6 Catching Up	128
7 Falling Behind	155
8 National Systems of Education and Training	180
9 National Systems of Innovation	200
10 The Role of Governments in Creating Wealth	225
Notes	243
Index	253

Acknowledgements

In writing this book I have benefited greatly from discussions with many people including Christopher Smallwood, John Kay, Keun Lee, Thomas Aubrey, Eoin O'Sullivan and Carlos Lopez-Gomez.

I would also like to recognise the part that the research and writing of Erik Reinert has played in the development of my ideas. In particular, his study of the history of economic thought stimulated much of the new thinking in this book. As John Maynard Keynes said, 'A study of the history of opinion is a necessary preliminary to the emancipation of the mind.'

I have also received a great deal of support and encouragement from David Teece, the Professor of Global Business at the Walter A. Haas School of Business at the University of California, Berkeley. His work on the dynamic capabilities of firms has greatly influenced my approach, and is one of the reasons why this book should be of interest to entrepreneurs as well as economists and politicians.

I would like to thank Daniel Davies and Paul Forty for the immense help they gave me in preparing this book for publication. Finally I would like to thank my secretary, Tracy Mattinson, for enthusiastically typing the endless and largely indecipherable drafts of the book, and Joe Burns for making the whole process of writing and publishing this book a smooth and effective one.

Figures

1.1 World GDP shares, 1000–2014   6
1.2 Labour productivity smoothed trend growth in G7
     countries; total economy, 1973–2013   7
1.3 The world's economic centre of gravity 1980–2007, and
     extrapolated thereafter at three-year intervals   9
2.1 Evolution of Japanese industrial structure   47
2.2 Economic complexity versus GDP per capita in 1985   52
2.3 Growth predicted from mismatch between economic
     complexity and GDP per capita in 1985   53
2.4 The 'flying geese' model: sequential structural
     transformation in East Asia   54
3.1 Technological opportunities in 51 industrial sectors
     of the US economy, 1899–1937   60
5.1 Japanese share of world motor-vehicle production, 1955–89 122
7.1 Labour-productivity growth in the US total economy,
     1988–2014 (year-on-year growth, %)   168
7.2 US trade balances for advanced technology goods and all
     goods, 1992–2016   170
7.3 R&D intensity: Funding as a share of US GDP,
     1953–2005   174
7.4 National R&D intensities: Gross R&D expenditures as a
     percentage of GDP, 2003   175
8.1 Progression pathways through education   198
9.1 References to scientific publications in US patents   205
9.2 Universities working with business   221

Tables

1.1 Extreme poverty by percentage of population, 1981–2015   8

3.1 Technology regimes for radical and incremental
    innovation in sectoral systems   64

3.2 Institutional framework architectures in Germany and the
    United Kingdom   74

7.1 Annual labour-productivity growth (in %), total UK
    market sector, 1999–2015   158

7.2 Contributions to labour-productivity growth (in %) by
    broad industry grouping, UK total market sector,
    percentage points per annum, 1999–2015   159

9.1 Academic spin-off firms in the UK   222

Preface

We are faced today with a world of opportunity and danger. Developments in science and technology are creating windows of opportunity for firms to innovate, create new competitive advantages and grow. At the same time, the UK and other Western developed countries face major competition in global markets from countries such as China, South Korea and Taiwan, and as a result the prospect of periods of economic stagnation.

In such a situation, policy-makers need a theory of economic growth that explains why the growth rates of countries differ, and what they can do to improve the growth rates of their own economies. However, neoclassical economics, which has dominated economic thinking in recent years, has failed to produce such a theory. In this book, therefore, I have sought to develop a new theory and test it in the laboratory of history.

The new dynamic capability theory that I put forward explains I believe not only some of the 'puzzles' of recent economic history, such as why the 'Asian Miracle' took place (Chapter 6) and why the G7 countries have experienced declining rates of economic growth over the last 25 years (Chapter 7), but also sets out in chapters 8, 9 and 10 what industry and governments in the G7 countries need to do to compete against China and other fast-growing Asian countries in 'a race to the top'.

It also shows why a belief in neoclassical economic growth theory has led to governments adopting flawed economic growth policies in four areas. Firstly, the theory's failure to recognise the importance of innovation and competitive advantage in the economic growth process means that the need for policies to stimulate innovation has not been high on governments' economic agendas.

Secondly, neoclassical economists have failed to understand that the windows of opportunity to innovate and create competitive advantage vary from sector to sector. As a result, the level of value-added per capita varies widely between different sectors of the economy, and therefore shifts of employment between sectors can slow down or speed up a country's rate of economic growth. This means policy-makers have tended to adopt horizontal policies that apply equally to all sectors, rather than policies that seek to build the competitive advantages of firms in specific sectors.

Thirdly, most neoclassical economists, because of their emphasis on market exchange, continue to see firms as black boxes, not realising the need for governments to support the building of their capabilities or the reform of their governance.

Fourthly, because neoclassical economists do not understand that many of the high value-added per capita jobs in an economy are produced by manufacturing firms, they have tended not to see the decline of the manufacturing sectors of an economy, and their replacement by low value-added per capita service industries, as a major problem.

To show how the new theory I set out is different, I have compared it with the original theory of economic growth set out by Robert Solow. Though a number of economists have suggested major modifications and refinements to the original theory, no revised theory has clearly emerged to take the place of the original theory. Equally, none of the revised versions deal fully with what seem to me to be the weaknesses of the original theory. A comparison of the two theories therefore seems the simplest and best way to explain the differences between them, even though very few economists today would probably fully support the original theory.

From my ringside seat in industry and government I have watched the failure of policy-makers and politicians to understand what is happening in their economies, along with their failure to develop effective policies to increase their growth rates. Where possible, I have sought to play a part in developing the policies that are needed. As a result, this book is firmly based on my experience of how firms innovate and create competitive advantage, and what governments can do to help them.

While, for example, I was Minister of Science and Innovation between 1998 and 2006, in what was then called the Department of Trade and Industry, I sought to improve the national system of innovation, and to increase the resources allocated to science and technology. What I managed to achieve while I was in government is set out, as an example of what can be done, in Chapter 9.

In 2007, after I left government, I was asked by the then Prime Minister Gordon Brown to produce a report on the science and innovation policies of the government. He asked that I look in particular at the role science and innovation can play in enabling a country such as the UK to compete against low-wage, emerging economies such as China and India.

In the report, I argued that there is a ladder of economic development, the rungs of which represent industries that require increasingly complex organisational and technological capabilities, and which developing countries have to climb if they want to raise the standard of living of their citizens. I also argued that to stay at the top of the ladder countries such as the UK and other Western developed countries need to innovate and upgrade their goods and services, and that if they do so they can continue to grow, increasing the standard of living of their citizens. I therefore called my report, 'The Race to the Top'.

Then, in 2015, at the request of the Conservative government's Minister of Skills, I chaired an Independent Panel on Technical Education, which put forward a major reform of the national system of technical education. This is now being implemented by the government, and is described in Chapter 8.

Finally, I believe that, in a market economy, the policies of government can only have a beneficial impact if they are understood by companies, and companies in turn take advantage of them. This book is, therefore, addressed not only to economists, civil servants and politicians, but entrepreneurs and businessmen who want to see their firms grow in today's highly competitive global economy. It is my hope that they recognise the world described in this book as the one in which they compete, that it is very different from the world of neo-classical economics, and that by working with government to develop their firms' capabilities and rates of innovation they can create an exciting and profitable future for their employees, their shareholders and their country.

1

The need for a new theory

What needs to be explained

There is currently an urgent need to develop a new theory of economic growth. This is because the world in the last twenty-five years has witnessed a dramatic change in the growth rates of its major economies. At the same time, the neoclassical theory of economic growth, which has been dominant over this period, has been unable to explain what is happening or to provide policy-makers with a framework with which to respond.

From 1820 to 1990, the share of world gross domestic product (GDP) taken by what are today's rich G7 countries (the United States, Germany, Japan, France, Britain, Canada and Italy) soared from about a fifth to almost two-thirds. In 1990, however, it started to fall rapidly and today is under one-half. Furthermore, the share of world income lost by the G7 has been largely picked up by just six developing countries, which have been labelled the I6 (Industrialising Six) and which grew strongly over the period 1990–2015 (China, South Korea, India, Poland, Indonesia and Thailand).

Starting around 1820, the rapid industrialisation of the G7 countries triggered a self-perpetuating spiral of industrial agglomeration, innovation and growth, which historians call the 'Great Divergence'. Now, over a period of just twenty-five years, this trend has been reversed, and the G7's share of world GDP is back to where it was in 1917, a change which economist Richard Baldwin has called the 'Great Convergence' (see Figure 1.1 overleaf).

Figure 1.1 **World GDP shares, 1000–2014**

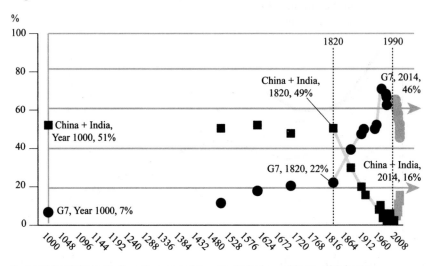

Source: Richard Baldwin, *The Great Convergence: Information Technology and the New Globalization*, The Belknap Press of Harvard University Press, Cambridge, Mass., 2016, p. 81; copyright © 2016 by the President and Fellows of Harvard College

Two other aspects should be noted about this dramatic reversal of the economic growth rates of countries. Firstly, the reversal was due not only to faster growth rates in some developing countries, but also to a slowing down in the growth rates of labour productivity of the G7 countries (see Figure 1.2). An economic theory that seeks to explain the overall reversal of economic performance must, therefore, explain not only the faster growth of some developing countries, but also the slower growth rate of the G7 countries.

Secondly, the contrasts across different regions of the developing world are as striking as the accelerating growth in a subset of countries. In 1950, both Africa and Asia were very poor, with African countries having higher incomes than their Asian counterparts because of their natural resources. In the immediate post-war period, economists believed that developing country incomes and future growth depended largely on natural resources. They therefore thought that Africa's prospects were quite bright, while Asia's were poor, as in the 1950s Asia was the poorest part of the world and was

Figure 1.2 **Labour productivity smoothed trend growth in G7 countries; total economy, 1973–2013**
% change, annual rate

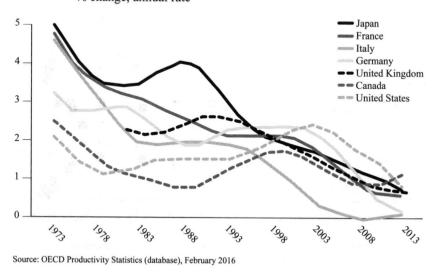

Source: OECD Productivity Statistics (database), February 2016

very low in natural resources compared with sub-Saharan Africa, Latin America and the Middle East. But, of course, what happened was very different.

Instead, Asia found a way to create competitive advantage in the global economy and grew at an unprecedented rate. For example, when China began market-oriented reform in 1978, it accounted for less than 1 per cent of global trade. By 2013, it had risen to become the world's leading trading nation, accounting for almost a quarter of annual international trade flows. In 1970, South Korea had a GDP per capita of $279 (a little under a dollar a day, and about the same as the poorest countries in Africa). Today, South Korea's GDP per capita is close to $30,000. In 1960, the small island state of Singapore, adjacent to Malaysia, was a fishing village with an average GDP per capita of $427. After becoming independent of Malaysia in 1965, the fishing village went on to become one of the largest ports in the world and a major financial centre. In 2017, Singapore had a GDP per capita of $55,000 – one of the highest in the world.

In contrast, African countries struggled with nation-building and governance, and saw a lot of variation across countries. The continent's high level of natural-resource wealth also proved to be a curse, with local politicians seeking to capture the wealth generated by natural resources rather than seeking to industrialise.

The dramatic shift in the economic growth rates of countries has led to a very welcome drop in the percentage of people in developing countries suffering from extreme poverty. Between 1990 and 2015 this percentage was reduced from 44 to 12 per cent, with the figure for East Asia dropping from 61 to 4 per cent (see Table 1.1).

Table 1.1: **Extreme poverty (less than $1.90 per day), by percentage of population; 1981–2015**

	1981	1990	1999	2010	2015
Europe and Central Asia	–	1.9	7.8	2.8	1.7
Latin America	23.9	17.8	13.9	6.4	5.6
East Asia	80.6	60.6	37.4	11.2	4.1
South Asia	58.1	50.6	–	27.2	13.5
Sub-Saharan Africa	–	56.8	58.0	46.1	35.2
Developing World	53.9	44.4	34.3	19.0	11.9
World	44.3	37.1	29.1	16.3	19.6

Source: World Bank, *PovcalNet*; Cruz et al. 2015. Reproduced in Johan Norberg, *Progress: Ten Reasons to look Forward to the Future*, Oneworld, London, 2016

This dramatic shift in the economic growth rates of countries has also led to major movement in the global economy's centre of gravity. According to economist Danny Quah's calculations, in 1980 the global economy's centre of gravity was located in the mid-Atlantic, reflecting how most of the world's economic activity then occurred in either North America or Western Europe.[1] By 2008, as a result of the continuing rise of China and the rest of East Asia, the centre of gravity had drifted eastward to a point just south of Izmir, Turkey, on the same

Figure 1.3   **The world's economic centre of gravity 1980–2007, and extrapolated thereafter at three-year intervals**

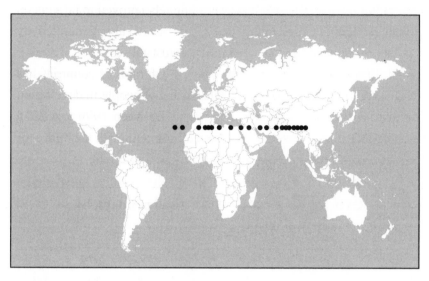

Source: Danny Quah, 'The Global Economy's Shifting Centre of Gravity', *Global Policy*, volume 2, issue 1, January 2011

longitude as Minsk and Johannesburg (see Figure 1.3). Furthermore, extrapolating growth in almost 700 locations, Quah calculates that in 2050 the world's economic centre of gravity will lie between India and China.

From the middle of the Atlantic to the Himalayas in fifty years; nothing on the scale and speed of this transformation of the world economy has been seen before in history.

The seriousness of the situation faced by the G7 countries due to this dramatic shift in the global economy should not be underestimated. While the 'catching up' of billions of poor people in the period from 1990 to 2015, and the resulting reduction in world poverty, was a huge step forward in the welfare of the world, we also need to recognise the impact it has had on developed countries. It not only slowed down their rates of growth but has had a dramatic impact on specific industrial communities and has led to the rise of populist political movements. We also need to understand that there is no economic law that says that all advanced countries will see their economies grow indefinitely, especially when they are being challenged by the rise of countries such as China today.

The reversal of the G7's share of world GDP, the rapid development of East Asia, and the recent slowing down of labour-productivity growth rates of the G7, are surely the dominant economic facts of the last fifty years. They are also facts that economic theory needs to be able to explain, in order that developing countries that have yet to participate in the global economy know what policies to adopt; and countries in the Western world know what policies to develop in order to revive growth in their economies. At present, the dominant academic 'neoclassical' theory of economic growth, based originally on the work of Robert Solow, does not give such an explanation.

While neoclassical economics is only one of several theories of economic growth, it has been the one that has dominated both economics textbooks and the advice given to policy-makers over the last sixty years. It has, however, failed to provide a convincing explanation for the 'East Asia Miracle', while the declining growth rate of the UK over the last twenty-five years has been declared 'a productivity puzzle'. We therefore need first of all to assess the ability of neoclassical economics to explain the growth performance of countries, and to advise policy-makers about how they can increase economic growth in their countries. If necessary, we need economists to develop a new theory to guide economic policy-makers in the difficult years ahead.

Two schools of thought

A useful first step in such an assessment is to look at how successful the theories and policies of economists belonging to the neoclassical school of thought have been, as opposed to those of the main alternative school. This is possible because the history of economic growth theory, unlike most scientific subjects, is not the history of a series of discoveries built one on top the other until it provides today's theory. On the contrary, it is the history of two different schools of thought which have been embraced at different points in time by economists. These two schools of thought are best described as the market-efficiency school of thought, which includes neoclassical growth theory, and the production-capability school of thought.

The market-efficiency school of thought includes the Physiocrats, Adam Smith, David Ricardo, Alfred Marshall, Paul Samuelson and Paul Krugman. The production-capability school of thought includes such figures as Alexander Hamilton, Friedrich List, the German Historical School and Joseph Schumpeter. The two schools of thought have held very different views of the world.

Firstly, according to the market-efficiency school of thought, wealth originates from material sources: land, physical labour and capital. The accumulation of these assets takes place in a static world through trade and war. According to the production-capability school, however, wealth originates from innovation and creativity, with the accumulation of assets taking place as a result of discoveries and innovations changing people's stock of knowledge and their tools. This accumulation occurs in a dynamic environment.

Secondly, the analytical focus of the two schools of thought is different. In the market-efficiency school, the focus of analysis is on barter and men and women as traders. In the production-capability school, the focus is on production and men and women as innovative producers.

Thirdly, because the market-efficiency school of thought was based on the trade and commerce conducted by the English, the English economists who played a large part in developing it came to see all economic activities as being qualitatively alike. This facilitated the use of models and mathematical formulations borrowed from physics, such as the concept of 'equilibrium', based on the science of thermodynamics as it stood in the 1800s. The production-capability school of economics, on the other hand, sought to use observable facts and experience as the starting point for theorising about economics, and used biological metaphors rather than those of physics. It was based on a qualitative and holistic understanding of the 'body' being studied, and incorporated important elements such as synergies between disparate yet interdependent parts that are not reducible to numbers and symbols.

As a result, while the production-capability school of thought sees different economic activities as offering different 'windows of opportunity' for achieving national welfare, the market-efficiency school of thought sees all economic activities as having the same potential.

Fourthly, the market-efficiency school of thought sees the market economy as a machine that, provided the 'invisible hand' is left alone, creates economic harmony. As a result, there is no role for government. This is because factors causing economic growth – such as new knowledge, innovation, the capabilities of firms, synergies and infrastructure – are kept outside the theory, or are eliminated by the use of an abstract concept such as the 'representative firm'. In the production-capability school of thought, however, these factors are seen as key to economic growth, and the government has an important role to play in developing them.

In his *Theory of Moral Sentiments*, Adam Smith makes it clear that tampering with destiny is not man's business:

> The case of the universal happiness of all rational and sensible
> beings, is the business of God and not of man … Nature has
> directed us to the greater part of these [means to bring happiness
> about] by original and immediate instincts … [which] prompts
> us to apply those means for their own sake, and without any
> consideration of their tendency to those beneficial ends which
> the great Director of Nature intended to produce them.[2]

Smith's view finds a parallel in contemporary economist Paul Krugman's view of the economy as a self-organising system: 'Global weather is a self-organizing system; so surely is the global economy'.[3] The implication is clear: man should not seek to interfere with the economy.

Finally, the production-capability school of thought sees no limits to progress, believing in the 'never-ending frontier of human knowledge'. In Smith's system, however, nations reach a stationary state in which they can advance no further because they have received that 'full complement of riches which the nature of its soil and climate ... allowed it to require.'[4]

It is here that we see the consequences of Smith's view that no new knowledge enters the system. The logical result is, of course, either a stationary state, as with Smith and David Ricardo, or an ecological disaster, as with Thomas Malthus. While economists of the market-efficiency school do not necessarily accept Smith's view of new knowledge, they find it difficult to incorporate knowledge into their models.

There are, as can be seen, profound differences between the two schools of thought, arising from two opposing conceptions of human nature, and the most basic human activity. Adam Smith and Abraham Lincoln, as Erik Reinert has pointed out,[5] neatly define the different views of human nature and the two resulting economic theories. The basis of the market-efficient view of economics was set out by Smith in *The Wealth of Nations*:

> The division of labour arises from the propensity of human
> nature to trick, barter and exchange one thing for another ... It is
> common to all men, and to be found in no other race of animals,
> which seem to know neither this nor any other species of
> contracts ... Nobody ever saw a dog make a fair and deliberate
> exchange of one bone for another with another dog.[6]

By way of contrast, in an 1858 lecture Abraham Lincoln described his view of human nature, which is the basis of the production-capability theory of economics:

> Beavers build houses; but they build them in nowise differently,
> or better now, than they did, five thousand years ago ... Man

is not the only animal who labours; but he is the only one who *improves* his workmanship. This improvement, he effects by *Discoveries*, and *Inventions*.

Of course, there are also inventions in Adam Smith, but they are created outside his economic system, and the term 'innovation' – which had been important in English economics from Francis Bacon's 'An Essay on Innovations' (*c*.1605) onwards – died out with Smith.

As has been made clear in recent years by Erik Reinert in his brilliant research on the history of economic thought, these two schools of thought have been embraced at different points in time by different economists.[7] For centuries, production-capability economic theory ruled alone. For example, Antonio Serra (whom Joseph Schumpeter noted as 'the first to compose a scientific treatise ... on economic principles and policy') sought to explain in his 1613 *Breve trattato*, or 'Brief treatise', why his home town of Naples remained so poor despite abundant national resources, while Venice, precariously built on a swamp, was at the very centre of the world's economy. Serra believed this was because the Venetians were unable to cultivate the land like the Neapolitans, and had therefore been forced to rely on their industry to make a living, harnessing the increasing returns to scale offered by manufacturing activities. In Serra's view, the key to economic development was having a large number of different activities, all subject to the falling costs of increasing returns.

The market-efficiency school of thought, however, is less than 250 years old, and has its roots in the Physiocrats (meaning those who adhere to 'the rule of nature'). Today's mainstream economics traces its ancestry back to the Physiocrats, who, in identifying national wealth with productive activity rather than the hoarding of gold, were revolutionary for their time. However, the Physiocrats had a doctrinal commitment to the view that only agriculture was a truly productive activity, with all other sectors 'parasitic' on rural labour. Their commitment to free markets in grain eventually discredited Physiocracy, as it led to food shortages and even famines during poor harvests in France.

Then, in 1776, Adam Smith, who had met with Quesnay and other Physiocrats during his sojourn in France in 1764–67, took over some of their teaching in the first edition of *The Wealth of Nations*. Smith also believed only agriculture was fully 'natural', which was why he was so offended by mercantilism. In mercantilist thought, not only are trade and manufacturing just as 'natural' as agriculture, they are also more productive in terms of wealth and power, and involve organisation by 'human institutions', in which Smith had little faith.

Smith also ignored the Industrial Revolution happening around him, which is why machine production, human entrepreneurship, technology and state promotion of manufacturing play no part in his thinking. He writes about the factory system, but purely in the context of his views on the division of labour: his famous discussion of a pin factory is an example in which mechanisation plays no role at all. To admit that technology harnessed natural forces, which was the critical insight of industrial production, would have established the primacy of manufacturing over agriculture, thus destroying the whole fabric of the 'natural order' by the application of knowledge. This was not something Smith could accept.

Because the greatest political economy controversies of the nineteenth century related to free trade, classical economists continued to ignore production, just at a time when doing so meant missing the greatest changes in the economy itself. They also did not study entrepreneurship, manufacturing technology, the factory system or the nature of economic growth.

Their way of thinking became so entrenched that it has been argued that it is still the preferred stance of mainstream neoclassical economists today, two centuries after Adam Smith's death. The production-capability school of thought did not, however, die out during this period, and had advocates in the form of Alexander Hamilton in the United States and Friedrich List in Germany.

Alexander Hamilton was the first Secretary of the Treasury in the United States and the main author of economic policies for George Washington's administration. In 1791 he produced his 'Report on

Manufacturers' for Congress, in which he quoted from *The Wealth of Nations* and used the French Physiocrats as an example for rejecting both agrarianism and physiocratic theory. Hamilton also refuted Smith's ideas of government non-interference, arguing this would be detrimental for trade with other countries, and thought that as the United States was primarily an agrarian country, Smith's ideas would put it at a disadvantage in its dealings with Europe. Among the ways that the government could assist in manufacturing, Hamilton mentioned levying protective duties on imported goods that were also manufactured in the United States and withdrawing duties levied on raw materials needed for domestic manufacturing.

Hamilton became the father of the American School of economic philosophy, which came to dominate the nation's economic policies. He firmly supported government intervention in favour of business, following in the footsteps of Jean Baptiste Colbert, the French politician who served as Minister of Finance from 1665 to 1683 under King Louis XIV, and whose *dirigiste* policies fostered enterprises in many fields. Hamilton opposed British ideas of free trade, which he believed skewed benefits to colonial and imperial powers, in favour of protectionism, which he believed would help develop the fledgling nation's emerging economy.

Hamilton also influenced the ideas of Friedrich List, a leading German economist with dual American citizenship, who was to argue for a German customs union from a nationalist perspective. List opposed the cosmopolitan principle in contemporary economic thought, as well as the absolute doctrine of free trade, which was in harmony with that principle. Instead, he further developed the infant industry argument, to which he had been exposed by Hamilton and the American economist Daniel Raymond.

List gave prominence to the national interest and insisted on the special requirements of each nation according to its 'circumstances', and especially the degree of its development. His theory of 'national economics' differed from the doctrines of 'individual economics' and 'cosmopolitan economics' espoused by Adam Smith and J. B.

Say. List also understood that innovation is the engine of economic growth, as demonstrated by the following quotations from his 1841 book *The National System of Political Economy*, which English economist Christopher Freeman rightly said could just as well have been called 'The National System of Innovation':

> The present state of the nations is the result of the accumulation of all discoveries, inventions, improvements, perfections and exertions of all generations which have lived before us: they form the mental capital of the present human race, and every separate nation is productive only in the proportion in which it has known how to appropriate these attainments of former generations and to increase them by its own acquirements.[8]

List also argued strongly that industry should be linked to the formal institutions of science and education:

> There scarcely exists a manufacturing business which has no relation to physics, mechanics, chemistry, mathematics or to the art of design etc. No progress, no new discoveries and inventions can be made in these sciences by which a hundred industries and processes could not be improved or altered. In the manufacturing state, therefore, sciences and arts must necessarily become popular.[9]

In addition, in a letter in 1827, List said:

> It is not true that the productive power of a nation is restricted by its capital of matter … Greater part of the productive power consists in the intellectual and social conditions of the individuals, which I call capital of mind.[10]

List was the father of the German Historical School of economics, an approach to academic economics and public administration that emerged in nineteenth-century Germany and held sway there until well into the twentieth century. Opposed by theoretical economists, its prominent leaders included Gustav van Schmoller (1836–1917) and Max Weber (1864–1920) in Germany, and Joseph Schumpeter (1883–1950) in the United States.

The German Historical School came into existence partly as a reaction to the laissez-faire ideas spreading across Europe at the time, and explicitly rejected economics as practised by the British Classical School of David Ricardo and John Stuart Mill. It held that history was the key source of knowledge about human actions and economic matters, since economics is culture-specific. As a result, equilibrium methods and analogies with physical science cannot be used to make generalisations over space and time. Thus, the school rejected the universal validity of economic theorems, arguing that economics should be based on careful empirical and historical analysis, rather than logic and mathematics. The school also preferred reality – historical, political and economic – to mathematical modelling.

Of these thinkers, probably the most important and interesting from our point of view is Joseph Schumpeter, who, in spite of his admiration for the logic, accuracy and elegance of the emerging mathematics-based economics, remained firmly rooted in the knowledge- and production-based academic tradition. Schumpeter also had many insights into the way capitalism works. As someone who has spent thirty-five years of my life in industry, I recognise the following three insights as giving an accurate representation of the world in which I have lived, and I have incorporated all three of them in the theory of economic growth set out in Chapter 2.

Firstly, he saw competition as a dynamic process of moving from one disequilibrium to another, rather than a process of moving towards equilibrium.

Secondly, he understood that we do not live in a world of perfect competition, and that the traditional theorist's focus solely on price is wrong. As he said:

In the capitalist reality as distinguished from its textbook picture, it is not [price] competition that counts but the competition from the new commodity, the new technology, the new source of supply, the new type of organisation (the largest-scale unit of control for instance).[11]

Thirdly, he saw the process of innovation as the engine of economic growth, remarking, 'without innovation, no entrepreneurs; without entrepreneurial achievement, no capitalist returns and no capitalist propulsion'.[12]

The Cold War, however, led to the almost total disappearance of the production-capability theory of economic growth, while at the same time the market-efficiency theory achieved a dominant theoretical position in the economic departments of universities. Three factors seem to have led to the near-disappearance of the production-capability theory in the post-Second World War era.

Firstly, the Cold War created an enormous demand for economic and political arguments that could be used to counter what was then seen as Russia's successful planned economy. The perfect markets of neoclassical economics provided an ideological defence line. While communism promised that what everyone would receive would be according to his or her needs, neoclassical economics rebutted this using Paul Samuelson's proof (1948, 1949) that international trade, under the usual assumptions of neoclassical economics, would produce factor-price equalisation.[13] Thus, if all nations in the future adopted free trade, the price of the factors of production, capital and labour would be the same all over the world, and all wage earners would be equally rich. Samuelson's proof depended, however, on not including three elements that are central to the production-capability theory of economic growth. They are the activity-specific nature of technology, the capability of firms, and innovation. If these elements are included, the uneven advance of technical change makes it possible for a country to be locked into a comparative disadvantage of being ignorant and poor.

Secondly, after the Second World War, science emerged with enhanced prestige, and in order to show that economics was equally scientific, economists appear to have adopted the view that it should in future be based on mathematical models. But it proved very difficult to build into mathematical models the three central features of the production-capability theory of economic growth mentioned above.

Thirdly, research and production during the Second World War produced a formidable amount of innovation which fed the post-war boom, and consequently there was little support for the argument that the government needed to stimulate innovation in order to create economic growth.

The economics profession, having also learned from John Maynard Keynes how to even out the ups and downs of the business cycle, was confident that it could produce a steady rate of economic growth, even though the ability to iron out the business cycle and Keynes's emphasis on the financial and monetary aspects of capitalism later turned out not to be adequate tools for the task.

While the Cold War led to an almost total disappearance of the production-capability approach, an important group of economists – led by people such as Christopher Freeman, Richard Nelson, Franco Malerba and Keun Lee – has continued to develop a production-capability theory of economic growth, though typically its members have worked in institutes of technology or departments of development. I have made great use of their research in this book.

What policies were successful

Having summarised briefly the history of the market-efficiency and the production-capability schools of economic thought, it is now possible to look at how successful they have been in guiding economic policy-making. If we look at the economic history of the two countries that have achieved global technological leadership in the last two centuries – the UK and the US – two historical facts clearly emerge. Firstly, they both adhered to the production-capability school of thought while moving from being poor to being wealthy. Secondly, only once they had achieved a global technological leadership did they switch from a production-capability theory of economic growth to a market-efficiency one.

It is one of the great myths of economic history that Britain, as the intellectual fountain of modern laissez-faire doctrines, developed without state intervention.[14] Britain entered the post-feudal age (the thirteen and fourteenth centuries) as a relatively backward economy. It relied on exports of raw wool and, to a lesser extent, of low value-added wool cloth (known as 'short cloth') to the then more advanced Low Countries, especially the towns of Bruges, Ghent and Ypres in Flanders, now part of Belgium.

Edward III (1327–77) is believed to have been the first king who deliberately tried to develop local wool-cloth manufacturing, but it was the Tudor monarchs Henry VII (1485–1509) and Elizabeth I (1558–1603) who, as described by the novelist Daniel Defoe in his 1728 book *A Plan for English Commerce*, transformed England from a country relying heavily on raw wool exports to the Low Countries into the most formidable wool manufacturing nation in the world.

Henry VII came to power in 1485 after spending his childhood and youth with an aunt in Brittany in France, where he had observed that the area was very wealthy due to the production of woollen textiles. He also observed that the wool and the material used to clean it (fuller's earth, or aluminium silicate) were both imported from England.

When Henry took over his destitute realm, whose future wool production was for several years mortgaged to Italian bankers, he decided on a policy of making England into a textile-producing nation rather than an exporter of raw materials. He imposed wool export duties, so that foreign textile producers had to process more expensive raw materials than their English competitors. He gave newly established wool manufacturers a tax exemption for a period, and monopolies in certain geographical areas for certain periods. He also sought to attract craftsmen and entrepreneurs from abroad, especially from Holland and Italy.

This early example of an industrial strategy turned out to be highly successful, as woollen cloth manufacturing was an industry experiencing rapid technical change. There was, therefore, the possibility of new learning and economies of scale and scope, and as a result it became a key industry for the country, accounting for at least half of Britain's export revenue during the eighteenth century.

This is not, however, the only example we find in Britain's economic history of government policies promoting manufacturing industries. Another important example was the 1721 reform of the mercantile law introduced by Robert Walpole, the first British Prime Minister, during the reign of George I (1714–27).

Up to this time, the main aim of the British government's economic policies was capturing trade, most importantly through colonialism and the Navigation Acts, which required that trade with Britain had to be carried in British ships. The policies introduced by Robert Walpole in 1721 were, however, deliberately aimed at promoting manufacturing industries. Introducing the new law, Walpole stated by means of the King's address to Parliament that 'it is evident that nothing so much contributes to promote the public well-being as the exportation of manufactured goods and the importation of foreign raw material.'

The 1721 legislation and its subsequent supplementary policies included lowering or even dropping altogether import duties on raw materials used for manufactures, raising significantly the duties on foreign manufactured goods, and extending subsidies ('bounties') to new items like silk products (1722) and gunpowder (1731), while increasing the existing export subsidies to sailcloth (1731) and refined sugar (1733).

Two other policies of the British government should also be mentioned. Firstly, regulations were introduced to control the quality of manufactured products, especially textile products, so that unscrupulous manufacturers would not damage the reputation of British products in foreign markets. Secondly, in 1719, acutely aware of the contribution of innovation to maintaining its competitive advantage in world markets, Britain introduced a ban on the emigration of skilled workers, particularly on 'suborning' or attempting to recruit such workers for jobs abroad. Subsequently, as increasing amounts of technology became embodied in machines, machine exports also came under government control. The current, belated attempts of the US to stop the flow of innovation to China is nothing new.

Faced with these attempts to prevent technology outflows by the advanced countries, the less developed countries tried illegally to gain access to advanced technologies. Entrepreneurs and technicians, often with the active encouragement of their governments – including offers of bounties for securing specific technologies – frequently engaged in industrial espionage.

By the end of the Napoleonic wars there was strong pressure from increasingly confident British manufacturers for free trade. There was a round of tariff reduction in 1833, but the big change came in 1846 when the Corn Laws were repealed and tariffs on many manufactured goods abolished. It is important to note, however, that the shift to a free-trade regime only came about when Britain's technological lead had already been achieved behind high and long-lasting tariff barriers.

As Friedrich List pointed out, Britain was the first country to launch an infant industry strategy, but its most enthusiastic exponent was probably the US. Around the time of independence, Southern agrarian interests opposed any protection, while Northern manufacturing interests, represented by, among others, Alexander Hamilton, the first Secretary of the Treasury (1789–95), were in favour of it.

In his 'Reports of the Secretary of the Treasury on the subject of Manufactures' (1791), Alexander Hamilton argued that competition from abroad and 'forces of habit' would mean that new industries that could potentially become internationally competitive ('infant industries') would not do so unless they were helped by government imposing import duties or, in rare cases, prohibiting imports. In line with this thinking, Congress passed a liberal tariff act in 1789, imposing a 5 per cent flat rate tariff on all imports other than hemp, glass and nails. This rose over the years, and by 1931 the average tariff level for manufactured products was 48 per cent. It was only after the Second World War that the US, having achieved world technology leadership, finally liberalised its trade and started championing free trade. Once again, a poacher had turned gamekeeper.

An obvious question is why did both the UK and the US, after lengthy periods when they strongly promoted their manufacturing industries, suddenly start preaching the value of free trade? The answer was provided by Friedrich List:

> It is a very common clever device that when anyone has
> attained the summit of greatness, he kicks away the ladder
> by which he has climbed up, in order to deprive others of
> the means of climbing up after him. In this lies the secret
> of the cosmopolitical doctrines of Adam Smith, and of the
> cosmopolitical tendencies of his great contemporary William
> Pitt, and of all his successors in the British Government
> administration.[15]

It was, of course, not only the UK and the US which used industrial, trade and technology policies to promote infant industries during their catch-up phase. Almost all newly developing countries did so, based on a production-capability theory of economic growth. There were what look like exceptions, such as Switzerland and the Netherlands, but they were countries who were already at or very near the technological frontier, and therefore did not need infant industry protection.

It is also difficult not to notice the similarities between the industrial, trade and technology policies of the successful East Asian countries and those used by newly developing countries in their catch-up phase. The export subsidies of the East Asian countries were, however, more fine-tuned and substantial, and they also integrated their human capital and learning-related policies more tightly with their industrial policies. In addition, there were serious attempts to upgrade their skill base and technological capabilities through subsidies to and public provision of education, training and R&D.

It should also be noted that the industrial policies of Japan, and later of countries such as South Korea and Taiwan, were based on the ideas of people such as Friedrich List and Joseph Schumpeter, and not Adam Smith and David Ricardo. Very few countries have ever developed by means other than innovation, learning and the growth of industrial production. The only exceptions to this rule have been unusual cases such as the Gulf states, where the natural-resource endowment has been so huge relative to the population that it is doubtful any policy lessons can be learned.

Equally, no state has managed to sustain a development strategy based on agriculture. Argentina came close in the nineteenth century but ended up as the only country thus far to have joined the First World and then left it. New Zealand might also be considered an exception to this rule, but the value-added milk products that form the basis of its exports to Asia often have a greater science and technology component to them than many manufactured products.

This historical assessment of the advice that economists have given to policy-makers can be summed up, I think, by saying that it is the production-capability school of thought that has proved most useful to policy-makers trying to increase the growth rates of their countries; while a harsh assessment would conclude that the market-efficiency school of thought, including neoclassical economics, has proved most useful to policy-makers trying to stop other countries from catching them up and competing against them.

Therefore, in the next section of this chapter, I will look more closely at why neoclassical growth theory has proved such a poor guide to policy-makers seeking to increase the growth rates of their countries, and why it is of so little use in explaining the growth performance of countries.

Neoclassical growth theory

Starting at the beginning of the twentieth century, neoclassical economists came to view the economic problem as being the optimal allocation of scarce resources rather than one of generating productivity to overcome conditions of scarcity. They thus came to believe that if the allocation of capital and labour by markets is efficient, then economic growth will follow.

This concentration on the more analytically tractable issues of stabilisation policy led them to ignore issues that had previously been of interest to growth economists, such as how firms are formed, how technologies are acquired, how industries emerge, develop or die, and what role governments play in the process. As American economist Richard Nelson has said, 'The premise of neoclassical theory is that, if the investments are made, the acquisition and mastery of new ways of doing things is relatively easy, even automatic.'[16]

In 1932, for example, we find a British economist, Lionel Robbins, summarising what he saw as the emerging neoclassical consensus: 'whatever economics is concerned with, it is not the causes of material welfare as such'. Instead, he argued that:

> economics is the science that studies human behaviour as
> a relationship between ends and scarce means which have
> alternative uses ... the technical arts of production are simply
> to be grouped among the given factors influencing the relative
> scarcity of different economic goods.[17]

Then in the 1950s, Robert Solow and others developed the so-called neoclassical growth theory, which was the starting point for most neoclassical growth theory in the years that followed.[18] In this model he used a production function where output (Y) is a function of the quantity of physical capital (K) and human labour (L), other things remaining equal. Among the 'other things' was technological change.

$$Y = f(K, L)$$

While increases in K and L in this model cause movements along the production function (curve), technological change – which he saw as exogenous, or outside the model – causes an upward shift in the curve, resulting in both K and L being more productively used.

When Solow discovered that 90 per cent of the variation in economic output was not explained by the amounts of capital and labour, he called the residual 'technical change'. The economist Moses Abramovitz pointed out, however, that the residual should more accurately be described as a 'measure of our ignorance'. Today, it is usually described as 'total factor productivity'.[19]

In time, Solow's theory became known as 'exogenous growth theory', because the variable for technical change was inserted exogenously, as a time trend:

$$Y = A(t) f(K, L)$$

It should in fairness be said that Solow's 1956 article did not put forth the model as an 'explanation' of growth so much as a criticism of, and alternative to, the non-equilibrium models of Harrod and Domar, which had argued that it was very unlikely that economic growth was compatible with sustained full employment of capital and labour. Solow's model did, however, describe the equilibrium approach to the economy in the long term, and so became the basis of neoclassical thinking about economic growth.

There have been many attempts to produce a more realistic neoclassical theory of economic growth by, for example, making technology endogenous (Paul Romer) or by including institutions as a key variable (Douglass North). But even with these changes it remains an unrealistic representation of the economic growth process in three key ways.

Firstly, it represents production as a simple process of combining non-specialised factors of production in such a way as to produce a number of products at a minimum cost. It does not see production as it is in the observable world; that is, as a complex process which involves innovation and the creation of competitive advantage, and which needs an entrepreneur to make it happen.

Secondly, it underestimates the heterogeneity of production activities within and across production sectors. It ignores the issue of both what is being produced (i.e. the product) and how it is being produced (i.e. the technologies and organisation used). As a result, it doesn't matter whether a firm is producing potato chips or microchips, a point of view still held by some neoclassical economists.

Thirdly, the framing of the economy as a series of transactions between individuals prevents it from including the capability of firms, which is clearly a collective process, as well as being an extremely important element in any realistic theory of economic growth.

As Nobel Prize-winning economist Herbert Simon pointed out:

> as soon as firms are elaborated to become more than simple
> nodes in a network of transactions, to be producers –
> transformers of factors into products – difficult and important
> questions arise for the theory. A large part of the behaviour of
> the system now takes place inside the skins of firms, and does
> not consist of market exchangers.[20]

As a result of these deficiencies, neoclassical economic growth theory continues to be of little value to policy-makers, providing no explanation of the level of total factor productivity, which is the key variable as far as the rate of economic growth is concerned. This is not surprising, as it does not include four elements which empirical studies of growth have shown to be important.

The first of these elements is the demand for a specific product or service. This demand for a specific product or service can be well known or latent. For example, when Steve Jobs produced the first Apple computer, it was not obvious that there was a huge latent demand for cheap personal computers, and it was an example of his entrepreneurial genius that he saw this was the case.

The second element is activity-specific technology, which can be used to produce a specific product or service, and the existence of which, together with the demand for the product or service, creates a 'window of opportunity'. A new window of opportunity can arise as a result of a new demand, a new technology, or both.

The third element is the capability of a firm, which enables it to apply the activity-specific technology to producing the product or service in order to meet market demand, thus creating a capability/market-opportunity dynamic.

The fourth element is the institutions of the country where the firm is located, which enable the capability/market-opportunity dynamic to operate effectively.

Only when these four elements are present and aligned do they produce the capability/market-opportunity dynamic which creates innovation and growth in an economy.

Because neoclassical economists have not been able to quantify these four elements and so include them in their mathematical models, they have not been able to explain why different sectors in an economy have different levels of value-added growing at different rates. This is a major problem because, as we shall see in the rest of this book, the growth rate of a country depends on what is happening to the value-added per capita in each of its different sectors as a result of the capability/market-opportunity dynamic, and on any shift in the distribution of economic activity across sectors. A new theory including these four elements therefore needs to be developed.

A new theory of economic growth

In Chapters 2, 3 and 4, I will put forward an alternative theory which I have called a 'dynamic capability' theory of economic growth. The fundamental way the dynamic capability theory of economic growth varies from neoclassical economic growth theory is that it does not assume the market economy is one of perfect competition, in which every firm is selling the same product at the same price as its competitors. This is a completely unrealistic view of the world, as can be seen by a quick trip to any shopping centre or car showroom. Instead, the dynamic capability theory assumes that, in a competitive market economy, firms compete by trying to gain a competitive advantage over their rivals, as this is what enables them to grow and enhance their profitability. It also assumes that this same type of competition exists between firms in different countries and is what determines in the long term what goods and services a country exports and imports.

The essential question that economic growth theory raises, therefore, is how do firms gain a competitive advantage over their rivals? There are two ways they can do this. Firms can either reduce the cost of their product or service through innovations in their production methods, or use innovation to make their product more attractive to their customers by better meeting their needs through enhanced performance, more functionality or improved design.

The ability of firms to achieve a competitive advantage in turn depends on the capability/market-opportunity I have just described. This will vary between sectors, and to understand the growth performance of a country one needs, therefore, to look at what is happening in its different sectors.

Finally, I will argue that there is a ladder of economic development, the rungs of which represent products that require increasing amounts of organisational and technological capability, and which produce increasing amounts of value-added per capita due to fewer companies being able to produce them. Developing countries can only compete on the lower rungs because of their lack of capability, and development for them depends on building their capabilities in order to take advantage of opportunities higher up the ladder. Their performance also, therefore, depends on a capability/market-opportunity dynamic.

After setting out the theory in more detail in Chapter 2, I will look in Chapters 3 and 4 at whether the capability/market-opportunity dynamic can be used to explain the economic growth performance of sectors, as well as cities and regions. Then, in Chapters 5, 6 and 7, I will treat the theory as a scientific hypothesis and test it in the only laboratory economics has for this sort of theory: the laboratory of history.

In a famous article in 1986, the eminent American economist Moses Abramovitz looked at the different economic growth dynamics of countries 'catching up, forging ahead and falling behind'.[21] To test the dynamic capability theory of economic growth I will, therefore, in Chapters 5, 6 and 7 see if it can be used to explain the growth performance of countries in these three categories.

These categories of course map onto the three groups of countries whose dramatic change of economic performance we observed at the beginning of the chapter: the forging ahead of the G7 countries between 1820 and 1990; the rapid catching up of a group of developing countries over the last twenty-five years; and the falling behind of the G7 countries over the same period.

Finally, in Chapters 8, 9 and 10 I will set out the policies that governments need to adopt in the fields of education and training (Chapter 8) and innovation policy (Chapter 9), and the role I believe governments need to play (Chapter 10) if they want to increase their rates of economic growth.

However, before looking in detail at the dynamic capability theory of economic growth, it is useful to make a number of general points about it. Firstly, it is wrong to believe that by building mathematical models one makes economic growth theory more scientific. On the contrary, I believe mathematical modelling has had a negative impact on our search for an explanation of the economic growth rates of countries due to the difficulty of quantifying and including such concepts as innovation and the capability of firms. In putting forward a new theory I will do so, therefore, purely in descriptive terms.

Secondly, the theory I will put forward is a production-capability theory, and I will argue that innovation is the engine of economic growth, and that innovation and its diffusion across national boundaries provides the explanation for the economic growth rates of countries rather than the accumulation of capital. Instead of looking at how resources are best allocated to the production of widgets, we will look at how widgets can be made more efficiently and how better widgets can be invented. As Joseph Schumpeter said, 'The problem that is usually visualised is how capitalism administers existing structures, whereas the relevant problem is how it creates and destroys them.'[22]

Thirdly, while the theory put forward in Chapters 2, 3 and 4 is a production-capability theory of economic growth rather than a market-efficiency one, no one should think that I am arguing for any kind of planned economy. A market economy with inclusive institutions enabling all citizens to participate is, I believe, essential for economic growth; a lesson which history clearly teaches us.[23]

Inclusive market institutions are those that allow and encourage participation by the great mass of people in economic activities, that make best use of their talents and skills, and that enable individuals to make the choices they wish. To be inclusive, economic institutions must feature secure private property, a system of law which gives everyone equal rights, and places in which people can exchange goods and services. They must also permit the entry of new businesses and allow people to choose their careers. The opposite of inclusive institutions is extractive ones, which are designed to extract income and wealth from one social group in order to benefit another.

Whether a country has inclusive or extractive institutions depends to a great extent on its political processes. This is for the simple reason that while inclusive institutions may be good for the economic prosperity of a country, some people or groups – such as the medieval feudal landowners in England or the sugar planters of colonial Barbados – will be much better off if they can benefit from extractive institutions.

These points are demonstrated by looking at the Industrial Revolution in England, which started at the end of the eighteenth century. On the eve of the Industrial Revolution, the governments of most European countries were controlled by aristocracies and traditional elites, whose major source of income was from landholdings or from trading privileges they enjoyed due to monopolies granted and entry barriers imposed by monarchs. In England in 1621, under James I, there were over 700 monopolies, covering everything from salt and butter to glass and writing paper.

These elites saw that, consistent with Joseph Schumpeter's idea of creative destruction, the spread of industries, factories and towns took away resources from the land, reduced land rents, and increased the wages that landowners had to pay their workers. The landowners therefore opposed industrialisation.

In England, however, industrialisation took off because events leading up to and including the Civil War of 1642–51, and the Glorious Revolution of 1688, had led to the abolition of monopolies and the establishment of more inclusive institutions. It was these institutions which enabled the great entrepreneurs of the Industrial Revolution, such as James Watt, Josiah Wedgwood, Richard Arkwright and Isambard Kingdom Brunel, to turn their ideas into commercial products, knowing that their property rights would be respected and that they would have access to markets where their innovations could be profitably sold.

On the other hand, in the Austro-Hungarian and Russian empires, the absolute monarchs and aristocrats were more firmly entrenched, and were, therefore, able to block industrialisation. As a result, their economies fell behind other European nations where economic growth took off during the nineteenth century.

Finally, this is a book about economic growth theory and not macroeconomics. While a stable macroeconomic environment is a prerequisite for economic growth, it should not be thought that simply by creating a stable economic environment this will automatically create a rapid rate of economic growth. To create rapid economic growth, policy-makers need to create an environment in which entrepreneurs can build up in their firms the organisational and technological capabilities required in order to take advantage of market opportunities. Only in this way will a rapid rate of economic growth be created.

The developed world faces a major challenge today in maintaining a steady rate of economic growth. I hope that by putting forward a new theory of economic growth, and testing it rigorously in the laboratory of history, I can help it meet this challenge, while at the same time not falling prey to the relevant and insightful criticism of economics provided by Colin Clark in the foreword to his book *The Conditions of Economic Progress* (1940), which is even more valid today than when he wrote it:

> I have left the academic world with nothing but regard for the intellectual integrity and public spirit of my former colleagues in the ... universities; but with dismay at their continued preference for the theoretical rather than the scientific approach to economic problems. Not one in a hundred – least of all those who are most anxious to proclaim the scientific nature of economics – seem to understand what constitutes the scientific approach, namely the careful systematisation of all observed facts, the framing of hypotheses from those facts, prediction of fresh conclusions on the basis of these hypotheses, and the testing of these conclusions against further observed facts. It would be laughable, were it not tragic, to watch the stream of books and articles, attempting to solve the exceptionally complex problems of present-day economics by theoretical arguments, often without a single reference to the observed facts of the situation ... The hard scientific discipline has yet to be learned, that all theories must be constantly tested and re-tested against the observed facts and those which prove wrong ruthlessly rejected.[24]

2

A dynamic capability theory of economic growth

The new theory

If neoclassical economic growth theory cannot explain what is happening in the global economy, and thereby provide policy-makers with a framework to develop new policies, we need to develop a new theory of economic growth which does. In order to be realistic, such a theory needs to be based on the many empirical studies of how firms increase their value-added per capita, and should incorporate key elements such as knowledge, capabilities and innovation.

A nation's standard of living in the long term depends on the ability of its firms to attain a high and rising level of value-added per capita in the industries in which they compete. A high level of value-added per capita is the basis of a nation's standard of living as it determines the wages and salaries of firms' employees and the returns given to firms' shareholders.

How, then, do firms increase their value-added per capita? Assuming they are not overmanned they can do it in two ways. They can increase their production efficiency by innovation or they can create a competitive advantage over their rivals based on a capabilities/ market-opportunity dynamic. The first will reduce the denominator, and the second will increase the nominator in the calculation of value-added per capita.

To create a competitive advantage, firms need to be able to

identify 'a window of opportunity' and have the organisational and technological capabilities to take advantage of it. If they can gain such a competitive advantage over their rivals, they can drive a wider wedge between the willingness of their customers to buy their product or service and the costs they incur in producing it, and in that way increase their value-added per capita.

Henry Ford's development of the production line is an example of using innovation to increase production efficiency. Steve Jobs development of the Apple iPhone is an example of using innovation to create competitive advantage.

Where there is perfect competition, as in neoclassical growth theory, it is not possible for firms to gain a competitive advantage over their rivals, enabling them to raise the willingness of their customers to pay for their product or service. The entrepreneur cannot influence the price of what he produces. He or she sees or reads on their mobile phone what the market is willing to pay and is a price-taker rather than a price-maker. This situation, however, is only found in a few commodity markets for agricultural or mining products. Business-people will often refer to a product becoming a commodity, meaning it should be avoided because it is not possible to create a competitive advantage and achieve a high level of value-added.

In most markets, however, competition is not the perfect competition of neoclassical economics, and in any country at any one time, opportunities will exist in specific industries for a firm to create a competitive advantage by differentiating its product or service and making it more attractive to its customers.

It should be noted, however, that when an entrepreneur creates a competitive advantage, and increases value-added per capita for a firm, he also creates a disequilibrium, which as soon as it is established sets in motion the competitive process that leads to its destruction. How long a competitive advantage is sustained depends on two character-istics of the capabilities involved: their durability and their imitability.

In the absence of competition, the longevity of a firm's competi-tive advantage will depend upon the rate at which the underlying capabilities depreciate or become obsolete. The increasing pace of technological change means that the useful life of most capital equipment and technological capabilities is becoming shorter. On the other hand, reputation, both brand and corporate, appears to depreciate relatively slowly, and can normally be maintained by low levels of replacement investment.

A firm's ability to sustain its competitive advantage over time will also depend on the speed with which other firms can imitate its strategy. To do so, a competitor will first need to establish what exactly is the competitive advantage of the successful firm, and how it is being achieved. It can then seek to acquire the resources required for imitating the competitive advantage of the successful firm, which if it can be replicated on similar terms means that the successful firm's competitive advantage will be short-lived.

Alternatively, the competitor can seek to replicate the successful firm's competitive advantage by internal investment. If the competitive advantage is based on highly complex organisational or technological capabilities, this can be extremely difficult to do. Complex technological capabilities are obviously difficult to emulate, but complex organisational capabilities can also present problems for a firm that wants to copy them.

Japanese car manufacturers were able to gain a competitive advantage by improving the quality of their cars through using quality circles. These did not involve sophisticated knowledge or complex operating systems, but because they require enthusiastic participation by the workforce, they have proved difficult for American and European firms to introduce successfully.

Another factor affecting the ability of firms to appropriate their competitive advantages is the use of advanced production tools, which are now commoditising the manufacture of many hardware products.[1] It used to be said that technology-intensive product manufacturers, such as automobile or white-goods firms, could capitalise on their long-standing engineering and design skills to maintain their leadership worldwide. Today, however, many young companies in many product segments, especially in China, seem to be able to develop world-class design and production capabilities in a short period of time, sometimes closing gaps with long-established leaders within a decade.

The reason for this change is that tacit knowhow that takes years to develop can now be embedded into the sophisticated production and automation tools used to design and manufacture products. These tools take things that are hard to do – for example, the production of electronic devices that have dimensions on the scale of tens of atoms – and makes them routine. This can lead to the rapid commoditisation of whole product areas, as all you need to be successful is the money to purchase the relevant tools. This makes it more difficult for firms to appropriate the benefits of an innovation for a long period of time. One way for companies to protect their proprietary advantages is to stop worrying about the commoditised parts of the value chain, and instead to focus on complex system design and protectable areas of the value chain.

Given both innovation in production methods and innovation as a product of the capability/market dynamic are central to the process of gaining competitive advantage, I think it is necessary to say up front what we mean by 'innovation'. Many people see innovation only in technological terms, as new products such as Apple's iPhone or as a new John Deere cotton harvester that is full of computer power and a precision GPS location system that is accurate to several inches. Others, meanwhile, see it only in terms of research and development actively done in universities, national laboratories and the research laboratories of firms.

Innovation is all these things, but it is also much more. The Organization for Economic Co-operation and Development (OECD) defines innovation as:

> the implementation of a new or significantly improved product
> (that is, a physical good or service), process, a new marketing
> method, or a new organisational method in business practices,
> workplace organisation or external relations.

By definition, all innovations must contain a degree of novelty, whether that novelty is new to the firm, to the market, or to the world. It must also be a viable commercial concept.

Sectoral and regional dimensions of economic growth

As well as understanding that the competitive advantage of firms is based on a capability/market-opportunity dynamic, we also need to understand that the 'windows of opportunity' for technical change, which enable firms with the necessary capability to achieve competitive advantage, are at any one time unevenly distributed among industrial sectors.

Technological knowledge is often visualised as moving forward as a technological frontier. This conveys an impression of orderly and even progress, like the 'frontier' being pushed from the east to the west coast in US history. But history shows that technical change takes place very fast in some sectors, while in others it hardly moves forward for centuries. This is why, as Erik Reinert has said, 'windows of opportunity create huge variations in economic activities and consequently also widely different opportunities for adding capital to labour in a potentially profitable way'.[2]

A key insight provided by history is that economic development at any point in time is sector-specific. The striking contrast between the historically successful, long-distance catching-up strategies of Britain, the United States, Germany and Japan, and neoclassical economic growth theory today, is that the strategies of these countries were sector-specific. Policy-makers rightly saw that the key to a successful economic strategy was to get into the right business areas, which almost always meant manufacturing.

The fact that, at any one time, the 'windows of opportunity' for technical change are unevenly distributed among different industries and industry segments, has been cleverly illustrated by Reinert with a comparison of the production of baseballs and golf balls in the world today.[3] The most efficient producers of baseballs for America's national sport are found in Haiti, Honduras and Costa Rica. Baseballs today are still hand-sewn, just as they were when they were invented, as all the engineers and all the capital of the United States have not managed to mechanise their production. Every baseball is stitched by hand with 108 stitches, and each worker is able to sew four baseballs per hour. There is no innovation, no differentiation, no increasing returns to scale, scope or experience, and no synergies with other economic activities. Competition is, therefore, similar to that of a commodity. As a result, even the wages of the most efficient baseball producers are appallingly low. In Haiti, they were around 30 cents an hour in 2007, with reports saying they were as low as 14 cents per hour in the mid-1990s.

Golf balls are, by comparison, a high-tech product, and one of the important producers, with 40 per cent of American production, is found in the Massachusetts town of New Bedford. Unlike with baseballs, R&D plays an important role in the production of golf balls, and while New Bedford is a high wage area, direct labour costs represent only 15 per cent of production costs due to the capital intensity of the production process.

These facts, coupled with the need for qualified labour, engineers and specialised suppliers, makes it unattractive for golf ball production to move to a low-wage country like Haiti. Production wages in the New Bedford area were, in 2007, between $14 and $16 per hour, and the differing wage level between the two industrial sectors of baseballs and golf balls can be attributed to uneven technological development.

It should also be noted that when innovations, products and processes mature and age, becoming technological dead-ends, the world market will automatically assign them to low-wage countries. This point can be illustrated, as Reinert has pointed out, by looking at the production of shoes in the United States between 1850 and 1936.[4]

In 1850, 15.5 work hours were needed to produce a pair of standard men's shoes. Then a productivity explosion took place in shoe production, with rapid mechanisation making it possible fifty years later, in 1900, to employ only 1.7 labour hours to produce an identical pair of shoes. During this period, St Louis, in Missouri, became one of the wealthiest cities in the US, based on its production of shoes and beer.

After 1900, the learning curve for shoes flattened out, and in 1936 only 0.9 hours were needed. As the learning curve flattened out, shoe production was moved to poorer regions, and the US, for a long time an exporter of shoes, now imports practically all its shoes.

As Reinert has brutally put it: 'Standard textbook economics which seeks to understand economic development in terms of frictionless "perfect markets" totally misses the point. Perfect markets are for the poor.'[5] The capability of a country's firms to take advantage of 'windows of opportunity' has also been eliminated as a factor in neoclassical economic growth theory, with, again, Reinert explaining:

> Economics has lost the art of organising the world by creating categories and taxonomies which characterised the birth of modern sciences during the Enlightenment. In doing that, all factors qualitatively differentiating a twelve-year-old and his shoeshine 'firm' based in a Lima slum from Microsoft as a firm have been eliminated. With it, an explanation as to why Bill Gates and his country are wealthier than the shoeshine boy has also been eliminated. The two of them have been averaged out as 'the representative firm'.[6]

The capabilities of firms which enable them to take advantage of the opportunities they face are, however, undoubtedly a critical factor in explaining the growth rates of sectors of an economy. In particular, whether firms have the dynamic capabilities which enable them to link their technological and organisational capabilities to a product or service demand is central to the theory of economic growth which is advanced in this book. This is why I have called this chapter 'A Dynamic Capability Theory of Economic Growth'. I will say more about the nature of dynamic capabilities in the next chapter.

The uneven nature of both 'windows of opportunity' and firms with the capabilities to take advantage of them, accounts for one of the most striking features ignored by neoclassical economists regarding the economic growth performance of countries: the existence of different levels, and different rates of growth and decline, of value-added per capita in different sectors. This is also an important factor to take into account when debating whether the decline in manufacturing as a proportion of the economy in G7 countries should be a matter of concern for policy-makers or not.

Columbia University economist Jagdish Bhagwati has dismissed anyone who says manufacturing is important as suffering from a 'manufacturing fetish',[7] while Christine Romer, former head of the Council of Economic Advisors for President Obama, said after she left the White House that there is no convincing rationale to treat manufacturing any different from services such as haircuts, and that any claim as to why manufacturing is different is based on 'sentiment'.[8] These views are based on the neoclassical economist's belief that there is no difference between car rental and car manufacturing as far as economic growth is concerned – they both employ people and produce economic output.

However, if we look at the historical record we find that agriculture has almost always produced low rates of value-added per capita; manufacturing has produced high rates of value-added per capita; while services has produced a few high value-added per capita sectors, such as financial and professional services, and IT, and many low value-added per capita sectors, such as the retailing trade, residential care activities, and food and beverage service activities.

This difference in the value-added per capita of sectors is not difficult to explain, and results from the ease with which competitive advantage can be created and appropriated, and production efficiency increased, in different sectors. In manufacturing, there have historically been many 'windows of opportunity' enabling firms to use their technological and organisational capabilities to create and appropriate competitive advantages. This has not been the case in agriculture, while only in a few service areas – such as financial and professional services, and IT – have windows of opportunity existed enabling firms to create competitive advantages through use of high-level skills and the spillover of knowledge in clusters.

This is the reason why, when we look at countries forging ahead (Chapter 5) and catching up (Chapter 6), we usually see manufacturing becoming a higher proportion of the economy and agriculture a smaller proportion; while in countries falling behind (Chapter 7), we usually see manufacturing becoming a smaller proportion and low value-added services a bigger proportion. A declining manufacturing sector should, therefore, be a matter of concern for G7 policy-makers.

Human capital and technological capabilities are not only unevenly distributed among the sectors of an economy, but also its cities and regions. America's new economic map, for example, shows growing differences between individual cities and regions. A handful of cities with innovative industries keep attracting high-skilled jobs offering high wages, while those cities depending on traditional manufacturing are stuck with low-skilled jobs and low average wages. This divergence of cities reflects the structural changes taking place in the world economy played out on the national stage.

What explains the different fortunes of cities is the same capabilities/market-opportunity dynamic that applies to sectors at the national level. If, therefore, we want to explain the economic growth performance of countries, we need to understand both the sectoral, and the city and regional systems of innovation, underpinning them. We will, therefore, look in detail at these two systems in Chapters 3 and 4.

A new theory of international trade

In addition to a new theory of economic growth, we also need a new theory of international trade. As we have seen in this chapter, the success of firms in their domestic markets is based on the competitive advantages they are able to build up over their rivals as well as their production efficiencies. It is difficult to see why competition between firms in different countries should be on a fundamentally different basis from that of firms in a single country. If we want, therefore, to explain the growth rates of countries, we need not only to understand the different costs and availability of factors such as capital and labour, but also the things which enable firms to differentiate their goods and services. It follows that a theory of international trade seeking to explain trade flows between two countries should seek an explanation in the comparative competitive advantages of the firms within them as well as their production efficiencies.

In this theory of international trade, the ways that firms compete with their foreign rivals should be seen as similar to the ways they compete with their domestic rivals, rather than being restricted to the limited types of factor-based advantage on which the theory of comparative advantage is normally based. Rather, the theory should reflect a rich understanding of competition that includes differentiated products, innovation, economies of scale, scope and experience, and synergies with other economic activities. Also, as in domestic competition, it should be understood that firms play a critical role in the process of creating competitive advantage.

International trade, therefore, both provides an opportunity to increase a nation's level of value-added per capita while also posing a danger that its value-added per capita will be reduced. International trade makes it possible for a nation to raise its value-added per capita by eliminating the need for its own firms to produce all the goods and services it wants. It can then specialise in those industries and segments where its firms have a high value-added per capita, and import those products and services where its firms have a low level of value-added per capita. In this way, it can raise its average level of value-added per capita.

On the other hand, if the high value-added per capita firms in a country lose out to foreign rivals, then the country's ability to sustain the growth of its value-added per capita will be impacted negatively.

Additionally, if firms transfer high value-added per capita activities abroad due to the environment there enabling such activities to be carried out more profitably (taking into account foreign wages and other costs), that will have a negative impact on the home country's level of value-added per capita. It is not overdramatising things to say that international competition in today's world economy is a 'race to the top'. For a higher-income country which fails to create new competitive advantages, the loss of higher value-added per capita industries could even result in an absolute decline in living standards.

This view of international trade, it should be noted, is one that neoclassical economists totally reject. Even Paul Krugman, who won the Nobel Prize for his insights into economic geography and how economies of scale shape the patterns of international trade, seems to be unable to take the implications of his own models on board. In a famous article, he claimed that 'the essential things to teach students are still the insights of Hume and Ricardo', and that 'if we can teach undergrads to wince when they hear someone talk about competitiveness we will have done our nation a great service'.[9] He also described the notion of 'high-value' sectors as silly.

Why does a distinguished economist such as Paul Krugman deny the importance of competitiveness? It could be because of the frequently uncritical and ill-defined use of the term, but I think that Erik Reinert was right when he said:

> The strong reaction against the term seems to be there because
> the implicit assumptions behind competitiveness contradict
> the very core of neoclassical thought. In a world inhabited by
> 'representative firms' operating under perfect information and
> with no scale effects – the orthodox assumptions of neoclassical
> theory – competitiveness is meaningless. Thus Krugman's
> view of a 'high value sector' as silly. Competitiveness is caused
> by factors which neoclassical economists traditionally have
> assumed away.[10]

This denial by neoclassical economists of the importance of competitiveness has led them to give poor policy advice to politicians. Firstly, they have not drawn strong enough attention to the impact the increasing competitiveness of developing countries has had on the growth rate of developed countries; and, secondly, they have not sufficiently stressed the need for developed countries, if they are to continue to grow, to raise their rate of innovation, and increase the competitive advantage of both their new and old industries.

A ladder of economic development

If we want to know why some countries grow faster than others, it is also important to understand that there is a ladder of economic development, the rungs of which represent different types of industry. It is a ladder developing countries have to climb in order to be successful – no developing country tries to start growing by creating a pharmaceutical industry, and no country has ever achieved a high GDP per capita by having a cheap garment industry. It is also clear that if one wants to explain why the growth rates of developing countries differ, it is necessary to understand that this ladder of economic development exists, and why the firms in some countries are able to climb the rungs of the ladder faster than others.

The existence of such a ladder has been known empirically for a long time, and over the years there have been a number of attempts to categorise the industries that each rung of the ladder represents. For example, the Japanese Economic Planning Agency in 1974–75[11] produced the following diamond-shaped diagram (see Figure 2.1), showing how Japan's exports had in the past been split between four different types of industry with different requirements for success, and how they hoped Japan's exports would have changed by 1985.

American academic Michael Porter, in his 1990 book *The Competitive Advantage of Nations*, has also sought to specify which industries the different rungs of the ladder represent,[12] arguing that there

Figure 2.1 **Evolution of Japanese industrial structure**

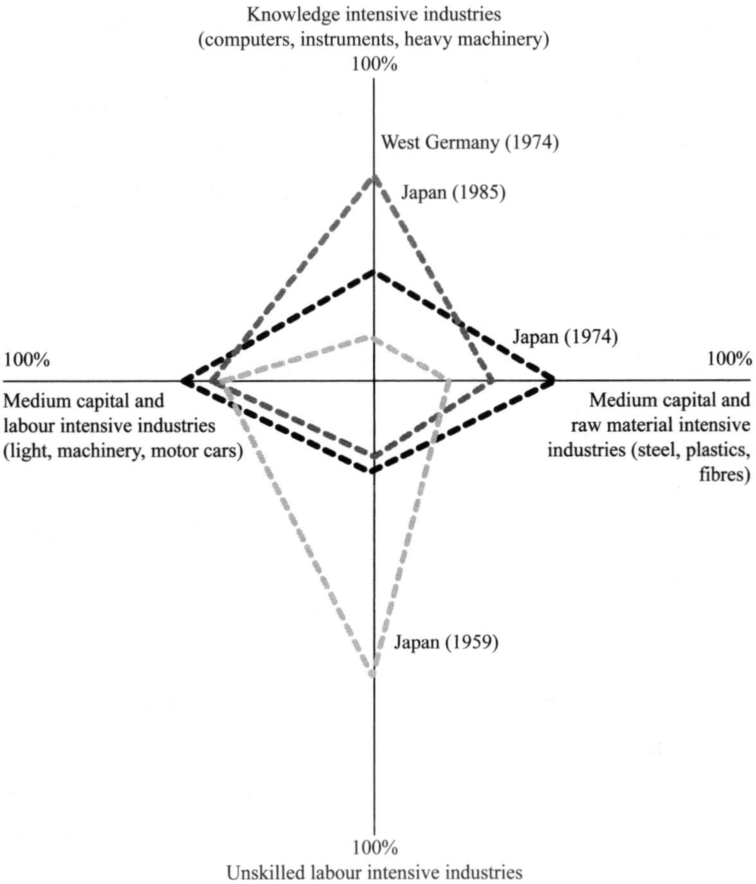

Knowledge intensive industries
(computers, instruments, heavy machinery)
100%

West Germany (1974)

Japan (1985)

Japan (1974)

100%

Medium capital and
labour intensive industries
(light, machinery, motor cars)

100%

Medium capital and
raw material intensive
industries (steel, plastics,
fibres)

Japan (1959)

100%
Unskilled labour intensive industries

Source: Japan Economic Survey, Economic Planning Agency, 1974–75; reproduced in Ira C. Magaziner and Thomas M. Hout, *Japanese Industrial Policy*, Policy Studies Institute, London, January 1980, p. 7

are four distinct stages of national competitive development: factor-driven, investment-driven, innovation-driven and wealth-driven; the last stage being one of economic decline.

In nations at the factor-driven stage, internationally successful firms draw their advantages almost solely from basic factors of production, whether they be natural resources, favourable growing conditions for certain crops, or an abundant and inexpensive semi-skilled labour pool. At the investment-driven stage, competitive advantage is based on the willingness and ability of firms to invest aggressively in modern, efficient and often large-scale facilities equipped with the best technology available in global markets.

At the third, innovation-driven stage, firms not only appropriate and improve technology and methods from other nations, but create them. A nation's indigenous firms push the state-of-the-art in product and process technology, marketing, and other aspects of competition; and thus price-sensitive, less sophisticated segments are gradually given away to firms from other nations. The driving force in the wealth-driven economy is the wealth that has already been achieved.

Finally, development economist Sanjaya Lall has divided the technological composition of developing countries' manufactured exports into five ascending categories: resource-intensive, labour-intensive, scale-intensive, differentiated, and science-based.[13] In broad terms, he calls the last three categories technologically advanced, and, additionally, the last two high-tech.

All these studies are describing the same underlying reality in slightly different terms. However, perhaps a more useful way of thinking about the rungs of the ladder of economic development is to see them as representing industries which require increasingly complex organisational and technological capabilities. On the bottom rungs are simple industries involved in, for example, the production of cheap clothes, the assembly of electronic components and the making of simple toys. On the top rungs are industries requiring complex organisational and technological capabilities that can only be acquired experientially, cumulatively and collectively; such as the aerospace, pharmaceutical and semiconductor industries.

In simple industries, such as the production of cheap clothes or the assembly of electronic components, it is difficult for any firm to gain a competitive advantage. Consequently, the value-added per capita of firms is low, and the wages and salaries they can pay is also low. On the other hand, in the case of firms in industries such as aerospace, pharmaceuticals and semiconductors, it is possible to build up significant competitive advantages, and, therefore, successful firms can achieve high levels of value-added per capita, and pay high wages and salaries.

This view is supported by some extremely interesting research by César Hidalgo and Ricardo Haussman on the role of knowledge and knowhow in economic development.[14] Before describing how they see this role, it is important to understand the differences between these two concepts. Knowledge involves understanding the relationships or linkages between entities, and being able, therefore, to predict the outcome of events without having to act them out. For example, we know that taking a drug will cure a person of a specific illness. Knowhow is different, as it involves the capacity to perform tacit actions; that is actions that cannot be explicitly described. For example, most of us know how to ride a bicycle even though consciously we don't know how we do it. Knowhow is the computational capacity that allows us to perform certain tacit actions, and can be accumulated at both the individual and collective levels.

Before knowledge and knowhow can be used to make new products and services, they have to be embodied in individuals and organisations. The knowledge and knowhow that a single individual can acquire is limited, as an individual can only absorb so much information. Therefore, the knowledge and knowhow to make complex products and services have to be embodied in a number of different individuals and co-ordinated by a firm's organisation.

The knowledge and knowhow of individuals may also be limited because experiential and social learning is involved, and the individuals in an organisation may not have had access to such learning. Knowledge and knowhow are experiential because we accumulate both mostly through practice, such as on-the-job experience. They are social because people learn from other people; children from their parents and workers from their co-workers. It is difficult to be a doctor without ever having worked in a hospital, and it is difficult to be a research scientist without ever having worked in a research laboratory.

This point about the difficulty of accumulating the knowledge and knowhow to make products and services is important for two reasons. Firstly, neoclassical economists tend to assume that demand and incentives are enough to stimulate the production of a product or service anywhere in the world, and if they don't it must be because the system of allocating resources is not working efficiently. However, while incentives and demand may be enough to motivate intermediaries and traders, the people who produce goods and services also need to know how to make them.

Secondly, if the ability to accumulate the knowledge and knowhow to make products and services is difficult, it is likely that countries will have accumulated varying levels of knowledge and knowhow depending on their economic history, and therefore the complexity of the products and services they can produce will vary.

To show that a ladder of economic development exists, however, we need also to be able to show that the varying capacity of countries to produce complex products and services correlates with their GDP per capita, and this the research of Hidalgo and Haussman very cleverly does.[15]

It is not easy to study the geographical distribution of knowledge and knowhow because knowledge and knowhow are difficult to see. Hidalgo and Haussman deal with this problem by looking at the geographic distribution of industries rather than the distribution of knowledge and knowhow. They do this on the grounds that the geographic distribution of industries can be seen as an expression of the knowledge and knowhow embodied in the networks of people and firms present in different locations. As they explain it, looking at industries instead of knowledge and knowhow is similar to what biologists do when looking at phenotypes (the physical and functional characteristics of an organism) as expressions of genotypes (the information embodied in an organism's DNA). And it enabled them, they argue, to determine what knowledge and knowhow was available in different locations. With this assumption in place, they set out to create an objective, data-driven measure of 'economic complexity'.

Taking a huge number of datapoints for products produced in different countries of the world (an 'industry-location matrix'), Hidalgo and Haussman theorised that products requiring a large input of knowledge and knowhow would tend to be exported from only a few countries. Some of the products exported by a large number of countries include simple garments, such as underwear, shirts and pants; while some of the products exported by a relatively few countries include optical instruments, aircraft and medical imaging devices. Such a simple scan suggests that industries requiring less knowledge and knowhow are present in more places, as one might expect.

However, the ubiquity of an industry does not give us a foolproof measure of the knowledge and knowhow required to make it, as among the products only exported by a few countries are mineral resources such as uranium ore. We can, however, distinguish between the rarity of uranium ore and the complexity of medical devices by looking at the diversity of products exported by countries exporting medical devices, which is greater than in countries exporting uranium ore.

A good measure of a high-complexity economy, then, is one that (a) produces a wide variety of goods; but (b) also produces a lot of goods that are not produced in many other places. Working from their industry-location matrices, Hidalgo and Haussman produced a set of indices of economic complexity based on the measurement of these two factors.

If the GDP per capita of countries in 1985 is plotted against this measure of the economic complexity of products as in Figure 2.2 overleaf, a good correlation is found. What makes such a measure of economic complexity most interesting, though, is its ability to explain changes in GDP per capital over long periods of time.

There are three possible positions that a country can occupy on Figure 2.3 (see page 53). Countries above the line have a GDP per capita higher than would be expected from the economic complexity of their exports. Countries below the line are countries with a GDP per capita lower than would be expected from the complexity of their

Figure 2.2 **Economic complexity versus GDP per capita in 1985**

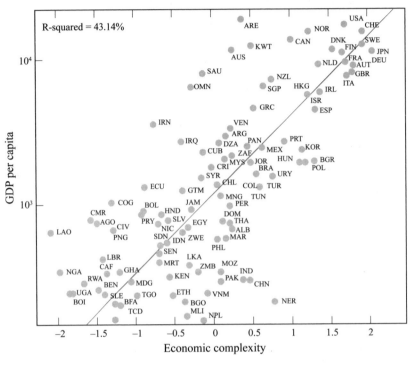

Source: César Hidalgo, *Why Information Grows*, Allen Lane, London, 2015, p. 159

exports. Finally, countries on the line are countries with a GDP per capita which is exactly what one would expect on the basis of the economic complexity of their exports.

If one then looks at how these gaps evolve over time, it can be seen that countries below the line, such as India and China, tend to grow faster than those on the line or above. This means that we can use the economic complexity of a country's exports to predict its increase in GDP per capita.

It is important to realise, however, that one cannot use the economic complexity of a country's exports over a period of less than five years to predict its economic growth. This is because such growth tends to be largely determined by periods of crisis, changes in

Figure 2.3 **Growth predicted from mismatch between economic complexity and GDP per capita in 1985**

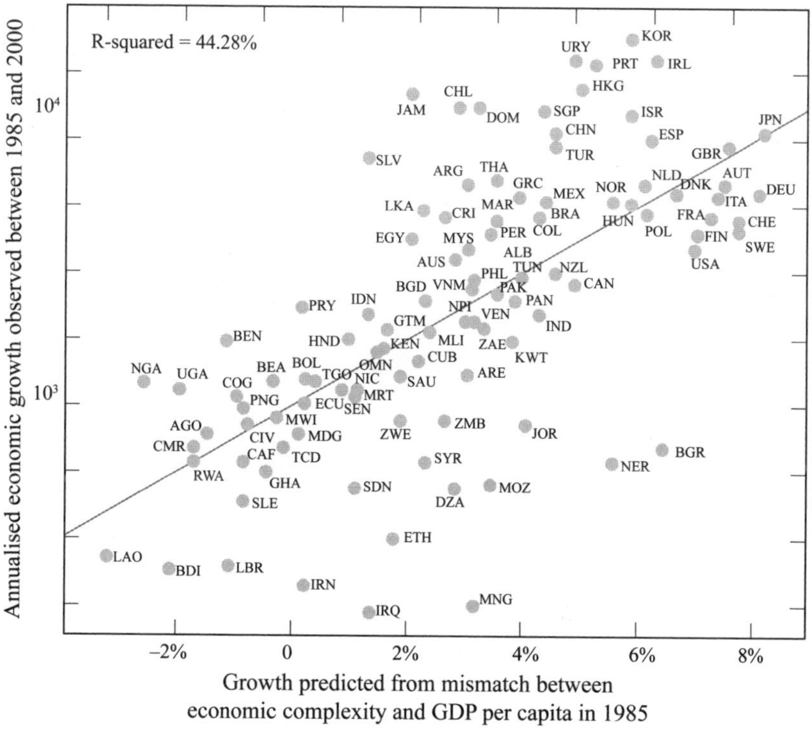

Source: César Hidalgo, *Why Information Grows*, Allen Lane, London, 2015, p. 160

commodity prices, and to some extent by variations in exchange rates. But over periods of ten to fifteen years the economic complexity of a country's exports is a good measure of its capacity to increase its GDP per capita.

As the firms in a country take advantage of the windows of opportunity for innovation to which they have access, they increase their value-added per capita, and the wages and salaries they pay their employees. And this in turn opens up a window of opportunity for countries with lower wages to exploit, provided they can develop the capability to do so. The new opportunity for these firms becomes

Figure 2.4 **The 'flying geese' model: sequential structural transformation in East Asia**

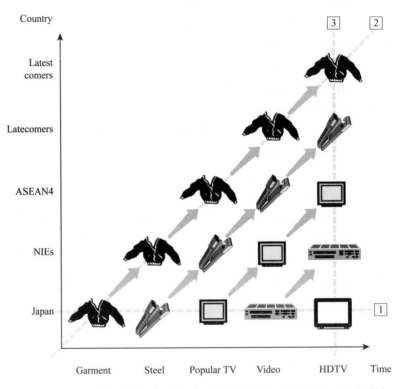

Source: www.grips.ac.jp/module/prsp/FGeese.htm. Reproduced in Erik S. Reinert, *How Rich Countries Got Rich… and Why Poor Countries Stay Poor*, Constable and Robinson, London, 2007, p. 141

a 'capability-destroying' challenge to the incumbents, unless the incumbents' capabilities allow them to introduce and exploit new opportunities of their own.

This is the dynamic behind the technological upgrading of countries in sequence, which was named the 'flying geese model' by the Japanese economist Kaname Akamatsu in the 1930s (see Figure 2.4). Saburo Okita, another Japanese economist and later Minister of Foreign Affairs in the 1980s, adopted the 'flying geese model' and argued that a poor country is able to upgrade its technology by jumping from one product to another with increasing knowledge content.[16]

In the case of cheap garments, the first flying goose was Japan's firms, which boosted their value-added and increased the standard of living of Japan to such an extent that production was taken over by South Korean firms, while Japanese firms moved into the more complex manufacturing of TV sets. South Korean firms then increased their labour costs, and cheap garments were for a while produced in Taiwan, until the same thing happened there and the production of cheap textiles moved to Thailand and Malaysia, and then finally to Vietnam. In this way, a whole group of countries used garment production to upgrade their production capabilities and standard of living.

In order to understand the ability of the firms and nations to innovate and grow, it is also necessary to understand the linkages between the capabilities of different industries. Beneath the surface of every product there are not just physical components, but a deeper set of hidden technological and organisational capabilities that enabled it to be created and produced. Today, for example, electronics account for about one-third of materials and labour involved in producing an automobile.

These capabilities are also not static. Instead, they evolve, and new ones are developed, which changes the possibilities of what a product can do. It is a mistake, therefore, to view innovation in any one industry in isolation from what is happening in other sectors. Such innovations do not take place in a vacuum. For example, innovation in steam locomotives depended on scientific insights from the field of thermodynamics, and advances in precision machine-tools, which came from the textile machinery industry. And advances in machine tools depended on major improvements in the production of high-strength steel to produce cutting tools that would not dull quickly.

The development of the personal computer also depended on advances in a number of areas, such as digital logic, semiconductor memories, software and high-precision manufacturing for disk drives, and displays. These interdependencies mean that the success of a particular sector in terms of its ability to innovate and grow is likely to be strongly shaped by its access to and connection with other sectors. This can be seen very clearly in Silicon Valley, which contains an array of the capabilities necessary for developing computer hardware and software, and accounts for the fact that the histories of many firms in Silicon Valley are interwoven. Steve Jobs worked at Atari, and Steve Wozniak worked at HP, before starting Apple. Also, Steve Jobs is famous for taking the concepts of the graphical user-interface and object-oriented programming from Xerox's Palo Alto Research Center.

This point about the capabilities underlying the products of a particular industry is very important when thinking about whether a new industry entering a country will be successful. A good mental image to use in such cases, as César Hidalgo has suggested, is a jigsaw puzzle. Bringing a complex industry into a new country is, according to him, like trying to move a jigsaw puzzle from one table to another. The more pieces are in the puzzle, the more likely it is to fall apart as one tries to move it. It is also easier, he points out, to move such a jigsaw puzzle if one only has to move a few pieces to another table, on which the remaining pieces of the same puzzle have already been assembled.

This analogy rightly suggests that the emergence of an industry is more likely to be successful in places which have already accumulated much of the required knowledge and knowhow. Business schools and regional development experts know this effect as 'diversification toward related varieties', which, as Hidalgo points out, is technical-speak for the idea 'that places producing curtains are pre-adapted to produce tablecloths but not expresso machines'.[17]

César Hidalgo also argues that the extent to which industries make use of similar capabilities can be measured using the concept of the product space. At the global level, it is possible to construct measures of product similarity by looking at products that are likely to be exported by the same countries. The assumption here is that if countries regularly export a pair of products, it reveals information about the similar capabilities the products make use of. In other words, if making shirts is similar to making blouses, then countries that export shirts will be more likely to export blouses.

In the case of domestic economies where data on the occupations employed by an industry are available, we can also connect industries that tend to hire a similar set of occupations. So we can say that mangoes are similar to bananas but not motorcycles, because mango-producing firms tend to hire workers in the same categories as banana-producing firms, while motorcycle manufacturers do not.

This information about the linkages between industries, together with a knowledge of the ladder of economic development, should give the policy-maker an understanding of the processes determining a country's rate of economic growth, and should enable him or her more easily to formulate policies to increase it.

The race to the top

There are those who see globalisation only in terms of price competition, and who, therefore, believe that the emergence of developing countries will inevitably result in a fall in wages, as well as lower social welfare and environmental standards, in developed countries. They fear that all countries will be involved in a 'race to the bottom'; with firms competing by seeking ever cheaper labour, land and capital, and countries competing by deregulating and shrinking social benefits. But any strategy for a developed country based on competing in low wages will end in a downward spiral, with each year bringing a new competitor. If the competitor today is the coast of China, tomorrow it will be the interior of China, Vietnam or India.

Fortunately, the reality of international competition is very different. While we live in a very competitive world, and countries need to understand that their standard of living largely depends on the ability of their firms to create products and services which have a competitive advantage in world markets, it is also important to understand that countries are not involved in a zero-sum game.

With a narrow view of national competitive advantage involving only factor costs and economies of scale, it is very easy for policy debates to degenerate into an 'us versus them' conflict. However, as I hope I have shown, a broader set of forces is at work, and if developed countries can rapidly innovate and create new high value-added products and services while ceding lower value-added products and services to developing countries, then all countries can increase their national standards of living. If the pie is bigger everyone can have a larger slice, and the 'race to the top' enables a country to climb out of a zero-sum confrontation with other countries at a similar stage of development.

I believe a strong case can be made for allowing developing countries to use tariffs to protect 'infant industries', but there can be no such case for developed countries using protectionism to help declining industries. Such protectionism only blunts incentives to reallocate resources into new products and firms that are competitive, and as a result slows down economic growth.

It is, therefore, important that developed countries see themselves as competing with developing countries in a 'race to the top' and not in a 'race to the bottom'. In a 'race to the bottom', cheap labour and a 'favourable' exchange rate may be seen as the best way to achieve competitiveness. By contrast, in a 'race to the top', the goal for firms is to develop products and services that command premium prices in international markets and can, therefore, support high wages. In this process of upgrading, neoclassical economists believe it is best if governments play no role, but history teaches us that governments can play a constructive role if they understand that their job is to help firms develop their capabilities, rather than to direct their strategies.

Developed countries should not think, however, that they have plenty of time to upgrade their economies. Countries such as South Korea and Taiwan, as we shall see in Chapter 6, have long ago moved up from the lower rungs of the economic ladder and are now often competing head-to-head with firms in developed countries, while many other countries are now following rapidly behind them.

3

Sectoral systems of innovation

The growth of high value-added per capita industries is the key to economic development, and the creation of competitive advantage by innovation is the way firms in an industry grow. If, therefore, we want an explanation of why the growth of the cotton industry played such a large role in the economic growth rate of Britain during the Industrial Revolution, or why the car industry played a similar role in Japan after the Second World War, we need to better understand the dynamics of sectoral systems of innovation. For present purposes, a sector is a set of activities that are unified by some related product group for a given or emerging demand, and that share a technology.

As we have seen, there are four elements which are important in understanding the dynamics of a sectoral system of innovation. They are the demand for its products or services; its activity-specific technology; the capability which firms need to have to apply the activity-specific technology; and the institutions of the country where the firm is located. It is only when these four elements are present and aligned that they produce the capability/market-opportunity dynamic which creates innovation and growth in an economy.

This is the reason why, when we look at the growth rate of an economy at a given point in time, we find that some sectors are growing, some are declining, and some are flat-lining. It is also the reason why an economy's rate of growth depends on the number of sectors which come into each category, and whether they are ones with a high value-added per capita or a low value-added per capita.

Figure 3.1   **Technological opportunities in 51 industrial sectors of the US economy, 1899–1937**

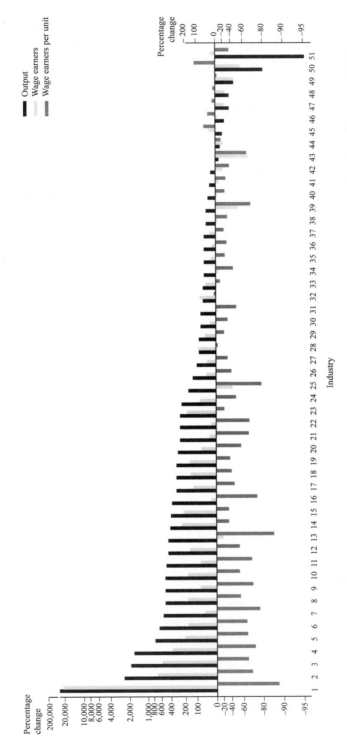

Source: Jan Fagerberg, Bart Verspagen and Nick von Tunzelmann (eds), *The Dynamics of Technology, Trade and Growth*, Edward Elgar Publishing, Cheltenham, 1994, pp. 180 and 181. Reproduced with the permission of the Licensor through PLS clear

Figure 3.1 reflects the distribution of technological opportunities in fifty-one industrial sectors of the US economy over the period 1899–1937. The growth in value-added per capita varies enormously, although we can assume that the same capital, skills and institutional variables were present over the whole spectrum of activity. And we can be absolutely certain that the US would not have taken world economic leadership if it had only been active in industries 27–51.[1]

This sector-specific aspect of economic growth is not one that neoclassical economic growth theory can explain, whereas the dynamic capability theory of economic growth can. If we want, therefore, to understand why at a given point in time a sector is growing, declining or flat-lining, we need to understand the state of the four elements within it, and whether they are aligned at that time or not. To do this, we need to know more about the nature of these four elements.

The demand of a sector

The demand of a sector is the demand customers have for a product or service in that sector. This demand can be latent or well known, and can be for a product or service that has better quality or greater functionality, or for a lower-cost version of an already existing product or service.

In Chapter 5, I will look at three countries where at a given point in time a sector gained a competitive advantage, forged ahead, and had a major impact on its country's economic growth rate. In all cases, a latent demand recognised by entrepreneurs was a critical element in the growth of the new industry. In Great Britain at the end of the eighteenth century it was the latent demand for cheap cotton clothing; in nineteenth century Germany it was the latent demand for cheap dyes; while in the United States at the beginning of the twentieth century it was the latent demand for a cheap and reliable motor car, and at the beginning of the twenty-first century the latent demand for easy access to cheap personal-computing power.

It has also been convincingly argued by Michael Porter that nations gain competitive advantage in industries or industry segments where home demand gives local firms a clearer or earlier picture of buyer needs than foreign rivals can have.[2] For example, in electrical transmission equipment, Sweden is a leader in high-voltage distribution (HVDC) equipment, used for transporting high voltage over long distances. This reflects a high relative demand in this segment compared with other countries, due to the remoteness of Sweden's energy-intensive steel and paper industries, as well as the fact that sources of electric power in Sweden are far removed from its southern population centres.

It might be thought that home demand would be made less significant by the globalisation of competition, but this has not been the case, with the home market having a disproportionate impact on a firm's ability to perceive and interpret buyer needs for a number of reasons. Firms are better able to see and understand, as well as act on, buyer needs in their home market, and tend to have greater confidence in doing so.

Understanding customer needs requires access to buyers, open communication between the buyers and a firm's top technical and managerial personnel, and an intuitive grasp of what buyers want. This is difficult to achieve with home buyers, but even more so with foreign buyers due to the distance from headquarters, and because the firm is not truly an insider with full acceptance and access. This is why product-development teams, as well as the managers who approve new products, are usually based in the home market.

Finally, as we shall see in more detail in Chapter 10, governments can upgrade the quality of demand their firms face. They have two valuable levers for doing this if they wish to do so. Firstly, they can use the government's purchases of goods and services to stimulate innovation; and, secondly, they can seek to raise the quality of products through the regulation of product standards and the processes by which they are made, such as those governing product performance, product safety, environmental impact and energy efficiency. Simply by designating a certain level of quality as 'export grade', the authorities in New Zealand helped its dairy industry achieve a dominant market share in Asian milk products.

Activity-specific technology

The specific pattern of innovative activity within a sector is largely determined by four dimensions of its underlying technology. These four dimensions are the level of opportunities; the appropriability of the innovations; the degree of cumulativeness of the knowledge and technology; and the nature of the sector's knowledge and skill-sets.

The level of opportunity produced by a technology is a key dimension, as it increases the probability of success for a given amount of resources. The appropriability of innovations relates to the possibility of protecting innovation from imitation and capturing profits from innovative activities. High appropriability reflects the existence of means, such as patents, to protect innovations from imitation, while low appropriability denotes an economic situation where there are widespread knowledge spillovers. The cumulativeness of knowledge is a measure of the degree to which new knowledge builds upon current knowledge. Finally, the nature of a sector's knowledge and technology determines the extent to which knowledge and skill-sets are generic to most firms in that sector, or whether they are firm specific.

The more the knowledge and skills of a sector are firm specific, the more likely it is that firms will use informal means of knowledge transmission, such as 'face-to-face' talks, personal teaching and training, mobility of personnel, and even acquisition of entire groups of people. Such means of knowledge transmission are, of course, extremely sensitive to the distance between agents. On the other hand, the more the knowledge and skills of a sector are generic, the more useful are formal means of knowledge communication, such as publications, licenses, patents and so on. In these circumstances, geographical proximity is unlikely to play such a crucial role in facilitating the transmission of knowledge and skills across agents. These differences in the dimensions of the underlying knowledge and technology of a sector are important, as they determine to a large extent whether the innovative activities of a sector follow a Schumpeter Mark I pattern, or a Schumpeter Mark II pattern.

A Schumpeter Mark I pattern of innovative activities is characterised by 'creative destruction', with technological ease-of-entry and a major innovative role played by entrepreneurs and new firms. On the other hand, a Schumpeter Mark II pattern of innovative activities is characterised by 'creative accumulation', as well as the presence of large established firms and barriers to entry for new innovators. Thus, high technological opportunities, high appropriability and low cumulativeness at the firm-level lead to a Schumpeter Mark I pattern, while low technological opportunities, low appropriability and high cumulativeness at the firm-level lead to a Schumpeter Mark II pattern.

These two sectoral systems of innovation are also typical of 'radically innovative' sectors, such as biotechnology and packaged software, and 'incrementally innovative' sectors such as machine tools, as summarised in Table 3.1 below.[3]

Table 3.1 **Technology regimes for radical and incremental innovation in sectoral systems**

	Radically innovative sectoral systems (e.g. discovery-based biotechnology or packaged software)	*Incrementally innovative sectoral systems (e.g. machine tools)*
Appropriability regime	High	Low
Level of technological cumulativeness	Low	High
Generic vs. firm-specific knowledge and skills	Generic knowledge	Firm-specific knowledge

In radically innovative sectors, such as the therapeutic discovery segment of biotechnology or packaged software, we typically find relatively tight appropriability regimes, meaning that their intellectual property protection is strong. We also find a lower level of technological cumulativeness, and that the knowledge and skill-sets of such sectors are generic; involving in the case of biotechnology relatively standard laboratory methods, and in the case of packaged software generic programming languages. Low technological cumulativeness is likely to encourage the entry of many firms, creating races between several of them to be the first to innovate and capture key intellectual property. Performance incentives, such as the widespread granting of shares or share options within a firm, are commonly used to create high-powered organisational environments.

On the other hand, in incrementally innovative sectors such as machine tools, we typically find relatively loose appropriability regimes, high levels of technological cumulativeness, and firm-specific skill-sets. The challenge for firms in these sectors is to maintain their lead in technological cumulativeness over other companies.

As organisational theorist David Teece has pointed out, when appropriability regimes are relatively weak, firms, in order to capture value from innovations, develop complementary assets that are specific to the firm and tied to the generic assets.[4] This often involves creating co-specialised assets used to customise products for particular clients, as often occurs in the machine tool industry, or strategies focused on marketing and distribution.

Firms developing co-specialised assets tend to create more complex organisational structures than firms innovating in areas where there are high appropriability regimes. The competitiveness of a firm may, therefore, be its ability to develop an organisational culture that enables different types of professional employees to work well together in cross-functional teams. From the viewpoint of employees, this is likely to involve them acquiring firm-specific and often tacit knowledge that it is difficult to then sell on the open labour market. This is likely to generate employee concerns that they will be exploited once they have made firm-specific knowledge investments and means that managers have to find a way of assuring them that this will not be the case.

The entrepreneur and firm capabilities

The third element of the capability/market-opportunity dynamic we need to understand when trying to explain the growth rates of individual sectors in an economy is the role of the entrepreneur and a firm's capabilities. The firm in neoclassical economic theory is a passive, nebulous organisation which has no place in it for the entrepreneur. Neoclassical economists see the central economic problem as that of meeting preferences as well as is possible given the available resources and prevailing technologies and institutions, and therefore do not see firm differences as an important variable affecting a nation's economic performance. Instead, they view the firm as a legal entity with a known set of feasible production plans, from which the manager has no difficulty in choosing the course of action that is best for the firm given its objective of maximising its profits. Firms can, therefore, be treated as 'black boxes', and what goes on in them can be ignored.

This view of the firm is unrealistic and misleading in two ways. Firstly, when entrepreneurs make decisions about innovations, they are faced not with a situation where there are risks and a set of known probabilities, but a world of uncertainty where they don't know what will happen, and in some cases have only a limited ability to describe the things that might happen. It is this uncertainty that gives rise to the profit opportunities that are the dynamic of the capitalist economy, and it is the ability of entrepreneurs to operate effectively in such an environment that defines their role, as opposed to that of the manager.

Secondly, as we have already seen, neoclassical growth theory does not assign any role to the capabilities of a firm, despite it being the capabilities of a firm that enable it to take advantage of the opportunities that arise. If we look at the performance of an individual firm, it clearly depends very heavily on its capabilities. It is difficult, for example, when studying the computer industry to ignore the different capabilities of Apple and IBM; or the different capabilities of General Motors and Toyota when examining the car industry.

It is very surprising that neoclassical economists have such a poor understanding of firm performance when almost all economists would agree that the business enterprise is the enabler and nexus of innovation in a private enterprise economy, and that the capability of firms to innovate and learn is of more importance in a private economy than static market efficiency. This view of neoclassical economists is also, I believe, one of the main reasons why neoclassical growth theory has proved to have so little value in explaining the different growth rates of countries, and why there has been so little effective governance reform of firms by policy-makers.

However, as we have seen in Chapter 2, the dynamic capability theory of economic growth assigns an important role to firms, and is based on a belief that the rate at which a country's economy grows depends on whether its firms have the capabilities to exploit the 'windows of opportunity' they see for innovation and technical change in their industries; as well as whether, over time, they are able to enhance their technological and organisational capabilities in order to climb the ladder of economic development, and move into higher value-added industries and industrial segments.

The business enterprise and entrepreneurship have been extensively studied, but so far research in these fields has had relatively little impact on economic analysis. But the 'dynamic capabilities' theory of the firm, which is drawn from the field of strategic management and has largely been developed and championed by David Teece,[5] can, I believe, provide critical insights into how firms develop capabilities in order to take advantage of market opportunities, and so create competitive advantages and grow.

According to the dynamic capabilities theory of the firm, an important analytical distinction must be made between ordinary and dynamic capabilities. Ordinary capabilities involve the performance of operational, administrative and governance-related functions necessary for the execution of current plans (doing things right). Dynamic capabilities, on the other hand, are higher-level activities which link the technological and organisational capabilities of a firm to a product or service demand, and which also develop new technological and organisational capabilities (doing the right things).

Dynamic capabilities are essentially entrepreneurial ones and can be broken down into three groups. First, the identification and assessment of opportunities to fulfil product or service demands by current or new technological and organisational capabilities; second, the development of new technological and organisational capabilities; and, third, the continuous renewal and transformation of the firm.

The theory of the dynamic capabilities of the firm has, therefore, put the entrepreneur back into the theory of the firm. This is a highly desirable development if governments are to understand and adopt policies based on how firms compete in a world of dynamic and imperfect competition, in which market disruption occurs regularly, thereby creating opportunities and threats to which businesses have to respond with entrepreneurial strategies.

The way the entrepreneur is seen is also very much in line with the way Schumpeter saw entrepreneurs. He saw them as being very different from managers, as he made clear in *The Theory of Economic Development*, when he said: 'Carrying out a new plan and acting according to a customary one are things as different as making a road and walking along it.'[6]

The dynamic capabilities model of the firm is also very different from the neoclassical model. As we saw in Chapter 1, neoclassical economics is the study of the allocation of scarce resources among unlimited wants, with the price system seen as the means of allocating resources efficiently, with the strongest wants indicated by the highest willingness to pay. In addition, neoclassical economics ignores the fact that much of the allocation of resources in an economy takes place inside firms under the direction of managers, and involves unpriced resources. Also, managers can change their resource base, diversify their activities, or divest assets. The relationship between managerial actions and the firm should, therefore, be seen in the same light as the relationship between prices and the market, in that they function to achieve co-ordination, resource allocation and adjustment.

Neoclassical economics also leaves out of its model of economic growth the design of new products and services, as well as the development of new production methods. As David Teece has pointed out:

> The response of most economists since at least Adam Smith, is to gloss over the fact that much organising must be undertaken by individuals before there are goods and services to exchange in markets. In Smith's famous pin-making example he offers no explanations of how the manufactured pin got invented and how the integration and co-ordination of non-traded manufactured pin sections (e.g. the wire, the head) took place inside the workshop in order to realise the fruits of specialisation. Smith can be forgiven because, apart from the military and the church, there were no large organisations to observe, and the Industrial Revolution was in its infancy. Modern economists cannot be so readily excused.[7]

For all these reasons, the neoclassical theory of economic growth is a very deficient one, and one that leads politicians and policy-makers to make poor policy decisions, which result in a lower rate of economic growth in their countries.

The dynamic capability theory of the firm also makes it clear that if firms are to be successful over a long period of time, their executives should be incentivised to build up and renew the technological and organisational capabilities of their firms, rather than focusing solely on short-term financial goals. This is, however, not the case in many firms today in the US and the UK, due to the corporate governance and executive remuneration systems that have been adopted, and the growth in the market for corporate control.

In the middle of the twentieth century, a group of economists came to hold the view that managers often spend shareholders' resources in ways that benefit themselves rather than the shareholders; a view that in the economics and finance literature came to be formalised as 'agency theory'. This led to changes in the composition of corporate boards, with a greater emphasis on monitoring principal/agent problems and accounting issues, and less on monitoring and assessing the long-term strategy of the firm. It also led to shareholder-value remuneration systems for top executives that tied their remuneration to the value of the firm's shares, and to an increase in the number of corporate takeovers.

This has had a disastrous impact on the building and renewal of capabilities by American companies, as has been shown by William Lazonick in a famous 2014 *Harvard Business Review* article entitled 'Profits Without Prosperity'.[8] In this, he argued that from the end of the Second World War until the late 1970s, a retain-and-reinvest approach to resource allocation prevailed at major US corporations. They retained earnings and reinvested them in increasing their capabilities.

A turning point came with the wave of hostile takeovers that swept the country in the 1980s. Corporate raiders often claimed, in line with agency theory, that the lazy leaders of targeted companies were failing to maximise returns to shareholders. This criticism prompted firms' boards of directors to try to align the interests of management and shareholders by making stock-based pay a much bigger element of executive compensation. This remuneration policy led, however, to a downsize-and-distribute regime of reducing costs and distributing the freed-up cash to shareholders through dividends and share buy-backs. The open-market share buy-backs not only lifted share prices, even if only temporarily, but also enabled firms to hit quarterly earnings per share (EPS) targets in executives' remuneration schemes.

The scale of these buy-backs has been enormous. If, as William Lazonick has shown, one takes the 449 companies in the S&P 500 index that were publicly listed from 2003 through 2012, during that period these companies used 54 per cent of their earnings (a total of

$2.4 trillion) to buy back their own stock. Dividends absorbed an additional 37 per cent of their earnings, leaving very little for investment in productive capabilities.

A similar situation has developed in the UK, and in both countries there is a need to reform what has become a very dysfunctional relationship between corporate boards and financial institutions. This has arisen because the short-term investment strategies of many investment managers mean they have no interest in exercising their rights as shareholders, and as a result we have 'capitalism without owners'. Given that a defining characteristic of capitalism is that the productive assets of a country are held by individuals who have a direct interest in making certain they are used efficiently over the long term, this is a major flaw.

The continuing failure of investment managers to get involved in the governance of the companies in which they invest has meant that the non-executive directors of these companies have effectively been appointed by management. The non-executive directors have not, therefore, been prepared to stand up to management; failing to put pressure on them to create and maintain competitive advantage by investing in product and process innovation as the only long-term source of shareholder value.

A possible way forward is the use of nomination committees, as happens in Sweden. Nomination committees are the body responsible for finding the right people to serve on boards, though Swedish nomination committees operate in a very different way to those in the UK. In the UK, the nomination committee is a sub-committee of the board, is made up of board members, and is usually chaired by the Chair of the Board. Candidates for the Board are proposed by the nomination committee to the Annual General Meeting, and in the normal course of events elected.

In Sweden, on the other hand, the nomination committee is a servant of the AGM. It is not made up of board members, but mainly of four or five of the largest company share-owners. It gets its mandate from the shareholders at the AGM, recommending to them who should join the board; the structure and amount of remuneration of each outside director; and procedural issues for the appointment of the following year's nomination committee. The remuneration of executive management is handled separately by the Board.

Today, the only way investment managers in the UK can influence boards strategically, or restrain them from paying themselves disproportionate rewards, is by reactive and ad hoc co-ordination with other shareholders. A UK version of the Swedish nomination committee would give them a low-cost and proactive way of exerting influence.

If, however, the US and UK governments do not take action to reform the current corporate governance institutions of their countries, it is likely there will be a decline in the capabilities of companies in both countries to create new competitive advantages, with an inevitable impact on the living standards of their citizens.

Institutions

The fourth element of the capability/market-opportunity dynamic affecting the success or failure of firms in a sector, are the institutions of the country where their key operations are located. Institutions include laws, values, standards and qualifications that shape the cognition and action of agents, and the interactions among them. Many institutions are national, such as the patent system, while others are specific to sectoral systems, such as sectoral labour markets or sector-specific financial institutions. Other examples of sectoral institutions include disclosure agreements and standards in software, and regulation in pharmaceuticals.

National institutions – such as the patent system, property rights or antitrust regulations – may have major effects on sectoral systems, with these effects differing from sector to sector. Equally, the same institution may take on different features in different countries, and in this way affect sectors in divergent ways across national systems. The well-known difference between the 'first-to-invent' and the 'first-to-file' rules in the patent systems of the United States and Japan has had major consequences on the behaviour of firms in the two countries.

As we have seen, a key idea behind research on sectoral systems of innovation is that sectors differ widely in their constellations of technological and market dynamics, and that sectors can be divided into 'radically innovative' sectors (such as biotechnology and packaged software), and 'incrementally innovative' sectors (such as machine tools) (see Table 3.1 on page 64). It is further argued that the firm-level capabilities required to be successful in these ideal typical sectors differ significantly.

The Varieties of Capitalism school of thought has taken this line of thought one stage further, arguing that national institutions affect the ability of firms to compete in 'radically innovative' and 'incrementally innovative' regimes. To make this argument they divide the national institutions of countries into two types: Anglo-Saxon or 'liberal market economies', and Germanic/Scandinavian 'co-ordinated market economies'.

The UK is a good example of a liberal market economy, while Germany is a good example of a co-ordinated market economy. The difference between the two institutional frameworks is summarised in Table 3.2 overleaf.[9]

Toyota Motor Company

In the next three chapters I will look at how the concept of a 'capability/market-opportunity dynamic' can be used to explain the performance of different sectors in countries forging ahead, catching up and falling behind. But before doing so, I think it is useful to validate the concept by looking at two case studies of the performance of companies. The first of these looks at the successful building of a distinctive production capability by the Toyota Motor Company in the period after the Second World War; while the second looks at the way leadership of the global shipbuilding industry has moved over time from one country to another.

Table 3.2 **Institutional framework architectures in Germany and the United Kingdom**

	Germany	United Kingdom
Labour law	Regulative (co-ordinated system of wage bargaining; competition clauses enforced); bias toward long-term employee careers in companies	Liberal (decentralised wage bargaining; competition clauses struck down by courts); few barriers to employee turnover
Company law	Stakeholder system (two-tier board system plus co-determinational rights for employees)	Shareholder system (minimal legal constraints on company organisation)
Skill formation	Organised apprenticeship system with substantial involvement from industry; close links between industry and technical universities in designing curriculum and research	No systematised apprenticeship system for vocational skills; links between most universities and firms almost exclusively limited to R&D activities and R&D personnel
Financial system	Primarily bank-based with close links to stakeholder system of corporate governance; no hostile market for corporate control	Primarily capital market system, closely linked to market for corporate control and financial ownership and control of firms
	Good at incremental innovation	Good at radical innovation

Peter Hall and David Soskice, in their book *Varieties of Capitalism*, also provide compelling evidence to support this view.[10]

Henry Ford's system of mass-production, together with market-ing and management techniques first introduced by Alfred Sloan at General Motors, drove the auto industry forward for more than half a century, and was eventually adopted in almost every industrial activity in North America and Europe. It only began to change when the Japanese developed a new way of making cars called 'lean manufacturing'.[11]

This new method originated at the Toyota Motor Company, which was founded in 1937. The company had barely gone beyond building a few prototype cars with craft methods when the Second World War broke out and auto production ended. After the war, Toyota was determined to go into full-scale car and commercial truck manufacturing. But the company faced many problems. The domestic market, while tiny, demanded a wide range of vehicles, including luxury cars for government officials, large trucks to carry goods to market, and small trucks for Japan's crowded cities. The demand for cheaper and better-quality Japanese automobiles was latent, requiring Toyota to innovate in order to realise it.

In addition, the native Japanese work force was no longer willing to be treated as a variable cost or as interchangeable parts, and new labour laws introduced by the American occupation had greatly strengthened the position of workers negotiating more favourable conditions of employment. Also, the outside world was full of large motor-vehicle producers anxious to set up operations in Japan, and ready to defend their established markets against Japanese exports. Taiichi Ohno, the production genius of Toyota, realised he needed a new approach, and started to put together the distinctive set of capabilities that came to be known as the Toyota Production System, or 'lean manufacturing'.

Under Ford's system of mass-production, assembly-line workers performed one or two simple tasks repetitively. Special repairmen repaired tools, special inspectors checked quality, and defective work once discovered was rectified in a rework area after the end of the line. The foreman did not perform assembly tasks himself but made certain the line workers followed orders. In contrast, Ohno grouped workers into teams with a team leader rather than a foreman, gave the teams a set of assembly steps, and told them to work together on how best to perform the necessary operations. The team leader would do assembly tasks and fill in for any absent worker, as well as co-ordinate the team. Ohno also gave the team the job of cleaning their area of the assembly line, minor tool repair, and quality checking. Finally, he set aside time periodically for the team to collectively suggest ways of improving the process. This system came in the West to be known as 'quality circles'.

When it came to rework, Ohno reasoned that the mass-production practice of workers passing on errors to keep the line running caused errors to multiply endlessly. He therefore placed a cord above every work station, giving workers rather than the senior line manager the responsibility of stopping the line immediately if a problem arose that they couldn't fix. The whole team would then work on fixing the problem.

Ohno also reorganised the way the final assembly plants were supplied with parts. The task of assembling the major components into a complete vehicle accounts for only 15 per cent or so of the total manufacturing process. The bulk of the process involves producing more than 10,000 discrete parts and assembling them into approximately 100 major components, such as engines, transmissions, steering gear and suspensions.

Under the original system of mass-production, the idea was to integrate the entire production system into one huge, bureaucratic command structure, with orders coming down from the top. But this proved impossible to organise effectively, and the world's mass-production assemblers ended up adopting widely varying degrees of formal integration, ranging – after the Second World War – from about 25 per cent in-house production at small specialist firms to 70 per cent at General Motors (GM) and 50 per cent at Ford.

At companies such as Ford and GM, the central engineering staff designed most of the 10,000-plus parts in a vehicle and the component systems in which they were embedded, and their suppliers were then asked to bid for them. This system of working to blueprints meant there was little or no incentive for suppliers to suggest improvements in the production design based on their own manufacturing experience, while suppliers offering standardised designs of their own modified to specific vehicles had no practical way of optimising these parts, as they were given practically no information about the rest of the vehicle. The pace of technological innovation for the component suppliers was limited by the automotive customer.

In the 1950s, to counteract these problems, Toyota began to establish a new, lean-production approach to components supply. This involved organising suppliers into functional tiers. First-tier suppliers worked as an integral part of the product-development team, developing new products, such as a steering, braking or electrical system. Each first-tier supplier then formed a second tier of suppliers, who were assigned the job of fabricating individual parts. As these suppliers were all specialists in manufacturing processes and not competitors in a specific type of component, it was easy to group them in 'supplier associations': a new form of sector-specific institution which exchanged information on advances in manufacturing techniques.

Finally, Ohno developed a new way to co-ordinate the flow of parts within the supply system on a day-to-day basis: the famous 'just-in-time' system, called 'Kanban' at Toyota. Under this system, parts are only produced at each step to supply the immediate demand of the next step. This is done using containers to carry parts to the next step. As each container is used up, it is sent back to the previous step and this becomes the automatic signal to make more parts. This simple system was enormously difficult to implement in practice because it eliminated all inventories, but it forced every member of the vast production process to anticipate problems before they became serious enough to stop the production line.

All these improvements took Toyota more than twenty years to perfect, but in time they led to huge increases in productivity and product quality, and made Toyota a world leader in the auto industry.

What makes this case study of Toyota's development of 'lean manufacturing' so interesting is that it validates the use of the capability/market-opportunity dynamic in explaining what happened in the Japanese car industry after the Second World War. Toyota saw there was a demand for cheaper and better-quality cars, and Taiichi Ohno developed a production system that gave them the capability to fulfil that demand. It should also be noted that his production system depended critically on the lifetime employment system, which was one of Japan's key institutions.

The worldwide shipbuilding industry

If we now look at how global leadership of the shipbuilding industry has moved between countries over the years, we find that it, too, validates the use of innovation and the capability/market-opportunity dynamic in explaining what happened.[12]

The first major actor in the modern shipbuilding industry was the United States. Before the 1830s, when steam-powered steel ships were introduced, sailing ships were the industry norm. Industry competitiveness depended on the cost and availability of raw materials, and the United States had abundant sources of timber along its Atlantic coastline. It also desperately needed to develop faster, speedier and more reliable merchant and naval fleets in order to carry goods and immigrants across the Atlantic and the Pacific. In this case, the demand for fast merchant ships was not latent, but constantly outstripped the capacity of shipbuilders to supply.

The early nineteenth century saw two technological breakthroughs in the shipbuilding industry: the introduction of the steam engine, and the use of iron and steel as shipbuilding materials. The steam engine, which had been invented by Thomas Newcomen and then perfected by James Watt, and which played a significant role in the Industrial Revolution in England, became widely used in ships in the 1830s, its adoption being pioneered by the British, French and Americans.

The use of iron in shipbuilding started in the late eighteenth century, but industrywide application awaited a time when an iron ship could be equipped with a steam engine. The first such ship to cross the Atlantic, the SS *Great Britain*, was built in 1843, and made her successful trans-Atlantic voyage two years later.

British shipbuilders quickly developed the new concept by building a series of iron steamships for merchant shippers and the Navy in the 1850s, and in 1862 pioneered steel shipbuilding. They also pioneered the use of diesel engines in the early 1900s, and as a result were able to sustain world leadership in shipbuilding technology through the Second World War.

However, in the latter half of the 1950s Japanese shipbuilders began to penetrate the world shipbuilding market, helped by a government scheme to provide shipbuilders with a steady flow of orders, and financial subsidies. Japanese shipbuilders also began to innovate in construction techniques and renovated their production facilities throughout the 1950s, building their capabilities to respond to technological change and customer demand. By the early 1960s Japanese shipbuilders boasted the biggest and most modern shipyards in the world. Japan managed to exceed Western Europe's total output in 1965, with a market share of 41.4 per cent, and since then Japan's share of the world market has remained at about 50 per cent.

Until the 1960s, shipbuilding had been one of the most conservative industries in introducing new technologies. Since the 1830s, when the substitution of iron steamships for wooden sailing vessels marked the beginning of modern shipping and shipbuilding, basic technology in the industry had remained virtually unchanged. In the 1970s, however, robotics were used to automate most of the welding processes, and there was also a shift in demand to building more homogenous vessels. At every stage, adoption of new technological developments depended on the capability of the shipyards to adapt.

As a result of these changes, market shares in the shipbuilding industry experienced yet another significant shake-up due to the emergence of developing countries at the expense of Western European countries. Japan and Western European countries accounted for 93.3 per cent of the world output of new ships in 1970, while the production output of the eighteen developing countries involved in the shipbuilding industry amounted to only 1.1 per cent. By 1982, the market share of developing countries had risen to 30.7 per cent of the total orders received.

I have included this lengthy description of the changes in global leadership of the shipbuilding industry because, firstly, it is so clearly a story of innovation and its diffusion across national boundaries; secondly, it validates the capability/market-opportunity dynamic as an explanation of economic growth; and, thirdly, it shows very clearly why economists, instead of wincing when they hear the word 'competitiveness', should see it as the key cause of the differing growth rates of countries.

4

City and regional systems of innovation

It is not only the sectors of an economy that differ in their rates of growth and decline, but also its cities and regions, and their rates of growth and decline, like those of sectors, can best be explained in terms of a capability/market-opportunity dynamic, and the speed with which they can reinvent themselves. This can be seen very clearly if we look at the American economy in the 1970s.[1]

After the Second World War through to the end of the 1960s, the industrial Midwest and Northeast, and the South and West, grew at about the same rate. However, while America as a nation enjoyed robust economic growth between 1975 and 1985, the growth rates of these two localised economies diverged.

Starting in the 1970s and through the mid-1980s, a struggling industrial belt from Western Massachusetts to Northern Wisconsin and down to St Louis down-shifted into slow growth. At the same time, regions such as the Rocky Mountains and the West boomed, growing respectively 37 per cent and 27 per cent faster than the nation. Buffalo, New York, a typical American city which had once helped power the country's industrial revolution, saw its jobs decline by 1 per cent; while Brownsville, Texas, saw its jobs grow by 75 per cent. Elsewhere, Syracuse, New York, saw its income grow at roughly half the rate of Santa Fe, New Mexico, with the former's jobs growing just 28 per cent compared to the latter's 124 per cent.

This divergence in the wealth of cities reflected structural changes taking place in the world economy played out on the national stage. Over the past half-century, the United States has shifted from an economy that achieved competitive advantage in traditional manufacturing to one that achieves competitive advantage in a range of innovative industries.

In the decade after the Second World War, America's most important industrial cluster in terms of jobs was not the Detroit auto industry but the New York garment industry. As recently as the mid-1980s, more than a million American workers were employed by US companies making clothing and garments. Today, that number has dropped by 90 per cent, and clothes sold by an American company have probably been manufactured in Vietnam or Bangladesh.

As traditional manufacturing jobs have declined, innovative sectors of the economy have grown. These include the high-tech sector – information technology, life sciences, clean-tech, new materials, robotics and nanotechnology – but also industries as diverse as entertainment and industrial design. Digital entertainment, for example, is a fast-growing part of the innovative sector, with revenues in the United States greater than the film and music industries combined. The feature all these industries have in common is that they are areas where firms can achieve competitive advantage by producing goods and services that are innovative and unique, and not easily copied by global competitors.

Innovative sectors have become the engine of economic growth despite being a relatively small part of the economy's output. To understand why this is the case, it is useful to make a distinction between the tradeable and the non-tradeable sectors of the economy. In a modern economy, most people work in local services as plumbers, nurses, real estate agents and hairdressers. These jobs serve the needs of a region's residents, are largely insulated from national and international competition, and are called the non-traded sector by economists. By contrast, the traded sector of the economy produces goods and services that are mostly sold outside the region and, therefore, need to be competitive in national and global marketplaces. It consists of most jobs in the innovative industries; jobs in traditional manufacturing; parts of finance, advertising and publishing; the agricultural industries; and the extractive industries, such as oil, gas and timber.

While the vast majority of jobs in a modern economy are in the non-tradeable sector, the wealth of a country is disproportionately and favourably impacted by the tradeable sector. There are two reasons why this is the case. The first is that labour productivity does not grow very much in the non-tradeable sector. The amount of labour to teach a class, paint a house, or sell real estate is much the same today as it has always been. By contrast, productivity in the tradeable sector has tended to increase over time as a result of technological progress. Today, it takes 75 per cent fewer worker hours to make a car than it did in 1950, while a constant stream of innovation causes labour productivity to grow even faster in high-tech industries.

A key reason for the divergence of the two American economies was the completion of the Interstate Highway System in the 1970s, which, together with jet travel, nationwide electrification and telephone access, enabled companies in tradeable sectors to locate almost anywhere in the United States. Couple this with the high costs of the 'rust belt', and it is not surprising that factories migrated away from the Northeast and the Midwest, to the South and West. This, of course, led to a transfer of wealth from one part of the country to another. The period also saw the emergence of new high-growth industries, such as electronics, aviation and instruments, which didn't need to be located at the ports or rail spurs in the Midwest and East.

The national process of industrial migration in the 1970s repeated itself, of course, at a global level in the 2000s. Container ships, air freight and the development of the Internet and fibre-optic cables started to link together not just state economies but also national ones, into a single integrated global economy. As a result, traditional industries such as textiles and furniture – which in the 1970s had migrated from Northern States to Southern States – in the 2000s moved abroad.

It is important to note, however, that not all Northeast/Midwest cities suffered a relative decline, a notable exception being Boston, Massachusetts, which looked as if it would decline but which reinvented itself a couple of times. With the arrival of the Cold War and the growth of defence spending, Boston achieved success in electronics with spin-offs from the Massachusetts Institute of Technology. It was also helped by a long-standing strength in financial services.

In the mid-1980s, Boston's industrial future was once again in doubt. The region's computer industry had been heavily involved in minicomputers, and firms such as Data General, Digital Equipment Corporation (DEC) and Wang all went into bankruptcy as the personal computer industry centred in Silicon Valley took off. But Boston, with its three long-standing assets – cutting-edge research universities, a large number of talented and well-educated residents, and a strong, risk-taking venture-capital industry – rebounded. By the 2000s, the region's IT industry had reinvented itself, Boston had become one of the world's leading hubs of biotechnology, and its financial services sector was still very strong. What enabled Boston to rebound again was its record of innovation. If Massachusetts was a nation, it would be the most innovative nation on earth, according to the Information Technology and Innovation Foundation's (ITIF) 'The Atlantic Century II' report.[2]

The example of Boston is important because it shows that decline at a city level is not inevitable, and that, if innovation is seen as the engine of economic growth and the right policies are adopted, cities can continue to grow even in the face of fierce international competition.

The need for a new theory of local economic development

The changing fortunes of cities in America raises two important questions. Why do new industries that increase the wealth of a country develop in specific cities and regions, and is there anything that policy-makers can do to encourage high value-added per capita industries to grow in their cities and regions? Two theories of local economic development have gained widespread currency among policy-makers in recent decades, but neither of them satisfactorily answer these two questions.

The first of these is the theory of clusters developed and made famous by Michael Porter.[3] Clusters, according to his definition, are regional concentrations of related firms and organisations, and the theory focuses on the agglomeration benefits to business from spatially concentrating economic activity. It was first articulated by Alfred Marshall in a famous passage from his book *Principles of Economics*:

> Where an industry has chosen a locality for itself, it is likely
> to stay there long: so great are the advantages which people
> following the same skilled trade get from near neighbourhood
> to one another. The mysteries of trade become no mysteries;
> but are as it were in the air, and children learn many of them
> unconsciously. Good work is rightly appreciated, inventions
> and improvements in machinery, in processes and the general
> organisation of the business have their merits promptly
> discussed: if one man starts a new idea, it is taken up by others
> and combined with suggestions of their own; and thus it
> becomes the source of further new ideas.[4]

The second theory, popularised by Richard Florida, is based on the link he saw between what he termed the 'creative class', which lives in a particular place, and that place's economic performance.[5] The measure used to calculate the size of the creative class in a particular place is based on a classification of job categories, with, for example, artists and engineers belonging to the creative class; and plumbers and secretaries being excluded. This theory of local economic development was embraced by many policy-makers around the world, with many deciding that the key to increasing their place's economic performance was to attract the creative class to move in.

The contrast between the two approaches is interesting. The cluster approach focuses on bringing complementary firms together at a specific place, while the creative-class approach focuses on bringing creative people to a specific place. But while both clusters and the creative class clearly contribute to local economic development, both theories fail for different reasons to describe the dynamic explaining why innovation clusters spring up in particular cities and regions. The dynamic initiating local economic development is more complex than either of these theories would suggest.

There is plenty of empirical evidence supporting the theory that clusters have a large impact on economic performance, and there are also good economic reasons why this is the case. There are three economic forces, which economists refer to collectively as the forces of agglomeration, that enhance the performance of clusters. These are thick labour markets, the presence of specialised service providers, and knowledge spillovers.

It has long been understood by economists that thick labour markets, containing many sellers and many buyers, are better at matching employers with workers. If you are a molecular biologist who specialises in a particular branch of recombinant DNA technology, you are more likely to find the firm that really wants, and will pay for, your skills if you move to a city such as Boston or San Diego, where many biotech firms are located. Employers also benefit from thick labour markets. A biotech start-up in Boston or San Diego will be able to increase its competitive advantage as it can find exactly the kind of molecular biologists it requires to fit its needs.

The presence of specialised services – such as advertising, legal support, technical and management consulting, and shipping – that are important to innovative firms, is another agglomeration force enhancing the performance of firms in a cluster. A good example is venture capital, which is vitally important for high-tech start-ups. Venture capital, in spite of modern communications and transportation, is still a very local business.

The third agglomeration force that supports clusters is knowledge spillovers. New ideas are rarely born in a vacuum, but spring from the flow and diffusion of knowledge among workers, and analysis of patent data has shown there is a strong local bias. Ideas flow more freely among people working in the same local area.

However, while these three agglomeration factors, the thickness of labour markets, the provision of specialised services and knowledge spillovers, are clearly important in supporting successful clusters, they cannot explain how or where regional clusters emerge in the first place. It is significant that Alfred Marshall, in the passage I have just quoted, talks about the impact of agglomeration 'when an industry has chosen a locality for itself'. Examining the positive feedback in an existing successful cluster does not explain how or where a cluster begins.

The second theory that seeks to explain the location of innovation clusters, that of Richard Florida, also fails to explain why clusters spring up where they do. Richard Florida argued that innovation clusters grow up where there is a strong 'creative class', and that local economic growth depends on a city or region attracting the creative class to it by making itself interesting and exciting to them. In *The Rise of the Creative Class*, exploring the rise of Seattle and Austin, Texas, as innovative clusters, Richard Florida wrote:

> Seattle was the home of Jimi Hendrix and later Nirvana and Pearl Jam as well as Microsoft and Amazon. Austin was home to Willie Nelson and its fabulous Sixth Street music scene before Michael Dell ever stepped into his now famous University of Texas fraternity house.[6]

However, there are two good reasons to think this theory is wrong. The first reason is that it confuses cause and effect. The history of successful innovation clusters suggests that in many cases cities become attractive to the creative class *because* they have fast-growing innovative firms, rather than the other way around. Seattle today is a culturally vibrant city, but in spite of its Jimi Hendrix connections, was not a particularly attractive place in 1979. Its economy depended heavily on old-style manufacturing and lumber, and about half of its manufacturing jobs were in transportation. It was a struggling city and people were leaving it in the thousands.

What transformed its fortunes was the arrival of Microsoft from Albuquerque, New Mexico, on New Year's Day 1979. The founders of Microsoft, Bill Gates and Paul Allen, did not, however, bring their company to Seattle because of its large creative class, but because they were both from Seattle and wanted to return to the place they had grown up. Today, Seattle is home to large numbers of the creative class, but that is because of the arrival of Microsoft, and not because a large creative class attracted Microsoft to it.

The second reason why one should reject Richard Florida's argument is that it makes the intellectual error of attributing the success of an innovation cluster to a single input. In a complex process such as economic growth, which requires a number of important inputs if it is to work, it makes no sense to attribute success to a single input.

A capability/market-opportunity theory of high-tech clusters

If neither of the two major theories of cluster formation can explain why or where clusters emerge, how do we develop a new theory? The best way of doing so is to step back from looking at current highly successful clusters, and instead look at clusters in the making; whether in Silicon Valley, in other high-tech clusters in the United States, or in other parts of the world.

If we do so, we find the processes of starting and sustaining a cluster have different explanations. Why a cluster emerges in a specific area is due to the same capability/market-opportunity dynamic as applies to sectors at the national level. Innovative clusters take-off in a particular place because a market-opportunity is created by a technology becoming available to fulfil a latent or well-known demand, and firms exist or are created that have the capability to take advantage of it. This explanation of clusters in the making is valid for Silicon Valley in the 1950s and 1960s, but also for other more recent, well-researched clusters in the United States, such as those in North Carolina, San Diego and Seattle; as well as those in places outside the US, such as Cambridge (England), Taiwan and Israel.

What all these clusters had in common in their early stages is that they took advantage of a market-opportunity created by new technology. In the Silicon Valley of the 1960s, in the other United States innovation clusters, and in Cambridge, England, it was the integrated circuit industry; in Israel it was the Internet and network-security markets; while in Scandinavia and Taiwan it was the hardware and equipment opportunities in new kinds of devices, such as cell phones and personal digital assistants.

The technological advance, however, need not come from the development of a new product category. The call centre cluster in Bangalore, India, came about because a fall in the cost of telecommunications, combined with a massive expansion in the need for technical support for PCs as they became ubiquitous, created a major opportunity. This was an opportunity that Indian firms in Bangalore took advantage of, having developed the necessary capability.

That it is new market opportunities created by technology that leads to new innovation clusters is not difficult to understand. Markets like information and communication technologies (ICTs) in the 1990s were ones where existing firms had built up significant competitive advantages, and where a direct assault was, therefore, unlikely to be successful. To be successful, entrepreneurs in a new innovation cluster had to find new sources of competitive advantage.

It is also interesting to note that there was often a strong complementarity between the technologies developed in new clusters, and existing ICT technologies sold mostly by US-based firms or US-linked multinationals. The reason for this complementarity is, of course, that it vastly increased the demand for the new entrants' inventions and advances. In this way, the new clusters could take advantage of the large and growing demand for the products of existing companies. It is also significant that the clusters in Ireland, India, Israel and Taiwan were regions that – because of their language, cultural connections or the presence of a diaspora – had easier potential interactions with the US market.

As well as taking advantage of the new market opportunities created by technology, what all the clusters described have in common is that they had all built up over a period of time the capabilities enabling them to take advantage of such opportunities when they arose. Nothing is more misleading for policy-makers than the idea that clusters can quickly take-off powered only by agglomeration economics. There is no magic recipe that says take one great university, add in large amounts of venture capital, sprinkle with sunshine and an entrepreneurial culture, and a high-tech cluster will spring up.

For a cluster to take-off, many years of investment in both human capital and firm and market building is required. The supply of highly skilled workers can come from a number of sources: in the case of Silicon Valley, Stanford- and Berkeley-trained scientists and engineers; in the case of Israel, military training and Russian émigrés; and in the case of Ireland and India, an educated population earning far less than world-standard wages.

If we take, for example, the case of Silicon Valley, we can see clearly how a capability/market-opportunity produced what is generally agreed to be the world's most successful high-tech cluster. There was, first of all, a rich market opportunity created by technology in the semiconductor business, and immediately available markets such as consumer electronics and defence. There was also the prospect of entirely new uses of semiconductors in information technology industries. Furthermore, the technological and market opportunities were separate from the existing tube-based electronics industry and provided an advantage to producers located far from existing sellers.

However, what is not usually appreciated is that Silicon Valley in the 1960s already had a history of investing in human capital, and firm and market building. The rise of Silicon Valley has attracted worldwide attention because it seemed to offer the possibility that a region with no prior industrial history could become overnight a leading-edge industrial economy. Unfortunately, this account of Silicon Valley's rise truncates its history, as well as divorcing it from the economic geography of the greater San Francisco Bay Area in which it is situated.

Most accounts of the region's history begin in 1955 when William Shockley, who had co-invented the transistor at Bell Laboratories in 1947, founded the Shockley Transistor Corporation in Palo Alto. The spin-off of Fairchild Semiconductor from Shockley Transistor, and the 'Fairchildren' companies which split off from it in turn, are widely believed to have been the original stimulus of Silicon Valley.

A more careful look at Silicon Valley, however, pushes its origin back to the formation of the Hewlett-Packard Company in 1938, and Varian Associates in 1948, within the incubator of Stanford University. According to this revision of the Silicon Valley story, the growth of electronics companies around Stanford University was due to the vision of Frederick Terman, the dean of Stanford University's School of Engineering during the Second World War, and the influx of military-financed research and development he brought to the area.

If we examine the industrial history of the San Francisco Bay Area carefully, though, we find there has been a vibrant electronics industry there since the earliest days of experimentation and innovation in the fields of radio, television and military electronics. The characteristics of the early Bay Area electronic firms also closely anticipate, on a much smaller scale, the structure of industrial organisation so widely hailed as being typical of Silicon Valley. From the start, these firms had the capabilities to apply new technologies to customer demand. They also had the capabilities and institutional structures to ensure they would be on the cutting edge of technology diffusion; as soon as something was invented in electronics, San Francisco's entrepreneurs would find out about it.

An important role for local venture capital; a synergistic relationship between local industry and the major research universities in the area; a product mix made up of electronic components, production equipment, advanced communications, instrumentation and military electronics; an unusually high level of interfirm co-operation; an acceptance of spin-offs; and a view of the region as existing mostly outside the sphere of influence of the ponderous, bureaucratic electronics firms and financial institutions of the East Coast – all these well-known Silicon Valley characteristics were already in evidence in the period 1910 to 1940.

I have described the history of Silicon Valley over the last one hundred years not in order to deny that Frederick Terman and William Shockley played important roles in its growth and success, but to undermine the 'instant industrialisation' myth that has been so central to the story of Silicon Valley's development, and has made it both so attractive and so misleading to planning bodies and government agencies.

High-tech clusters such as Silicon Valley are based on a capability/market-opportunity, and the capabilities that are essential to their growth and success cannot be built up overnight. The lesson for planners and economic developers is to focus on long-term, rather than short-term, developmental trajectories. Silicon Valley was the fastest growing region in the United States during the late 1970s and early 1980s, but its success depended on a long history of industrialisation and innovation in the larger San Francisco Bay Area.

It also needs to be recognised that the growth of clusters depends on entrepreneurs spotting a market opportunity and putting together the capabilities necessary to take advantage of it. This may involve an element of chance. We have already seen that Seattle became a high-tech cluster largely because Microsoft went there, but there are other examples of growth taking off in a particular place due to chance, with the history of the biotech industry an interesting case in point. In 1973, Herbert Boyer and Stanley Cohen invented a recombinant DNA technique that had an immense impact in life-science research. As a result, dozens of private biotech labs sprang up all over the United States in places such as Houston, Long Island, Cambridge, Philadelphia, Northern New Jersey, Miami, Palo Alto, Los Angeles and La Jolla.

Today, though, the industry is largely concentrated in three areas: the Boston–Cambridge metropolitan area, the San Francisco Bay Area, and San Diego. Why were biotech firms so successful in these areas and not in others? A possible explanation might be that being close to a top biology department in a top university was the critical factor. However, when biotech companies first appeared in the 1970s, there were at least twenty excellent research universities with world-class biology departments or research hospitals in the United States. They were all attractive locations, but not all developed major clusters. The answer to this question can be found in a 1998 article by sociologist Lynne G. Zucker and economist Michael Darby,[7] in which they argue that the location and success of private biotech companies is explained by the presence of academic stars; that is researchers who have published the most articles reporting specific gene-sequencing discoveries. The data produced by Zucker and Darby is impressive, suggesting that stars are more important than proximity to venture-capital firms or government funding. As with Microsoft and Seattle, the academic star researchers who drove the biotech revolution were responsible for creating industry clusters in Boston, San Diego and San Francisco simply because those places happened to be where they wanted to live and work.

There are two reasons that explain the impact of stars. The first is that scientists and researchers in private-sector start-ups need to be physically close to frontier academic research in order to be at the cutting edge; regularly attending academic seminars and engaging in informal discussion in order to develop new ideas. Secondly, stars are often personally involved in the creation of leading private-sector start-ups.

Thus, the Boston–Cambridge metropolitan area, the San Francisco Bay Area, and San Diego, got lucky. Where the stars lived at the time biotech emerged in the mid-1970s was, to some extent, a matter of chance. It could have been any of the 187 American cities with a university, or at least any of the twenty cities with a top biology department. But what happened as these clusters became established was not random. Agglomeration began to have an impact, with the result that their share of industry jobs keeps increasing.

The same element of chance can be seen in the motion-picture industry. At the beginning of the twentieth century, film was the exciting new thing, competing with theatre to establish itself as a respectable medium of entertainment and facing major technological and managerial challenges. In 1913, the year before the First World War broke out, the movie industry was largely concentrated in New York, where the major studios and the biggest stars were located, with smaller outposts in Chicago, Philadelphia, Jacksonville, Santa Barbara and Los Angeles. By 1919, however, 80 per cent of American movies were made in California. Charlie Chaplin and countless other stars had moved west, and the forces of agglomeration started to have an impact.

The conventional explanation for this sudden geographic change is that the motion-picture industry needed to be based in Los Angeles because of its good weather, as New York's cold winters presented technical challenges for outdoor filming. This, though, would appear to be a case of after-the-fact rationalisation. Los Angeles is not the only city in America with a good climate, and Berlin, London, Paris and Moscow have all remained important film capitals despite not having mild winters.

A much better explanation has been proposed by UCLA geographer Allen Scott, who has pointed to the influence of Thomas Ince and D. W. Griffith, both of whom had a huge impact on the business and aesthetic practices of Hollywood production companies at this time, propelling them to the leading edge of the industry.[8]

Thomas Ince played a key role in the development of the full-blown studio system. He arrived in Southern California in 1911 and set up a studio to produce cowboy films for the New York Motion Picture Company. He was the first producer to get the industry to abandon the simple set of craft practices on which it had been based, and to industrialise the whole film-making process. Instead of improvisation, Ince developed much more methodical procedures based on the continuity script. Radically, he separated conception from production, and broke the shooting process down into disconnected segments that were later put together at the post-production stage. The continuity script became like an industrial blueprint, enabling an advanced division of labour to take place; as well as expanding the capability of production companies to control the entire film-making process, exerting discipline over the behaviour of talent workers such as writers, directors and actors.

If Thomas Ince was the person who changed the managerial practices of Hollywood, D. W. Griffith was the person who changed the whole conception of cinematic entertainment. He is credited, among other things, with developing the close-up, flashback and fade-out techniques in cinematography, and in 1915 achieved great success with his Los Angeles production of the film *Birth of a Nation*. The film is reported to have cost $85,000, making it five times more expensive than any previous film, but it subsequently earned gross revenues of over $18 million, far more than any other motion picture of the silent era.

The dramatic surge in Hollywood's business fortunes and reputation, which came as a result of the work of Thomas Ince and D. W. Griffith, pushed the entire Hollywood complex to the undisputed forefront of motion-picture productions. The Californian studios built capabilities that simply did not exist in the film industry elsewhere. After 1915, Hollywood ceased to be an extension of New York's motion-picture industry, instead becoming a highly productive cluster with its own dynamic. As a result, the forces of agglomeration began to have an impact. The number of workers and establishments in the Hollywood motion-picture industry shot up, and in 1919, 80 per cent of the world's motion pictures were being made in California. By the late 1920s, the studio system of production was firmly established, and Hollywood was at the beginning of the golden age that would continue through the Second World War until the late 1940s.

A further factor enabling Hollywood to overcome the first-mover advantages of New York were the activities of the Motion Picture

Patents Company, popularly known as the Trust. The Trust was a sector-specific institution that, whatever advantages it may have had for the industry at the start, became a barrier to its advance. It was set up in 1908 largely by motion-picture companies in the New York–New Jersey metropolitan area. The Trust functioned as a holding company for the patents owned by its members, and this effectively gave it monopoly control over what was then the most efficient equipment for both shooting and projecting films. As a result, the Trust was able to exert massive control over the production, distribution and exhibition of motion pictures in the US, which created a strong desire on the part of independent motion-picture producers to put as much distance as possible between themselves and the Trust.

The massive power of the Trust also encouraged its members to believe that their competitive advantage lay more in cultivating monopoly power than in improving the quality and appeal of their films, whereas the new production companies of Hollywood concerned themselves with film content and appeal. The members of the Trust resisted producing feature films, instead concentrating on less demanding short films, and opposed the emerging star system; whereas the new Hollywood production companies concentrated more on producing feature films and promoting individual stars.

This description of the birth of Hollywood makes it clear that the growth of the film-making industry in Los Angeles, as opposed to other parts of the US, cannot simply be attributed to the physical attributes of Southern California. A dominating motion-picture cluster might have sprung up in many places in the US in the early years of the twentieth century. While Southern California's warm, sunny climate and diversity of landscapes undoubtedly played a part in making it a favoured place for the motion-picture industry, the rise of Hollywood can largely be attributed to the innovative system of production which evolved under the chance leadership of people such as Thomas Ince and D. W. Griffith.

Looking back, the location of the computer industry in Silicon Valley; the biotech industry in the Boston–Cambridge metropolitan area, San Diego, and the San Francisco Bay Area; and the movie industry in Los Angeles, seem inevitable. But this is not how people saw these cities before these industries settled in them. The location of these industries in these cities was the result of entrepreneurial decisions which could not have been predicted by industrial leaders or governments. This is not to say, however, that industrial leaders and governments can play no part in the development of industrial clusters.

The strategic management of place

Having established that the growth of high-tech clusters depends on a capability/market-opportunity dynamic, we now need to ask what role the state can play in creating high-tech clusters. The idea of clusters as a policy tool has proved very popular with policy-makers across the world; with national and local governments in Germany, Brazil, Japan, South Korea, the Spanish Basque country, and France, among others, seeking since the end of the 1980s to foster their development.

These initiatives have not, as a whole, been successful. In their authoritative and detailed study, *Building High-Tech Clusters: Silicon Valley and Beyond*, Timothy Bresnahan, an economics professor at Stanford University, and Alfonso Gambardella, a management professor at Duke University, reported on how high-tech clusters had emerged in countries as varied as Israel, India, Ireland, Sweden and Taiwan. They concluded:

> our overall research design took seriously the proposition that
> government policy leading and directing cluster formation might
> be an important part of the cluster formation story, although we
> ultimately reject that proposition. [9]

While initiatives by governments to create high-tech clusters have not generally been successful, even on the basis of the evidence that

Bresnahan and Gambardella produce in their study, the statement above is too sweeping a judgement. It is, therefore, worth looking at two high-tech clusters which have been very successful, and in which governments clearly played a part, to see what lessons can be learned. The first of these high-tech clusters is the Research Triangle Park in North Carolina,[10] and the second is the Hsinchu region in Taiwan.

In 1950, there were only five states in the United States that had a per capita income lower than North Carolina and South Carolina. Both these states were relatively rural, and to the extent that they had any form of economic strategy it was one based on unskilled, low-waged labour manufacturing such products as tobacco, textiles and shoes. Today, South Carolina still ranks among the poorest states in the United States, while North Carolina has become one of the wealthier places in the country. In 2011, South Carolina's per capita GDP was $30,620, barely above Mississippi and West Virginia. By contrast, North Carolina generated a per capita GDP that was nearly one-third higher, at $38,847.

What accounts for this divergence in economic performance? The answer is that in 1956 Governor Luther H. Hodges gathered together North Carolina's business leaders in order to kick off a new economic strategy based on knowledge and human capital. He then implemented this strategy through far-sighted investments in universities, research centres and infrastructure. He also led a programme of educational reform, built vocational schools, and embarked on a persuasive industrial recruitment and incentive programme. In South Carolina, on the other hand, there was no such economic growth initiative, and the state continued to be dependent on low-productivity manufacturing and agriculture.

At the centre of North Carolina's new economic strategy was the Research Triangle Park, which was created by the state's university, business and government leaders, and which became one of the most successful planned science parks in the world. The 7,000-acre 'Triangle' is linked to the state's universities, which are less than thirty miles apart: North Carolina State University in Raleigh (NCSU), the

University of North Carolina at Chapel Hill (UNC–Chapel Hill), and Duke University in Durham.

These three universities acted as the pillars of the region's knowledge-based economy, providing world-class research facilities as well as a critical mass of scientists, researchers and technicians. As a result, research-oriented companies began to locate in the region, and over time a large number of clusters developed in the region. These included not only biotechnology/pharmaceuticals and communications, but also plastics, chemicals, fibres, medical devices, analytical instruments, and education and knowledge creation.

There are three features of the Research Triangle story that contributed to its success. Firstly, it was not simply a government initiative but one involving business leaders and academics. It is essential that business leaders take a leading role in economic development, with active government participation in a privately led initiative likely to have a much better chance of success. Companies will always be better at identifying the opportunities open to them, as well as the obstacles and constraints in their path. Also, letting the private sector take the lead makes such initiatives less political, while at the same time taking advantage of the private sector's usually better implementation ability. Secondly, the government did not seek to take entrepreneurial decisions, but provided enabling policies in the areas of physical infrastructure, R&D, and education and training. And, thirdly, the policy was a long-term one, based on a shared understanding that the sources of competitive advantage are productivity and innovation, and not low wages, low taxes or a devalued currency.

It took twenty years to build a large corporate R&D presence in the Research Triangle, and another twenty years for it to produce significant economic developments. The Research Triangle Institute opened in 1958, but it was not until the late 1980s that the biotechnology/pharmaceutical cluster took off. In both cases, it was necessary for local leaders to assemble a critical mass of facilities and institutions, as well as waiting many years to see the economic benefits.

Turning now to the very successful Hsinchu region in Taiwan, we again find that, in taking advantage of the opportunity created by the IT revolution, the government provided the necessary enabling conditions for industry rather than taking entrepreneurial decisions; worked closely with industrial leaders; and took a long-term view based on a shared understanding of the sources of competitive advantage.

In 1962, Taiwan's GDP per capita was US$172, less than that of Ghana. Today, Taiwan is a prosperous country, with its companies producing the majority of the world's notebook computers, motherboards, monitors, optical scanners, power supplies, and a range of other electronics related products. In addition, the island's semiconductor foundries account for two-thirds of the global foundry output.

So how did this small, and initially very poor, island of 24 million people come to overtake other Asian economies in global technology competition? At the start, Taiwan's political leaders made substantial investments in technical education. The annual number of higher-education graduates grew from less than 10,000 in 1961 to almost 200,000 in 1996, with 40 per cent of these degrees in engineering. The capabilities of Taiwan's public research institutions were also upgraded. Taiwan's Ministry of Economic Affairs established the Industrial Technology Research Institute (ITRI) in 1973 to provide joint research, technical services and advice to Taiwan's small and medium-sized enterprises (SMEs). A major opportunity for ITRI, based in part on advice from overseas Chinese experts in the United States, was the semiconductor industry, and in 1974 ITRI officials created the Electronics Research and Service Organization (ERSO), a subsidiary devoted to research in semiconductor manufacturing and commercialisation. By 1987, ERSO had a staff of over 1,700 and a budget of about US$100 million.

Then, in 1980, based on visits to Silicon Valley in the 1960s and 1970s, and advice from the region's community of US-educated Taiwanese engineers, the National Science Council (NSC) sponsored the Hsinchu Science Park in order to attract foreign and overseas Chinese investments in research-oriented companies. The park was located near to two leading technical universities, National Chiao Tung and

Tsinghua, and ERSO's labs were moved to the area. In the early 1980s, the Ministry of Finance also created the institutional framework for a Taiwanese venture-capital industry in order to provide funding for the research-intensive production it wanted to attract to the science park, as well as to stimulate the development of a public capital market.

As a result of these initiatives, the 1980s saw the emergence of an indigenous IT industry. There were two separate clusters of entrepreneurship: a large number of small firms and start-ups in the Taipei area began cloning PCs and components; while at the same time a small number of integrated circuit (IC) manufacturing and design start-ups were spun out of the government-funded semiconductor research institute (ERSO) in Hsinchu Science Park.

It was not until the 1990s, however, that local firms began to differentiate themselves on the basis of innovation and skills, rather than low-cost labour. This shift was due to the impact of government policies, growing production experience, and 'learning by doing'. But the most significant change was the 'reversal' of the brain drain in the early 1990s, when thousands of Chinese engineers who had been educated and worked in the United States were encouraged to return to Taiwan either to start their own companies, or work for start-ups or established companies. These returning engineers, many of whom had worked for more than a decade in Silicon Valley, played an important role in assisting Taiwanese companies to move towards the world's technological frontier in the manufacture of ICs, PCs and related components, as they brought with them technical and organisational skills, entrepreneurial experience, and connections with leading-edge IT markets in the United States.

For most of the 1980s, less than ten engineers a year were attracted to the Hsinchu Science Park. By 1989, though, 2,840 Taiwanese engineers had returned from the US to work there. The importance of these returnees can be gauged by the fact that, in 1999, of the 284 companies in the science park, 110 had been founded by US-educated engineers, many of whom had significant managerial or entrepreneurial experience in Silicon Valley.

A final similarity between Silicon Valley and the Hsinchu region should be noted. Taiwan's PC and IC industries are geographically clustered in a pattern that closely resembles that of Silicon Valley, with the majority of the island's approximately 10,000 IC- and PC-related firms located within the 50-mile region linking the Taipei metropolitan area and the Hsinchu Science Park in the northwest. This separation of Taiwan's high-tech industries from Taiwan's traditional industries in the south has enabled new institutions to be created to support them, and agglomeration to have an impact.

The cases of the Research Triangle Park in North Carolina, and the Hsinchu region of Taiwan, demonstrate that governments working with business leaders can play a role in assisting the development of high-tech clusters. However, this role involves providing the enabling conditions for companies rather than taking entrepreneurial decisions. To be successful, governments need to take a long-term view and have a shared understanding with industry on the sources of competitive advantage. Governments should not support individual companies or try to take entrepreneurial decisions. These decisions should rather be taken by entrepreneurs and investors who understand the markets and the companies involved, and have 'skin in the game'.

The reinvention of cities

We have seen that the economic growth of cities and regions can best be explained in terms of a capability/market-opportunity dynamic, and the speed with which they reinvent themselves. To speed up the national rate of economic growth, and reduce city and regional inequalities, governments at a city or regional level need, therefore, to develop policies that help cities reinvent their economies by creating high value-added per capita jobs in advanced manufacturing and knowledge-intensive business services (KIBS). This is something they have not done in the past, instead often seeking to replace low value-added jobs in cotton mills and dockyards with low value-added jobs in call centres and distribution sheds.

There are four ways that the national government in England, in the absence of a regional tier of government, can give cities such support. Firstly, they can match the training of skilled workers in further education colleges and the new Institutes of Technology with the needs of local industries. This should be easier with the new national system of qualifications for technical education (T Levels) that the government is currently implementing (see Chapter 8). It does, however, require that the process of matching be delegated to the city level.

Secondly, support should be given to the creation of institutions supporting innovation. This can take the form of institutions such as the Sheffield Advanced Manufacturing Research Centre, which has attracted companies such as Boeing, Rolls Royce and McLaren Automotive to open high-tech manufacturing operations in Sheffield, as it can help them develop their manufacturing capabilities. It should also, though, involve the development of science parks linked to universities in order to develop the next generation of high-tech companies in areas such as software, digital businesses and biotechnology.

Thirdly, support should be given to high value-added per capita clusters within regions. It is important, however, that support be given only to clusters already in existence. There is nothing more pointless or wasteful than regional or local governments deciding they want to be world leaders in, say, nanotechnology, when they do not already have a significant presence in that industry. What could be done instead is shown in a report done by McKinsey and the Centre for Cities, which reviewed the position of clusters in the UK.[11] Using a rigorous methodology which made use of the most recent gross value added (GVA) data from 2013, the study identified thirty-one economically significant clusters in the UK. These clusters contained 8 per cent of the UK's businesses, but generated 20 per cent of the UK's GVA. They were also an important source of well-paid jobs, employing four million people (one in seven of the working population), and paying average salaries that were typically higher than those in the surrounding area.

The clusters identified were spread across the country and included the creative industries and financial services in London; the large area in Northamptonshire that is home to a concentration of Formula 1 motor-racing teams and thousands of specialist motorsport suppliers; the aerospace industry in the North West; the chemical industry around Hull; the Midlands automotive cluster; oil and gas in Aberdeen; and financial services in Edinburgh. The study looked at five cases in depth and found three major barriers to growth in each of them. Each cluster faced specific infrastructural challenges holding back growth; the education and skills systems were not producing the required concentration of specialist skills; and clusters were not being as successful as some of their global peers in tapping into local innovative universities. These clusters were therefore clearly cases where targeted interventions would have a large pay-off. Unfortunately, the UK government has not taken up the challenge, either because it doesn't know how to do so organisationally, or because it is frightened of being accused of 'picking winners'.

Fourthly, governments at the national or regional level need to deal with the scars of industrial legacy in cities. In the days when labour was cheaper and railways played a major role in the transport of goods, factories were usually located in city-centre multi-story buildings, in order to be near railway stations. Today, manufacturing firms prefer to operate in single-story buildings on the edges of cities, while KIBS prefer to be located in city-centre offices in order to form the knowledge networks needed to facilitate innovation. This requires a massive re-development of city centres, as well as land remediation.

These four policies will not, in themselves, guarantee the creation of high value-added per capita jobs. However, they will help produce the conditions in which entrepreneurs can create high value-added per capita jobs, by developing the capabilities of their firms to take advantage of the market opportunities that arise.

This model of city economic development can be illustrated by looking at the history of Manchester in the twentieth and early twenty-first century. As we shall see in the next chapter, in the nineteenth century, the city of Manchester was a major producer of cotton goods, as well as being an important trade centre. Manchester and its surrounding Lancashire mill towns were responsible for spinning 32 per cent of global cotton production in the late nineteenth century.

In 1911, 22 per cent of the city's jobs were in textile production. Textile production also helped support a logistics industry for moving goods, which employed over 8 per cent of all workers. In the inter-war period, textiles and logistics as the key drivers of Manchester's growth began to falter as a result of the Great Depression and growing competition from international trade. The city had around 80,000 more jobs in 1951 than in 1911, but most of these were in the chemical and electrical engineering industries. There was a 60 per cent increase in jobs in engineering and electrical goods between 1911 and 1951, by which time the sector employed the same number of workers as the textiles industry.

The thirty years after the war were, however, disastrous for Manchester. Between 1951 and 1981, jobs in engineering and electrical goods nearly halved, and jobs in the textile industry declined by 86 per cent. As a result, Manchester was in a desperate situation. The city, however, acted proactively. The Central Manchester Development Corporation was created in 1988 in order to redevelop the city centre, converting neglected buildings into offices and constructing new office buildings, which, together with a period of strong national economic growth during the 1990s, helped the creation of jobs, particularly in KIBS. Manchester is now experiencing a process of reinvention, having seen a 24 per cent growth in jobs between 1991 and 2013, including 77,000 more jobs in private sector, knowledge-intensive service industries. In 2013, Manchester still had 90,000 fewer jobs than it did in 1951, but it has successfully reinvented itself for the twenty-first century.

The problem experienced by those cities that have struggled over the last century has not been the inevitable decline of extraction, logistics and manufacturing employment, but rather their failure to support the growth of jobs in new industries, The regional policies of the various political parties in England have done little to help cities reinvent themselves, either attempting to limit the decline of low-skilled manufacturing employment or encouraging its expansion in poorly performing cities. Governments in future will need to adopt a new set of policies to stimulate the growth of new high value-added per capita jobs, in the ways outlined above.

*

In the previous three chapters, I have set out a new theory of economic growth. In the next three chapters, I will test the theory to see if it can be used to explain the performance of countries forging ahead, catching up and falling behind.

5

Forging ahead

In the last two hundred and fifty years, three countries – Great Britain, Germany and the United States – have forged ahead of other countries by creating world technologically leading industries. In this chapter, I will look at the years when these dynamic changes took place, because it is at these moments that the input to the economic growth process, or the feature of the economic growth process enabling the country to forge ahead, should be most obvious.

I will look specifically at four case studies: the growth of the cotton industry in Great Britain at the end of the eighteenth century and the beginning of the nineteenth century; the rise of the German chemical industry at the end of the nineteenth century; the rise to world leadership of the American car industry at the beginning of the twentieth century; and the forging ahead of the American computer industry in the second half of the twentieth century. All these cases illustrate the main argument of this book, which is that the rapid forging ahead of new industries in the last two hundred and fifty years has not been caused by changes in the flexibility with which capital and labour resources can be moved around the economy, but by innovation and the capability/market-opportunity dynamic that I outlined in Chapter 2.

The British cotton industry

Looking first at the cotton industry, economic historians generally agree there was a fairly sharp acceleration of British industrial output in the last two decades of the eighteenth century, and that this growth was not balanced across all industries, but was characterised by exceptionally fast growth in the cotton industry, and to a lesser extent the iron industry.

The share of cotton in the total value-added of industry grew from 2.6 per cent in 1770 to 17 per cent in 1801.[1] Also, exports of cotton textiles reached 60 per cent of output in 1820, becoming the single biggest commodity in nineteenth-century trade. Furthermore, it continued to account for over 30 per cent of British manufacturing exports in 1899, when Britain was still by far the biggest exporter.

The growth of the cotton industry enabled Britain to forge ahead of its great trading competitors: Spain, Portugal and the Netherlands. We therefore need to ask whether innovation and the capability/market-opportunity dynamic outlined in Chapter 2 can provide us with an explanation of how Britain became the world's leading industrial country at this time. To answer this question, two further questions need to be asked. Did a latent demand exist in the cotton industry for British firms? And did British firms have the organisational and technological capabilities to fulfil this demand?

The latent demand for the cotton industry arose, surprisingly, from the fact that from around 1100 to the middle of the eighteenth century, Britain was a major woollen clothes-maker, due to the high quality of the wool it produced. Cotton, on the other hand, remained a small industry, its output negligible in size in comparison with the high-quality, cheap and brightly coloured cotton fabrics brought from India by the East India Company.

In time, these imports from India came to be a serious threat to the woollen industry, and Acts of Parliament in 1701 and 1720 made illegal the use and wearing of Indian and Chinese silks, and the use of Indian cotton cloth. So, a product that was popular among the British people was effectively banned. Consumers started looking for any firm that could produce a reasonable imitation of Indian cotton, and this led to enormous latent demand for the cotton and linen industries already existing in Manchester.

At the same time, a burst of technical invention took place which, when combined with the demand for cotton goods, created a 'window of opportunity' for British industry. John Kay's invention of the flying shuttle made weaving much faster, and, once it became widely adopted in the 1760s, a single loom could devour the thread from at least half-a-dozen spinning wheels. This led to an urgent need for a faster method of spinning, and from 1771 to 1781 there was a rapid increase in the productivity of spinning due to the invention of James Hargreaves's spinning jenny, and Richard Arkwright's water frame (so called because it was driven by water power). In the ten years from 1781 to 1791 there was a further acceleration due to the invention of Samuel Crompton's mule, so named because of its combination of the jenny and the frame, and the expiration of Arkwright's patent. As a result of these technical inventions and their diffusion, there was a dramatic reduction in the number of operative hours to process (OHP) 100 lbs of cotton.[2]

	OHP/100 lb cotton
Indian hand spinners (eighteenth century)	50,000
Crompton's Mule (c.1790)	1,000
Power-assisted mules (c.1795)	300
Roberts's automatic mule (c.1825)	135
Most efficient machines (1990)	40

How, though, did the British cotton industry acquire the organisational and technological capabilities to take advantage of this opportunity?

Firstly, the fact that Britain was a major woollen clothes-maker meant it already had a considerable knowledge of spinning and weaving techniques.

Secondly, the great entrepreneurs of the day transformed the textiles industry by replacing a cottage system of production with a factory system of production. While the term factory had been used for centuries to mean a collective place of productive work, in the modern sense of a site where goods are manufactured by a variety of devices powered by a single energy source, the factory is an eighteenth-century innovation. It provided a new model of how productive work could be organised, showing how mechanised machinery within a large factory could provide major gains in productivity over hand-operated devices in small workshops.

In 1721 in Derby, England, the first successful example of a factory that had all the characteristics of a mechanised modern factory was built by John and Thomas Lombe on an island in the River Derwent.[3] It was a silk-spinning mill, and had a large workforce engaged in co-ordinated production using powered machinery, in this case driven by a twenty-three-foot-high water wheel. But the great age of factories came with the mechanisation of cotton spinning in the 1770s and 1780s, starting with the opening in 1772 of Richard Arkwright's purpose-built, water-powered mill at Cromford in the Derwent Valley. In 1782, there were two cotton mills in the Manchester area. By 1830 there were ninety-nine, and by 1835 there were 1,262 cotton mills across the UK, 683 of them in Lancashire.

With these innovations in place, the economics of agglomeration played a key role in building up the capabilities of the cotton industry workforce. Pools of specialised skilled labour grew up in various Lancashire towns: Bolton (fine yarns); Oldham (coarse yarns); Blackburn and Burnley (coarse cloth). A similar situation existed in the supply of skilled mechanics able to maintain and improve the local machinery. The impact of these economies of agglomeration on the sustainable competitive advantage of Britain's cotton industry was considerable. As William Mass and William Lazonick have pointed out:

By the 1870s cotton industries around the world could readily purchase British plant and equipment and even British engineering expertise. But no other cotton industry in the world could readily acquire Britain's highly productive labour force; no other industry in the world had gone through the century-long developmental process that had produced the experienced, specialised and co-operative labour force that Britain possessed.[4]

The economics of agglomeration can also be seen in the machine-building industry. The skills of early millwrights were based on the skills of the mechanics who had built corn mills and windmills, but with the increased specialisation and sophistication of machinery, special and cumulative skills became increasingly important here too. As a result, Lancashire benefited from high levels of machine utilisation, as well as lower initial costs of machinery.

The highly concentrated Liverpool cotton exchange also provided Lancashire with an exceptional advantage in relation to material costs. Foreign buyers were able to buy cotton cheaper in Liverpool than anywhere else in the world, in much the same way that flower-buyers flock to the Amsterdam flower market today. From 1830 onwards, the Manchester ship canal and the railway from Liverpool meant transport costs were low, and Lancashire spinners did not have to bear the heavy warehousing costs of more distant competitors. The whole system functioned much like an early 'just-in-time' system.

Finally, Lancashire benefited from a worldwide marketing network. Over time, the British cotton industry exported yarn and cloth to all parts of the world. This needed not only a transportation network to move yarn and cloth from various specialised cotton towns to destinations across the globe, but also information concerning the types of yarns and cloths that buyers in the various markets wanted and could afford. In the early 1870s, a worldwide network of cables emanating from Manchester was completed, and in the early 1880s this communication network was enhanced by telephone. Lancashire was not only at the centre of a worldwide transportation system, but also a worldwide information system.

The history of the British cotton industry in the last two decades of the eighteenth century and the beginning of the nineteenth century shows clearly that its extraordinary growth was due to innovation and a capability/market-opportunity dynamic. An attempt by the British government to protect the woollen industry by banning the import of Indian cloth provided the small-scale cotton industry in Manchester with massive latent demand for cheap cotton clothes, ensuring its investment in new technology would be profitable. At the same time, conditions in Britain enabled the industry to quickly build up its technological and organisational capabilities in order to fulfil this latent demand, creating a long-term sustainable competitive advantage in world markets. And because this resulted in a large high value-added per capita industry, this sustainable competitive advantage had a major impact on the growth rate of the economy.

The German chemical industry

Turning next to the chemical industry at the end of the nineteenth century, we find that German firms forged ahead of their British competitors in the new organic chemical industry as a result of innovation and a technological capability/market-opportunity dynamic. In 1850, Britain led the world in the production of inorganic chemicals, such as chlorine, bleach, caustic soda and sulphuric acid. The main reason for this dominance was the large domestic demand from industries such as textiles, soap and glass, which in turn can be traced back to the large domestic market, and the high levels of per capita income in Britain at the time.

Then, in 1856, the Englishman William Perkin discovered the first synthetic dye (aniline mauve), an event which is generally considered to have launched the modern organic chemical industry.[5] This is an industry in which Britain could have become a world leader. The world's largest market for dyes was the British textile industry, and it remained so until after the Second World War. As well as the first discovery of a dye being made by an Englishman, dyes were made from coal, of which Britain had a plentiful, high-quality supply. But while organic dyes were first discovered and commercialised in Britain, within twenty years Germany overtook Britain in their production, and by the 1880s dominated the organic chemical industry. In 1880, German firms accounted for nearly half the total world output of synthetic dyes, and by 1913 their dominance was even greater. Of the total world output of 160,000 tons, Germany produced 140,000.

To explain how German firms achieved dominance, it is necessary to understand that the organic chemical industry was one of a number of industries – such as food, oil, electrical machinery, primary materials and transportation equipment – which began in the last quarter of the nineteenth century to utilise technologies that had the potential to produce large economies of scale and scope. But to be successful in these industries, firms had to make use of a new type of organisation, which the historian Alfred D. Chandler Jr has called 'the modern industrial enterprise'.

In these new capital-intensive industries, production units achieved much greater economies of scale or scope; that is, as the volume of materials processed increased, their cost per unit dropped much more quickly than in the old labour-intensive industries. Such potential cost advantages could not be realised, however, unless a constant flow of materials through the plant or factory was maintained to ensure effective capacity utilisation. This, in turn, required careful co-ordination not only of flow through the processes of production, but also of the flow of inputs from the suppliers and the flow of outputs to the retailers and final consumers. Such co-ordination did not happen automatically, instead requiring the constant attention of a managerial team.

The differentials in the potential economies of scale and scope of different production technologies explain not only why large hierarchical firms appeared in some industries and not in others, but also why they appeared suddenly in the last two decades of the nineteenth century. It was only with the completion of modern transportation and communication networks – railroads, telegraphs, steamships and cables – and the organisational innovations essential to operate them as integrated systems, that materials could flow into a factory or processing plant, and finished goods move out, at a speed and volume that achieved substantial economies of throughput. Transportation that depended on the power of animals, wind and currents was not fast, regular or certain enough to maintain the level of throughput necessary to achieve the new technologies' potential economies.

The reason German firms in the organic chemical industry were able, at the end of the nineteenth century, to forge ahead of their British competitors, is that they made the necessary investment in production, marketing, distribution and research; and also developed the managerial hierarchies necessary to run them.

In the 1870s, the German firms Bayer, BASF, Hoechst, AGFA and two others invested in larger production units for aniline and alizarin dyes. This investment increased throughput and drove the price of alizarin dye down from 270 marks/kilo in 1869 to 23 marks/kilo in 1878. In the 1880s, these firms also extended their marketing organisations throughout the world.

Then, in the late 1870s and early 1880s, three firms – Bayer, BASF and Hoechst – began to build much larger plants in order to exploit the economies of scope by producing many dyes and pharmaceuticals from the same set of intermediates, an investment that permitted the reduction in the price of alizarin to 8 marks/kilo by 1886. At the same time, they started offering salaries which quickly brought back to the country the German chemists who had gone to work in Britain. When they came back they worked in the new research laboratories, which for many decades to come would make German companies the world leaders in the development of new products and processes based on organic chemistry. In the organic chemistry industry, as in other industries of the era that started using technologies with the potential to produce huge economies of scale and scope, the first firms to make the necessary investments, and develop the managerial hierarchies to manage them, acquired powerful first-mover advantages in costs.

First movers had other advantages as well. In the more technologically complex industries, the first firms to install research laboratories and train technicians in product-specific development skills had a similar advantage, often reinforced by patents on both new products and processes. Their head-start in developing capabilities in all functional areas also meant they were often well down the learning curve in each of the functional activities before newcomers had started up their operations. As a result, in those industries where scale and scope provided cost advantages, the number of players remained small and there was little turnover among leaders.

The analysis presented here makes clear that innovation and a capability/market-opportunity dynamic played the critical role in creating competitive advantage and growth in the firms investing in technologies with the potential to produce large economies of scale and scope at the end of the nineteenth century. It also makes clear why the window of opportunity for investing was short-lived; and why once the window was closed it was difficult to reopen because so many of the continuing cumulative innovations occurred within established enterprises.

This explanation of how German firms in the organic chemical industry were able to forge ahead of their British competitors raises a further question of interest to policy-makers: Was there any feature of the environment in Germany which made it easier for its firms to make the necessary investment in production, marketing, distribution and research; and to develop the managerial hierarchies necessary to run their new enterprises?

One explanation put forward is that Germany's university system had a much stronger science base, particularly in organic chemistry, and appears to have been more responsive to the needs of industry than universities in Britain. It is undoubtedly the case that German universities turned out more capable researchers, and more of them, than British universities. By the 1930s, the German system of higher education was arguably the best in the world. Germany also pioneered the idea of the research university, and Liebig's laboratory in Giessen attracted students from many parts of the world, including Britain.

While German chemical companies clearly benefited from an

excellent supply of trained and skilled chemists and engineers, we should be careful of accepting a simple supply-side explanation. The scientific community was already international at this time, and communication of research findings was quite quick. A number of distinguished German chemists worked in Britain and many got industrial experience with British firms. For instance, August Hoffman taught for many years in London and was William Perkin's professor. If the supply-side was important, so too was the demand-side. Chemists enjoyed much higher prestige and salaries in German firms; and while the supply of English chemists was low, so was demand for them. The difference in access to scientific and technological knowledge is unlikely, therefore, to be the entire story.

The most important reason why the strong science base was important is that it affected the willingness of German firms to invest in the commercialisation of science-based innovations. German managers understood that science and technology could provide them with competitive advantages as important as access to markets, raw materials and capital; and this understanding arose from the fact that many of them were trained and skilful chemists who enjoyed relationships of mutual respect with leading university professors. In other words, the main impact of the strong university research-base was that it improved the capabilities of the managers of German companies.

Therefore, in the case of the German chemical industry we can again see that the growth of the industry was driven forward by innovation and a capability/market-opportunity dynamic. We can also dismiss in this case the argument often put forward that British firms failed because they did not have access to financial capital. It is not possible to argue that a lack of financial capital was the reason why British firms did not invest in the new organic chemicals industry because London was the largest and most sophisticated capital market in the world, and German and American firms financed their subsidiaries in London.

The American automobile industry

The rise to world leadership of the American car industry was also due to innovation and a capability/market-opportunity dynamic. The United States did not lead Europe in the early days of the automobile industry – in fact, almost all the early inventions and innovations were made in Germany and France. By 1905, however, hundreds of small companies were producing automobiles in the United States, as well as the main European countries. They all used craft techniques and general-purpose machine-tools scattered in small machine-shops. The craft workers were highly skilled and co-ordinated by the assembly entrepreneur.

This situation was, of course, dramatically changed by Henry Ford, who saw the huge opportunity that existed due to the latent demand for a cheap, utilitarian car that any man earning good wages could own. He also saw that if he was going to produce cheap, utilitarian cars, there would need to be a major breakthrough in production systems, and this he achieved with the development of mass-production.

This built on earlier work on the interchangeability of parts that took place in the United States in the middle of the nineteenth century and was labelled by British engineers the 'American System of Manufacturing'. The concept of the interchangeability of parts was brought from France by Thomas Jefferson, and developed at the federal armouries at Springfield, Massachusetts and Harper's Ferry, West Virginia.

Before the concept of interchangeability, products were each made separately by highly skilled craftsmen, and no two were exactly alike. During the American War of Independence, for example, small weapons – such as muskets, rifles and pistols – were produced in this way. This made it difficult to repair weapons in the field, which was a major problem for the continental army, which had limited resources.

As a result, the US government initiated a fifty-year drive to push the federal armouries at Springfield, Massachusetts, and Harpers Ferry, West Virginia, to invest heavily in developing a new approach to manufacturing weapons with interchangeable parts. This involved developing single-purpose, specialised machines arranged in a sequential production system, and required the use of gauges, fixtures and inspection devices to achieve standardised parts. Over time, this made possible huge increases in productivity. The production potential of the new system was revealed in the first year of the Civil War. In 1862, the Springfield Armory produced over 100,000 arms; nearly a tenfold increase from 1861.

The federal armouries and the privately owned Colt Armory, established in Hartford, Connecticut, in 1855, also developed a set of capabilities that fed numerous other early manufacturing industries, such as sewing machines, textile machinery, furniture, locks, clocks, bicycles, locomotives and machine tools. Eventually, this included automobiles as Henry Ford's development of mass-production was built on earlier work on the interchangeability of parts.[6]

To achieve complete and consistent interchangeability of parts, Ford first insisted on the same gauging system being used all the way through the entire manufacturing process for every part. He also benefited from recent advances in machine tools, which enabled them to work on pre-hardened metals. The warping that had occurred as machine parts were being hardened had previously been a major obstacle to standardising parts. Once the warping problem was solved, Ford was able to develop innovative designs that reduced the number of parts needed and made them easy to attach.

Ford's first efforts to assemble his car, beginning in 1903, involved setting up assembly stands on which a whole car was built, often by one fitter. In 1908, on the eve of the introduction of the Model T, a Ford assembler's average basic cycle (the amount of time he worked before repeating the same operations) was 514 minutes, or 8.56 hours. This involved him getting the necessary parts, filing them down so they would fit – as Ford hadn't yet achieved perfect interchangeability – and then bolting them in place.

The first step Ford took to make the process more efficient was to deliver the parts to each work station. Then, around 1908, when he finally achieved perfect part interchangeability, he decided that the assembler would only perform a single task, and move from vehicle to vehicle around the assembly hall. Finally, in a stroke of genius in the spring of 1913 at his new Highland Park plant in Detroit, Ford introduced the moving assembly line, which brought the car past the stationary worker. This innovation cut the cycle time of the worker from 2.3 minutes to 1.19 minutes, cutting the minutes needed to assemble the engine, for example, by 62 per cent. Henry Ford now had a car that was designed for manufacture and was also user-friendly. Anyone could drive and repair it without a chauffeur or mechanic. And the price came steadily down.

In 1908, the price of the Model T was $850. As Ford developed his system of mass-production, the price fell to $600 in 1913, and $360 in 1916. As a result of the price reduction, sales of the Model T increased fifty times over, while market share increased from 10 per cent in 1909 to 60 per cent in 1924. Profits on net worth were sometimes as high as 300 per cent per annum, and the US attained a dominant position in world export markets.

This was 'fast history', and has many similarities with the extraordinary growth of the semiconductor industry half-a-century later. There were the same price reductions, rapid changes in market shares, sudden profits from innovating firms, and the same world export-dominance for the leading country until imitators caught up. It is also another impressive example of how a firm, having achieved a huge competitive advantage, is able to grow rapidly at home and abroad, making a significant contribution to the growth rate of its country.

As a result of Ford's huge success, other American firms had to introduce the assembly line, become small niche players, or go out of business. A few of them were, however, amalgamated into a company, General Motors (GM). Under the leadership of Alfred Sloan, GM provided a challenge to Ford by adopting a strategy based on a greater range of models, more frequent model changes, and steady incremental improvements coming partly from production engineers but also from large R&D activity. Sloan also famously introduced a divisionalised corporate structure, with the various divisions taking responsibility for specific segments of the market. This was necessary to manage the complexities his strategy had introduced into the business.

Due to these innovations, the American mass-production of cars marched from success to success for decades. The US car companies dominated the world automobile industry, and the US market accounted for the largest percentage of the world's auto sales. In 1955, for the first time, 7 million cars were sold in the United States. The three giant companies, Ford, GM and Chrysler, accounted for 95 per cent of all sales, and six models accounted for 80 per cent of all cars sold.

However, 1955 was also the year the downhill slide began. The share of market claimed by imports began to rise steadily, and US companies could no longer depend on their early perfection of mass-production to maintain their leading positions. A major reason for the three American firms losing their competitive advantage was that, by 1955, mass-production had spread widely across the world.

Many people had thought that the Americans would lose their lead much earlier, in the years after the First World War. Henry Ford was very open about his techniques, and even before the First World War there was a steady stream of visitors to Highland Park, including André Citroën, Louis Renault, Giovanni Agnelli of Fiat, and William Morris, founder of the Oxford Motor Company and its subsidiary MG; as well as Herbert Austin, founder of the Austin Motor Company.

William Morris visited Highland Park in 1914 and returned to England determined to immediately copy mass-production techniques in his own factory. He faced, however, major difficulties, which show why new firm capabilities giving an industry in one country a huge competitive advantage are not always immediately copied by the same industries in other countries.

The war interrupted production and a hand-powered assembly line was not in place until 1919. Under this system, cars rode on rail-mounted dollies, with automobiles pushed along to the next station by hand, meaning the whole line ran at the speed of the slowest worker. The assembly line was not powered until 1934, twenty years after Ford's first powered line in Detroit.

Morris also continued to pay all his workers on a piece-rate system until after the Second World War, despite all tasks being linked together in a continuous line. As a result, the main concern of the workers was to work as fast as they could to meet the day's quota and qualify for a bonus, and then knock off. It is not difficult to imagine the consequences of this system for the quality of the finished product.

Morris stuck with piece rates because he could think of no other way to get his employees to work. He also found it difficult to develop managers who wanted, and were able to operate, a Ford-style mass-production system. This meant he could only run his plant indirectly, with the aid of shop stewards who mediated between him and his workers on the pace of work and piece rates. Herbert Austin faced a similar situation, and also stuck with piece rates as the best way of motivating his workers.

As a result, British plants never matched the productivity or quality of US plants, and it was not until a financial crisis in 1980, sixty-seven years after the introduction of the powered assembly line at Highland Park, that Rover (formerly British Leyland, and the successor to the merged Austin and Morris companies) finally adopted standard hourly rates and set out to match the productivity of the Americans. By then, it was too late.

The main reason for America's loss of dominance in the world automobile market was the meteoric rise of the Japanese automobile industry, which I described in Chapter 3. By the 1960s, Japanese firms had, on average, gained an enormous advantage over mass-production elsewhere by adopting the principles of lean production. This enabled them to achieve a commanding share of the world automobile market (see Figure 5.1 overleaf), and this, in turn, had an impact on the growth rate of the American economy and the prosperity of the city of Detroit, the automobile capital of America.

Figure 5.1 **Japanese share of world motor vehicle production, 1955–89**
Share, %

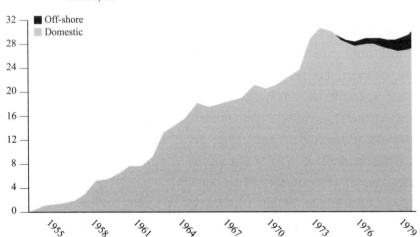

Note: Includes both domestic and offshore production.
Source: *Automotive News Market Data Book*. Reproduced in James P. Womack, Daniel T. Jomes and Daniel Roos,
The Machine that Changed the World, Rawson Associates, New York, 1990, p. 69

The American computer industry

The last sixty-five years has, for the computer industry, been a period
of rapid and dramatic change, continuous product innovation, and a
number of major breakthroughs. It is also a period that demonstrates
clearly how the growth of industries is driven by innovation and a
capability/market-opportunity dynamic; and is a good case study of
how firms are able to gain competitive advantage, as well as how they
maintain or lose it in competition with other firms.

The history of the computer industry over this period needs to be
divided into three overlapping phases if we are to understand what
happened.[7] The first phase ran from the late 1940s to the late 1980s,
and can best be characterised by the sale of mainframes and the dominant leadership of IBM. The second phase ran from the late 1950s to
the late 1980s, and saw the appearance of new market segments, and
the arrival of minicomputers, workstations and microcomputers. The

third phase, in the 1990s, saw the entry into the mainframe market of networks of small computers, and a capability-destroying challenge to IBM's leadership. When products using a new technology are introduced into a market, this inevitably destroys the value of the capabilities used in the previous generation of products, unless they can be used elsewhere.

What is most striking about the three phases, however, is that through all three of them one country – the United States – was the world's technological and commercial leader. This was due to an ever-increasing array of technological capabilities and an extraordinary record of product innovation.

The conditions and early entrants in the pioneering period, which led to the emergence of a mainframe computer industry, were very similar in the United States and Europe, with Japan lagging behind. In the 1940s, universities in both the United States and Europe were active at the scientific and prototype levels; and during the 1950s, the three types of entrants – office equipment producers, electronics firms and new firms – had similar capabilities and faced similar challenges in each country.

The electronics-based firms faced the challenge of either building or acquiring a business-equipment marketing capability, including a substantial field sales-force, or finding a way to succeed without it. Firms with business-equipment capabilities, on the other hand, had to acquire the technological capabilities necessary to compete in the new computer market. Both types of companies in the US were pioneers in computers during the 1950s, on the basis of sectoral demand underpinned by government contracts, primarily from the Department of Defence.

However, in the 1950s and early 1960s, IBM, which had previously been the leader in punch-card machines, emerged from this contest as the world leader in mainframes, and remained so for thirty years. It stayed ahead by a strategy of almost continuous product development. In the 1950s and early 1960s, IBM introduced highly successful families of computers, such as the 701 (1952), 650 (1954) and 1401 (1960). Each of these new families involved the company in the development of new computer technology; not only processing power but also peripherals. IBM linked this continuous R&D effort with the development of advanced manufacturing capabilities, excellent marketing capability, and management structures that kept technology and market aligned.

By 1960, IBM had produced fifteen different non-military computer systems, at a time when no other company had developed more than three or four. These fifteen systems used different types of components, peripherals and other auxiliaries, and in 1961 IBM's senior managers made an extremely bold move. They decided the company would build a new generation of computers, covering a broad range of price and performance markets. All the hardware and software would be compatible, and IBM would make its own hardware: printers, disk drives, and other peripherals, as well as semiconductors. The latter would not be based on transistors, but on recently invented, though still untested, integrated circuits.

Developing the machine turned out to be a huge project, so much so that the whole venture came to be known as a 'bet the company' initiative. IBM had to make use of virtually all its financial, technological and human resources, and by 1964 had spent more money on software development than it had planned to spend on the entire project. In 1967, though, it produced a flood of new products which made existing machines obsolete. The 360 was an immediate and huge success, and more than a thousand orders were made in the first month. By 1969, IBM had captured 70 per cent of the world market for general purpose computers.

The 1970s saw IBM continuing to dominate the mainframe segment and producing a new family of computers: the System 370. This made a further considerable technical advance, much of it capability destroying with respect to IBM's own capabilities. As with the System 360, IBM was prepared to give up added-value on its existing product lines as part of a strategy to strengthen its long-term competitive position.

The history of the IBM 360/370 computer systems shows what

an impact innovation and the achievement of competitive advantage can have on economic growth. Worldwide revenue brought in by US computers and their related products rose from £2.5 billion in 1965 to £10 billion in 1970; $21 billion in 1971; and to $37 billion in 1974; giving a compound annual growth rate of 33.5 per cent.

We need now to look at the second phase of the computer industry's development, which saw the arrival of minicomputers, workstations and microcomputers. In the early 1960s, the availability of new types of semiconductor components – integrated circuits – facilitated the introduction of minicomputers. This in turn stimulated new types of demand for computers in research laboratories; for the monitoring and control of industrial processes in manufacturing plants; and for technical problem-solving. A large number of specialised minicomputer firms also entered the market, such as the Digital Equipment Corporation (DEC); Data General; two Massachusetts firms, Prime Computer and Wang; the California instrument maker Hewlett-Packard; and IBM itself.

The early 1970s then saw the invention of another new technology at the components level – the microprocessor – which, over time, permitted the development of smaller and more user-friendly computers to satisfy new types of demand, such as family, hobby, educational and small business uses. These 'microcomputers', or 'personal computers', were far less powerful, but also far cheaper than the machines discussed thus far.

In 1977, three firms in different parts of the country introduced their initial products: Apple Computer in California; Radio Shack in Texas; and Commodore in Pennsylvania. But the industry was still in its infancy when, in the spring of 1980, IBM's management decided to take advantage of this new opportunity. With a brilliant, flawlessly executed strategy, reflecting its capability for new product development, IBM gave a huge boost to the new industry. In doing so, though, it helped develop a product which would in time destroy the worldwide dominance of the mainframe, in which IBM and its clones were the leaders.

The management of IBM understood that the capabilities needed for designing, producing and marketing its microcomputer, or personal computer (PC), were very different from those needed for mainframes. It therefore set up an autonomous business unit and in the summer of 1980 tasked it with building a global enterprise within a year. This it did, and by the autumn of 1981 IBM's plant at Boca Raton, Florida, was producing a machine every forty-five seconds.

In 1984, the third year of full production, the revenues of IBM's PC unit were $4 billion, revenues that were at the same level as the seventy-fifth largest US industrial company. In 1985, revenues levelled off at $5.5 billion. But while the IBM PC was a highly successful product, the fact it used outside suppliers of peripherals, components (Intel) and software (Microsoft), meant that it was easy to clone, and IBM was not able for long to appropriate the value-added per capita it had created. The minimum-efficient scale of production was also not high enough to create an effective barrier to entry. Start-ups and established firms swarmed into this huge new market, and by 1986 there were some 200 firms producing IBM PC clones.

By the end of the decade, IBM's market share had dropped to 22.3 per cent of the personal computer market worldwide; and by 1992 it was down to 17.2 per cent, followed by Apple with 12.3 per cent, and Compaq with 9.2 per cent. This sharp drop in market share was due to the decision of IBM to open the PC architecture. This speeded up its entry into the market and enabled it to get the benefits of setting the industry's standards, but it also made imitation incredibly easy. IBM's competitive advantage, therefore, rapidly disappeared.

The development of microcomputers and minicomputers did not, however, destroy the existing capabilities of established mainframe producers in the mainframe market segment. On the contrary, it opened new demand segments requiring different types of capability, different types of firm organisation, different customers, and a different user–producer relationship. It also brought new firms into the computer industry.

*

What is significant about the bursts of economic growth described in this chapter, is that each of them was caused by innovation and a capability/market-opportunity dynamic. In each case, firms in the economically successful country were able to gain a huge competitive advantage over firms in other countries by acquiring new organisational and technological capabilities. They were also able to maintain that lead for a period because firms in other countries found it difficult to imitate the capabilities they had acquired.

It might be argued that the four cases in this chapter have been specially selected to prove the point I want to make. But it is not difficult to argue that these four cases are among the top ten economic growth stories of the last 350 years. They are also significant for what they don't show. In none of the cases, for example, does it appear that the ability to access capital gave firms a competitive advantage. These cases are also not examples of a sudden improvement in allocative efficiency leading to economic growth. They are production-capability stories that show how innovation creates competitive advantage and is, therefore, the engine of economic growth; and as experiments in the laboratory of history they provide very clear results.

6

Catching up

Economic reform

In the last twenty-five years, a number of countries have dramatically caught up with the world's technological leaders. In this chapter, I want to test whether innovation and the capability/market-opportunity dynamic can be used to explain their performance.

In Chapter 1, I argued that the industrial take-off of a country requires, as a necessary but not sufficient condition, that the country has an inclusive market economy. In seeking to explain the rapidly increasing share of world trade captured by the catching-up countries since 1990, it is clearly important to note that three of them (China, India and Poland) became inclusive market economies at that time.

In the case of China, the economic reforms introducing market principles were begun in 1978 by Deng Xiaoping, and were carried out in two stages. The first stage, in the late 1970s and 1980s, involved the de-collectivisation of agriculture and the introduction of the household-responsibility system, which divided people's communes into private plots. Farmers were able to keep the land's output after paying a share to the state. The first stage also opened up the country to foreign investment and permitted entrepreneurs to start businesses. However, most industry remained state-owned. The second stage of reform, in the late 1980s and 1990s, involved the privatisation and contracting out of much state-owned industry. As a result, the state sector's share of industrial output dropped from 81 per cent in 1980 to 15 per cent in 2005.

Economists estimate China's GDP growth from 1978 to 2013 at between 9.5 per cent and approximately 11.5 per cent. Since the beginning of Deng Xiaoping's reforms, China's GDP has risen tenfold. Per capita incomes grew at 6.6 per cent a year, while between 1978 and 2001 those suffering from absolute poverty declined from 41 per cent of the population to just 5 per cent.

Turning to the case of India before the process of economic reform began in 1991, the country's economy was largely closed to the outside world. The Indian currency, the rupee, was inconvertible, and high tariffs and import licensing prevented foreign goods from entering the country. The Five Year Plans of the country resembled central planning in the Soviet Union; and steel, mining, machine tools, water, telecommunications, insurance and electrical plants, among other industries, were effectively nationalised in the mid-1950s. In addition, elaborate licences, regulations and accompanying red tape commonly referred to as the Licence Raj, were required to set up businesses in India between 1947 and 1990.

However, in response to a financial crisis, Prime Minister Narasimha Rao, and his Finance Minister Manmohan Singh, initiated in 1991 a programme of economic liberalisation. The reforms did away with the Licence Raj, reduced tariffs and interest rates, ended many public monopolies, and allowed automatic approval of foreign direct investment in many sectors. As a result, by the start of the twenty-first century, India had made good progress towards becoming an inclusive market economy; with a substantial reduction in state control of the economy and increased liberalisation.

The annual growth rate of the Indian economy stagnated at around 3.5 per cent from the 1950s to the 1980s, with the growth of per capita income averaging 1.3 per cent. During the same period, Indonesia's annual growth rate was 9 per cent; Thailand's was 9 per cent; South Korea's was 10 per cent; and Taiwan's was 12 per cent. As a result of liberalisation in 2006, India recorded its highest GDP growth rate of 9.6 per cent; making it the second fastest growing major economy in the world, behind only China.

Finally, in Poland, after the failure of the Communist government in the June 1989 elections, a programme of reform was drawn up and in December 1989 passed by the Sejm (the lower house of the Polish parliament), and signed by the President. This drastically limited the state's influence over the economy and abolished price-fixing for many products, allowing them to be dictated by the market instead of the Central Statistical Office.

If we are to understand the changing pattern of world trade over the period 1990–2015, then as well as noting that three of the catching-up countries became functioning market economies at the start of this period, we also need to note the obvious fact that two of these three countries – China and India – have huge populations. As a result, when their economies began to grow fast, they had a huge impact on the pattern of world trade. At the start of this period, China had just 3 per cent of world manufacturing. By the end, it had almost a fifth.

The fact that three of the catching-up countries became market economies at the start of the 1990–2015 period is part of the explanation as to why the pattern of world trade shifted so dramatically, and there will no doubt be some economists who argue that no other explanation is needed. However, there are plenty of countries in Africa that were market economies during this period, but did not catch up. 'Getting the prices right' is not enough.

A further explanation is, therefore, required to understand how the catching-up countries increased competitive advantage in key sectors of their economies; and the question to be asked is whether innovation and the capability/market-opportunity dynamic I outlined in Chapter 2 provides an answer. I think it does, and that it convincingly explains why the 'Asian Miracle' took place – something neoclassical economists have singularly failed to do.

To demonstrate that the capability/market-opportunity dynamic provides an explanation, we need to show that major changes in the world economy opened up many windows of opportunity for the catching-up countries, while other major changes in the world economy enabled their firms to build up their capabilities in order that they could take advantage of these opportunities.

Windows of opportunity

If one looks at the world economy during the years 1990 to 2015, it is not difficult to identify the factors that opened up windows of opportunity for the developing world, as well as the factors enabling their firms to increase their capabilities in order to take advantage of them. The factors that opened up windows of opportunity for them were trade liberalisation, new forms of transportation, and the growth of global value chains (GVCs).

At the end of the Second World War, the Allies – especially the United States and the United Kingdom – started to design the post-war economic architecture, determined to avoid the international governance vacuum that had emerged after the First World War. One of the key institutions that they set up to avoid a governance vacuum on trade was the General Agreement on Tariffs and Trade, or GATT as it became universally known. To achieve GATT's mission of fostering living standards and sustainable development, its members set out to establish some basic 'rules for the road' for international trade. They also committed themselves to trade liberalisation, negotiating reciprocal and mutually advantageous reductions in tariffs, and by the early 1990s had brought down world trade tariffs from the high levels at which they were set after the Second World War to reasonably low levels.

The second factor opening up 'windows of opportunity' for the developing world was new forms of transport. The period between the end of the Second World War and 1990 saw continuous technological improvements in ships, trains and trucks, which significantly reduced the cost of moving goods, but did not overcome the age-old problem of loading and unloading goods. A major breakthrough, however, came in the 1960s with 'containerisation', and the impact of this development grew exponentially in the 1970s and 1980s.

Before containerisation was developed, ships were loaded by hand. This was not only costly, but meant imported goods could remain for weeks in port. It also meant that the length of time imported goods stayed in port was highly uncertain, and this created major problems for anyone running an international production network. Containerisation made shipping both cheaper and more reliable by putting goods into standard-size steel containers. This meant goods did not have to be individually handled, resulting in a significant drop in the cost of moving goods. It has been estimated by economists that containerisation boosted trade far more than all the tariff cutting between 1947 and 1994.

Containerisation was not the only change in the 1970s and 1980s that opened up windows of opportunity for the developing world. Air freight first became commercially viable due to the surplus of planes available after the Second World War, but it was only in the mid-1980s that it really got going, with the rise of Federal Express, DHL and UPS. It stimulated and was stimulated by the development of international production networks, as it allowed manufacturers to be confident that intermediate goods would flow among distant factories almost as surely as they flow between factories within a nation. Today, 40 per cent of the parts and components imported into the United States are imported by air.

This is not because air cargo is cheaper. In fact, air cargo today is many times more expensive than sea freight, though it has been getting cheaper. The key advantage of sending products by air is speed. European freight sent by sea, for example, takes an average of twenty days to reach US ports, and a month to reach Japan. Air shipments take a day or less, and there is much greater certainty about the time they will take – a fact which, as we have seen, is of great importance for firms managing international production networks.

The third factor that significantly increased the windows of opportunity for developing countries was the growth of GVCs. In the late 1980s, revolutionary advances in the transmission, storage and processing of information dramatically lowered communication costs.

The price of telephone calls dropped, cellular usage exploded, and in the 1990s the Internet lowered the cost of moving ideas even more.

These cheaper communication costs interacted with two other trends – the spectacular fall in the price of computing power and the equally impressive rise in fibre-optic transmission rates and bandwidth – to cause the death of distance for digitised ideas. As a result, manufacturing stages that previously had to be done within walking distance could now be performed in different countries without a significant loss of efficiency or timeliness.

This change enabled G7 countries to take advantage of the very large wage differences that had grown up during the Great Divergence between, for example, the United States and Mexico; and between Japan and China. The offshoring of manufacturing to Mexico and China did not make economic sense when co-ordination had to be done by phone, faxes or overnight express mail. But the revolutionary advances in information and communication technology made it profitable for G7 countries to offshore some stages of production to low-wage countries.

The offshoring of production by the G7 countries opened up many new windows of opportunity for developing countries. When a developing country enters a GVC it can free-ride on the industrial base of the company that has set up the GVC, meaning it has to become competitive in only a single stage of the production network rather than in all stages.

The growth of GVCs did not reduce the need for firms in developing countries to upgrade their capabilities, and to become proficient in producing more complex parts of GVCs or in entering higher value-added sectors, but it provided more windows of opportunity for them to do so.

The importance of GVCs to developing countries can be seen not only in the performance of the countries, but also in their policy-making behaviour. When the GVC revolution started picking up steam, many developing countries decided that trade barriers were harming their chances of getting their share of offshored jobs, and around

1990 started enthusiastically cutting tariffs. The reason for this policy change was simple. Developing countries that are part of international production networks typically import some parts, and then re-export them after some processing. If it is seen to impose a tariff on imported parts it will harm its perceived competitiveness, making it less likely to be selected to become part of an international production network.

In the late 1980s, developing countries not only cut tariffs, they also developed a new relationship to foreign direct investment (FDI). Up to this point, they had had a love/hate relationship with FDI. Though they liked foreign investment, they feared the impact it might have on the performance of their own companies. In almost all developing countries, the balancing of these pros and cons had led to regulation of FDI. This attitude changed, however, in the late 1980s, and can be seen in the growth of bilateral investment treaties (BITs). These mainly consist of concessions to rich-nation firms seeking to invest in the developing country that signs the BIT. The concessions take the form of disciplines put in place to govern interactions between private foreign investors and host governments. For example, they often limit the developing country's ability to impose controls on capital flows, and give foreign investors the right to submit disputes to international arbitration rather than local courts. In these cases, the perception of potential demand led to the creation of institutions.

The interesting thing about the signing of BITs is the speed at which they grew in the late 1980s and early 1990s. In 1985, there were eighty-six BIT signers. By 2000, the number had doubled, almost entirely due to the increase in developing countries joining the trend.

The capabilities of firms

As we have seen, between 1990 and 2015 many windows of opportunity opened up to developing countries. However, these windows of opportunity would have been of no value to them if their firms had not at the same time been able to build up their capabilities so as to take advantage of them. Here, again, there were three factors that helped them: the growth of GVCs; the movement of people; and the management of technology diffusion by governments.

The growth of GVCs not only provided developing countries with many windows of opportunity, but also had a significant impact on the global distribution of technological knowledge, knowhow and market information. This resulted in a combination of low-wage labour and advanced technology, which made the firms involved very competitive. The offshoring of the production of Apple computers from Texas to China, for example, is essentially a story of American technological knowledge and knowhow moving to low-wage workers in China.

However, the way developing countries used GVCs to tap into foreign technology and market information differed significantly. For example, Singapore largely used internal transfer from the headquarters of a foreign firm to its subsidiary in Singapore. By contrast, Taiwan and, especially, South Korea, relied mostly on external transfer through mechanisms such as Original Equipment Manufacturing (OEM), an important organisational innovation that greatly facilitated learning and technological upgrading in developing countries.

Under an OEM contract, products are manufactured in line with a customer's specification produced by a transnational corporation (TNC), which then markets the products under its own brand name, such as 'Nike' or 'Apple'. This was the mechanism used by many US and Japanese firms from the 1970s onwards, particularly in the ICT sector, when contracting out their production to Korean and Taiwanese firms. It was a mechanism which allowed the latter countries to build up their basic production capabilities in areas such as electronics, as the TNCs usually helped with the selection of equipment; the training of managers, engineers and technicians; as well as giving advice on financing and management. They did this because their reputation depended critically on the quality, delivery and price of the final product.

In time, many OEM contracts evolved into a more advanced 'own design and manufacturing' (ODM) stage, as Korean and Taiwanese firms gradually acquired more advanced capabilities in process engineering and product design. A final step firms could take if they acquired the capabilities to produce and market products under their own brand names was 'own brand manufacturing' (OBM), but to do this they had to acquire significant capabilities in marketing, as well as make very substantial investments in distribution. It was, however, potentially a very rewarding step, as a great deal of value-added is generated at this stage.

The mode of technology transfer affects the need for independent local effort, though some learning is always involved. Internalised technology transfer provides access to state-of-the-art technologies, along with brand names and entry into global markets. It is, therefore, a very effective way to transfer and operationalise new technologies for export competitiveness. On the other hand, externalised technology transfer, such as an OEM, involves greater effort and risk on the part of the recipient country, and may not allow access to the most valuable new technologies held by innovators. But there are good reasons why countries adopt externalised transfers of technology. In most medium to large economies, local enterprises account for the bulk of industrial activity, and their competitiveness depends on externalised technology transfer. Externalised technology transfer involves greater effort but yields greater learning benefits, and, therefore, makes upgrading easier.

The second factor that helped firms in developing countries build the capabilities needed to take advantage of windows of opportunity that opened up to them from the 1970s onwards was the movement of people. In all cases where developing countries have successfully built up new capabilities, they have relied extensively on the cross-border flow of people. These flows have involved both citizens from the catching-up country going abroad to learn and then returning home; and citizens from the advanced countries establishing themselves in, or simply visiting, the developing countries as advisors, professors, or as technical personnel for local and foreign firms.

British technicians played a central role in the diffusion of knowledge about their home country's manufacturing techniques when they migrated to the United States or continental Europe during the late eighteenth and early nineteenth centuries. Equally, the training of Japanese nationals abroad and the recruitment of foreign technical advisors made a significant contribution to the development of Japanese industry in the late nineteenth and early twentieth centuries. In more recent times, the success of the Korean and Taiwanese semiconductor and electronics industries can partly be attributed to a similar movement of people, as can the success of a range of other industries in China and India.

However, whereas in earlier years the cross-border flows of people were the result of individuals' search for economic and professional opportunities abroad, more recently business enterprises have become an increasingly important vehicle for such movements. In addition, over the last quarter-century, the transnational flow of people has been significantly increased by the greater number of young people going to universities abroad in the relevant fields of engineering and applied science. As a result, national policy debates have broadened out from discussing the costs of brain drain to the opportunities offered by the process of brain circulation.

These developments have taken on increased importance in recent years due to the widespread shift in the computer industry during the 1980s and the 1990s from vertically integrated corporations controlling all aspects of hardware and software production, to the more flexible manufacturing systems of Silicon Valley, based on firm-level specialisation and extensive outsourcing. This decentralised system depends heavily on the co-ordination provided by cross-cutting social structures and institutions. While Silicon Valley's entrepreneurs innovate in increasingly specialised niche markets, intense communication among them ensures the speedy and often unexpected recombination of these specialised components into new products. This decentralised system in a fast-changing environment provides significant advantages in terms of speed and flexibility over the more integrated traditional model.

As recently as the 1970s, only the world's largest corporations had the resources and capabilities to grow internationally. Today, though, the new transportation and communication technologies described earlier in this chapter allow even the smallest firms to set up GVCs and tap into overseas expertise, cost savings and markets. As a result, start-ups in Silicon Valley today are often global actors from the day they are set up.

The resource that is in short supply in this new environment is the capability to locate foreign partners quickly, and to manage complex business relationships across cultural and linguistic boundaries.[1] This is obviously a particularly difficult problem when products, markets and technologies are rapidly changing. However, first generation immigrants – such as Chinese and Indian engineers who were educated in the United States and gained experience in Silicon Valley – are obviously well placed to play a central role in this environment, as they have the necessary language and cultural skills, as well as the technical knowledge. They can potentially create social networks enabling even the smallest producers to locate and maintain mutually beneficial collaborations across great distances. The proliferation of such relationships can, over time, lead to the creation of transnational technical communities that play a significant role in transferring technological knowledge and market information to newly industrialising and rapidly upgrading countries.

The most obvious example of such a transnational technical community is the one the government of Taiwan helped create in Hsinchu Science Park. As already seen in Chapter 4, the science park contained many returnees from the US, who by 1999 had created 110 of the 284 companies in the park. At the same time, a growing number of these highly mobile, Taiwanese-born, US-educated engineers began to work in both the US and Taiwan, regularly commuting across the Pacific. As they travelled between the two regions they carried technical knowledge, as well as contacts, capital and information about new opportunities and markets. In this way, they have formed a transnational technical community that has played a significant role in accelerating the flow of skills, knowhow and market information between the two regions.

The third factor that helped developing countries build up their capabilities was the management of technology diffusion by governments.[2] Clearly, a major factor in the rapid economic growth of countries such as South Korea, Taiwan and Singapore was the advanced technological capabilities they were quickly able to develop in addition to those they had acquired as a result of participating in GVCs. These advanced technological capabilities were not acquired by conventional approaches to innovation and R&D. Instead, in order to enable their firms to compete successfully in world markets, the industrially successful countries of East Asia devised methods to acquire and internalise technology developed elsewhere.

The creation of new ways of learning from other countries meant that firms were no longer forced to learn from foreign firms on their own. These new methods should be seen as part of a country's 'national system of economic learning' (NSEL), in contrast to the 'national systems of innovation' (NSI) in advanced countries. Three types of vehicle have been used by developing countries as a means of diffusing technological knowledge to their firms: the use of large already established firms in their own country; the use of public-sector laboratories and institutions linked to R&D consortia of small firms; and the use of multinational corporations (MNCs).

The Korean approach, which was modelled on its perception of what Japan did, especially in the latter's industrial colony of Manchuria in the 1930s, was to use large firms that had already been created in the early years of industrialisation. As will be seen later in the chapter, the Korean policy approach in the semiconductor industry was to encourage existing large firms – which had already developed an ability to import technology – to enter this high-risk area in the 1980s, using technology acquired from foreign companies.

A second approach was the one used by the Taiwanese government. As there were many small and medium-sized firms in Taiwan, and an absence of large firms, the government made use of public-sector agencies. In the case of the electronics industry, as we will again see later in this chapter, the public body used was the Industrial Technology Research Institute (ITRI), which had been set up to provide public support for R&D, and research consortia formed with Taiwanese firms.

A third approach, pioneered by Singapore, was the use of multinational corporations. The Singapore government believed the local entrepreneurial base was too weak to lead the process of industrialisation, and instead encouraged MNCs to take on that role. Multinational corporations are the world's best source of technological competences, and Singapore pioneered the approach of offering them favourable conditions to locate their activities in their country, thereby raising the overall skill and technological capabilities of their national firms.

The Singapore government also sought to upgrade the activity of the MNCs according to its strategic priorities, by directing their investments into higher value-added activities, and encouraging existing affiliates to upgrade their technologies and functions. This was a very active policy involving extensive interventions in skill creation; encouraging R&D and technology institutions; infrastructure development; supplier support; and attracting, targeting and guiding investment. It was also very successful.

Sectoral dynamics

In the first part of this chapter, I have shown that the catching-up countries, which grew so strongly between 1990 and 2015, had many windows of opportunity open to them, and that there were a number of ways they could acquire the technological capabilities and market information necessary to take advantage of these opportunities. But it is a central argument of this book that the capability/market-opportunity dynamic that drives economic growth in catching-up countries is activity-specific and operates at a sector level, and, therefore, if we want to understand fully why some countries catch up faster than others we need to look at a number of sectors in the fast-growing countries.

The following few pages, therefore, give three examples of fast-growing sectors in different countries. Two of these are high-tech sectors in fast-growing developing countries: the semiconductor industry in South Korea, and the electronics industry in Taiwan. The third is the worldwide wine industry, which in recent years witnessed catching up by sectors in both developed and developing countries. I have included the worldwide wine industry as it shows that competitive advantage can be created in agricultural products that require complex processing, and because it shows that catching up can take place in both developed and developing countries.

Before I look at these three examples of catching up, though, it is necessary to describe in more detail the different windows of opportunity that can open up to firms, and the different paths taken by catching-up firms in comparison with those taken by the leading firms in their sector.

The concept of 'windows of opportunity' was first used by Carlota Perez and Luc Soete[3] in 1988 to refer to the role new techno-economic paradigms can play in enabling latecomer firms to overtake incumbents. They pointed to the difficulties faced by firms in developing countries when trying to compete against well-established firms in developed countries that benefited from economies of scale and experience curves. The only way it appeared firms in these circumstances could grow was to choose mature products and combine them with the low wages of a developing country. However, given that mature products are precisely those that have exhausted their technological dynamism, such a strategy carries with it the risk of getting trapped in a low-wage, low-growth, development pattern. An effective catching-up process can only be achieved, they argued, by acquiring the capacity to participate in the generation and improvement of technologies, as opposed to the simple 'use' of them.

This meant that such firms would have to be innovators or early imitators of new products and processes. Perez and Soete asked under what conditions this would be possible. To be able to answer this question, they claimed, it is necessary to reject the traditional notion of technological change as a global and more-or-less continuous process. If technology is understood as a cumulative unidirectional process, development will always be seen as a race along a fixed track, where catching up will be merely a question of relative speed. Speed is undoubtedly an important factor, but as Perez and Soete said: 'History is full of examples of how successful overtaking has been primarily based on running in a new direction'.[4] They, therefore, argued that catching up takes place when firms are in a position to take advantage of 'windows of opportunity' temporarily created by technological or other transitions.

There are two very clear reasons why such 'windows of opportunity' are favourable times for catching up. The first is that incumbents and latecomers are in the same position of having to learn a new technology. Secondly, the incumbents may get caught in an incumbent trap. Firm leaders are often complacent and do not wish to write off the capital they have invested in the old technology. They may, therefore, respond slowly to new 'windows of opportunity'.

The concept of 'windows of opportunity' can be developed further by linking it to the building blocks of a sectoral system of innovation.[5] If we do so, we can identify three different types of window: technological windows, demand windows, and institutional windows. A technological window of opportunity occurs when a major technological change takes place; for example, the move from the analogue era to the digital era in consumer electronics. A demand window opens up when a new type of demand occurs, there is a major shake-up in local demand, or a new set of consumers appear, such as happened in the case of demand for low-cost cars in India. Finally, an 'institutional/public policy window' can be opened through public intervention in an industry, or drastic changes in its institutional conditions. For example, in achieving leadership in the worldwide mobile-phone industry, Nokia took advantage of the European regulatory strategy that sought to rapidly replace the analogue standard with the GSM digital standard for mobile phones.

The ability of latecomer firms to take advantage of windows of opportunity depends, of course, on their capabilities. It also depends on the action taken by the institutions supporting them in their country, including types and levels of networks; the education and training system; the national system of innovation; financial institutions; and public policy.

Three different patterns of catching up by latecomer firms have also been identified.[6] Firstly, there is path-following catching up, which means latecomer firms follow the same path as that taken by their forerunners, but do so in a shorter period of time. Secondly, there is stage-skipping catching up, which means latecomer firms follow the path to an extent, but skip one or more steps, and in doing so save time. Thirdly, there is path-creating catching up, which means that latecomer firms create a new path, having previously followed the path of their forerunners. The second and third of these patterns have been described as leapfrogging.

With these different patterns of catching up in mind, as well as the various windows of opportunity, we can now look in more detail at the three examples of fast-growing sectors previously mentioned, in order to understand fully how the capability/market-opportunity dynamic operates to produce a rapid rate of growth.

In looking at these three cases, the unit of analysis used is the industry or sector. This is based on the assumption that, in an industry, the firms from a particular country share a common ecosystem, involving: national or local networks; infrastructure; a university–industry system; human capital; financial organisation; and other institutions of that country. While the unit of analysis is the sector, the focus will be on the leadership of the firms belonging to the sector in the country being examined.

The electronics industry in Taiwan

From 1970 to 2000, Taiwan built up its electronics industry by enhancing the capabilities of its firms so they could take advantage of the technological windows of opportunity open to them. Its path of development over this period was a path-following one.[7] During the 1960s, Taiwan quickly diversified away from primary products to manufactured products, and by the 1970s it was ready to follow Japan's example and pursue knowledge-intensive sectors such as electronics.

United States, European and Japanese firms competed fiercely in the 1960s to sell consumer items such as radios, calculators and TV sets; as well as communication products, computers and components, particularly semiconductors. Seeking to gain competitive advantage, US electronics and semiconductor firms invested in low-cost manufacturing operations in East Asia, to which they first transferred production of components, then assembly of products, and, finally, test and assembly operations for both semiconductors and final electronic goods.

The major policy instrument used by the Taiwanese government at this stage was a local content obligation that forced foreign producers to upgrade the capabilities of local suppliers of parts and components. In 1965, local content rules were imposed for black-and-white TV sets at a level of 50 per cent, gradually rising to 90 per cent in 1974. This direct intervention by government was designed to foster the development of a local parts-and-components industry.

The Taiwanese government also established the world's first export-processing zone in 1968, the manufacturing equivalent of nineteenth-century free ports. This opened the way for considerable investment from US, Japanese and European firms in the production of electrical and electronic components, and in the 'back end' of the semiconductor cycle, which includes testing, packaging and assembly.

Then, in 1973, the government created the Industrial Technology

Research Institute (ITRI) to provide public support for R&D. ITRI's first laboratory, the Electronics Research and Service Organization (ERSO), was dedicated to creating technological capabilities in the electronics sector.[8] A major vehicle used by ITRI in order to keep Taiwanese firms abreast of new technologies in electronics has been R&D consortia. Taiwan's rapid economic growth has been based not on giant firms, as in Japan and South Korea, but on small and medium-sized enterprises where entrepreneurial flexibility and adaptability have been key to their success. The co-operation between the public and private sectors in ITRI's research alliances has enabled Taiwan's firms to build up their capabilities and overcome the scale disadvantages of small firms.

The basic model of the Taiwanese consortia brings together many small firms in a collaborative alliance with each other and with one of ITRI's operating laboratories, with ITRI providing the institutional vehicle for acquiring the needed technology. In their reliance on public-sector laboratories to provide the core institutional vehicle for R&D co-operation, Taiwan's R&D consortia are similar to their counterparts in North America, Europe and Japan. However, they differ in that their goal is the rapid adoption of new technological standards, products or processes developed elsewhere, rather than doing more R&D.

These R&D consortia are an interfirm organisational device that Taiwan has successfully developed from early cases where government contributed all the funds, and research tasks were formulated in terms that were too generic and overly ambitious for companies to take advantage of. The R&D alliances formed in the 1990s were more focused, more tightly organised and managed, and involved participant firms much more directly in co-developing a core technology or new technological standard that companies could incorporate into their own products.

The power of Taiwan's public–private R&D consortia was demonstrated in one successful industry intervention after another. Taiwan's current dominance of mobile (laptop) PCs, for example, can be attributed at least in part to a public–private-led consortium that rushed a product to world markets in 1991. Taiwan's strong performance in communication products such as data switches, which are used in PC networks, can also be attributed to a consortium that worked with ITRI to produce a switch to meet the Ethernet standard in 1992/93.

The effectiveness of these consortia can be judged by their ability to move fast. In 1995, when IBM introduced a new PC based on its Power PC microprocessor, Taiwanese firms produced a range of computing products based on the same processor just one day later. They were able to do so because they had set up an R&D consortium, involving both IBM and Motorola – joint developers of the Power PC microprocessor – as external partners. There can be no doubt that Taiwan's R&D consortia were a very effective vehicle for both catching-up industry creation and technological upgrading.

By 1990, due to such policies as the R&D consortia, the electronics industry in Taiwan accounted for no less than 12.2 per cent of the country's manufacturing output, as well as a significant proportion of the country's exports. The sector continued to expand as a result of a consistent set of policies towards IT products, components, semiconductors, and industrial electronics; and by the end of the century, electronics contributed 25 per cent of Taiwan's manufacturing value-added. By this point, Taiwan was also producing 5.5 per cent of the world's semiconductors, as well as most of the world's computer terminals and peripherals, and had become the world's sixteenth largest economy.

The DRAM industry in South Korea

The semiconductor industry consists of three main segments: microprocessors; memories used for information storage; and ASICs (application-specific integrated circuits). The memory market, which includes DRAMs (dynamic random-access memories), is characterised by rapid technological progress, with new generations of product brought to the market every three or four years. This opened up technological windows of opportunity for latecomers.[9]

South Korea became involved in the semiconductor industry from the middle of the 1960s, when major US semiconductor firms relocated their assembly processes to East Asia in order to take advantage of cheap labour there. While Japan sought to catch up with the US at the beginning of the 1960s, South Korea, lacking the capability to compete with the leaders, joined this high-tech industry as a provider of low-cost, unskilled labour for assembly processes. It imported 100 per cent of the equipment, materials and technologies it needed directly from foreign MNCs; and exported 100 per cent of the products it assembled through MNCs' global marketing networks.

However, in the early 1980s South Korea launched a strategy to catch up. By that time, the Korean *chaebols* – family-controlled, diversified business groups – had built up their management and financial resources as a result of the country's Heavy and Chemical Industrialisation Drive of the 1970s. They had also acquired significant mass-production capabilities by means of their consumer-electronics businesses. Having witnessed the Japanese success in overtaking the US in the DRAM industry, the Koreans wanted to emulate it. They began by investing heavily in the semiconductor industry, turning out their first commercial DRAM product, a 64K DRAM, in 1984.

The Korean catch-up strategy was basically a repetition of the Japanese one. First, Korean semiconductor manufacturers adopted an unbalanced growth strategy by focusing on DRAMs, as the Japanese industry had done before them. After rapidly narrowing the technological gap with the Japanese, Korean companies again emulated the Japanese by adopting what has been described as a 'dynamic catch-up strategy'. This involved developing a 4M DRAM and a 16M DRAM almost simultaneously.

It should be noted that this strategy of simultaneous catch up in overlapping generations of products requires extremely high levels of investment. The Korean *chaebol* were able to sustain these due to their ownership structure. Unlike the Japanese *keiretsu*, which is a loose federation run by professional managers, the Korean *chaebol* maintain a centralised co-ordination system, with power concentrated at the top, mainly with the owner-family. Once a strategic decision is made, therefore, the *chaebol* can concentrate its resources on an investment race and win.

The Korean manufacturers also sought to increase their competitive advantage by reducing production costs and mass-producing better-quality products. While it took three years for the forerunners to mass-produce 16M DRAMs after development concluded, it only took Samsung two years, making the company the first in the world to mass-produce the 16M DRAM in 1991.

How did Samsung manage to develop the capabilities to produce such an outstanding performance? In the 1970s, several FDI and OEM firms started wafer processing and absorbed low-level technology, with the technology capability being provided by foreigners. The late 1970s to the early 1980s was the period of high-level technology absorption, with all foreign companies selling their shares to Korean firms, and Korean *chaebols* such as Samsung taking over these firms.

Under its own initiative, Samsung started producing 64K DRAM chips in the 1980s. It was helped in this task by being able to buy 64K DRAM design technology from Microelectronic Technology, a small US-based venture company, and manufacturing technology from Japan-based Sharp. A couple of years after starting to produce DRAMs using purchased manufacturing technology, Samsung chose to develop its own design technology for 256K or higher DRAMs. In this process, the role of overseas R&D outposts in Silicon Valley and returning scientists and engineers was critical, and Samsung's 256K DRAM, developed by its Silicon Valley team, was assessed to be better than the Japanese counterparts. Throughout, government industrial policy lagged behind the progress made by private initiatives. Only in 1986 did the government initiate the formation of a semiconductor R&D consortium, with Samsung, LG and Hyundai participating to develop successive generations of memory chips.

As a result of its efforts, Samsung emerged as the world's number one producer of DRAMs in 1992, and the number one producer of memory chips in 1993. On a national basis, South Korea emerged as the number one memory producer in 1999. After a dip in its production, mainly due to a financial crisis at Hynix, South Korea re-emerged as the number one memory-producing country in 2002, and has maintained its leadership ever since.

The growth of the Korean DRAM industry is, therefore, a good example of an industry driven by a capability/market-opportunity dynamic. The frequent generation changes in production technologies opened up technological windows of opportunity for the Koreans, who were also able to conduct a massive ramping up of investment during the changes, and as a result achieved a similar or higher level of performance as the incumbents.

By contrast, the impact of the 'demand window' that existed was marginal, although demand for memory chips was growing for all players. The Koreans were, however, helped by an institutional window of opportunity that opened in the US at the conclusion of the Semiconductor Trade Agreement (STA) in 1986. The STA effectively established a floor price for DRAMs in the US market. The selling price of 256K DRAMs not only stopped decreasing, but even increased slightly for almost three years after the introduction of the STA, which helped both Japanese and Korean firms.

As far as the pattern of development is concerned, the catching-up pattern of South Korea regarding DRAMs was a 'stage-skipping' one. However, it is perhaps better described as a 'compressed' one, as Samsung did not 'skip' or attach less importance to 4M DRAMs, but rather developed the 4M and 16M DRAMs simultaneously; and it was the mass-production of 4M DRAMs that was mainly responsible for the change in market leadership from Japanese producers to Samsung.

The worldwide wine industry

Until the end of the 1980s, the international wine market was dominated by Old World countries such as France and Italy.[10] Since then, though, they have been challenged first by affluent New World countries such as the US and Australia, and later by less developed countries such as Chile, Argentina and South Africa.

The scale of the challenge to the Old World producers from the New World producers can be seen in the world export figures for wine. In volume terms, the share of world trade by European exporters has declined from almost 95 per cent in the late 1980s to 71 per cent in 2007. This reflects the fact that during the late 1980s the original challengers – the US and Australia – were joined by a second group, made up of developing countries. Among these, the Chilean wine industry stands out in export terms, rapidly overtaking the US, and then catching up to the market leader, Australia.

The performance of the New World countries looks even more impressive when one looks at the value of exports, the growth of which shows how these countries have raised the quality of their wines. For example, since the early 1990s, premium exports have contributed to 97 per cent of the growth in value of Australia's wine exports. Chile and South Africa still specialise in lower-quality segments, but the unit value of their exports has gradually been converging with the world average, and has more than doubled in absolute terms since the 1990s. As a result of quality upgrading and volume expansion, the value of exports from Chile increased from US$72 million in the first half of the 1990s, to almost US$400 million in 2004. In South Africa, meanwhile, they increased from less than US$200 million in the second half of the 1990s to more than US$500 million in 2004.

Here again we see the wine sector in different countries driven by a capability/market-opportunity dynamic. But in this case the window of opportunity was a demand one, and the catching-up path a path-creating one. Since the 1980s, there has been a transformation in consumer attitudes to wine-drinking in European countries with an existing wine culture, such as Italy, France and Spain, as well as in other affluent countries with a growing wine culture, such as the UK, the US and the Scandinavian nations. Due to increasing wealth and foreign travel, people became more sophisticated in their tastes. This led to wine becoming more popular as a drink, in turn giving rise to a preference for the cabernet, sauvignon, merlot and chardonnay varietal wines typically produced in the New World.

At the same time, there was a major consolidation of distribution at both the wholesale and retail levels, which had a major effect on competition in the wine market. In the US, the twenty largest wholesalers control 20 per cent of the market, while supermarkets and hypermarkets account for more than 40 per cent of retail wine sales. A similar trend is emerging in all affluent countries.

The diffusion of wine-drinking to a large number of relatively inexperienced consumers, who purchased wine mainly in supermarkets, resulted in an increased emphasis on marketing and consistent 'product building'. Also, wholesalers and supermarkets prefer to stock only the top-selling brands, rather than small or new labels. This sales strategy obviously has a damaging impact on wine industries that have small and micro wineries, such as in Italy.

In order to respond to the window of opportunity opened by the changing demand for wine, wine producers developed a new set of capabilities. These were based on a more scientific approach, aligned to their marketing strategies. Because scientific knowledge in the field is rapidly diffused to wine producers worldwide, competitive advantage is not built on the appropriability of research output, but on the alignment of R&D with both production and marketing requirements.

California, among New World producing areas, has been the pioneer in introducing this new scientific approach, with its research programmes largely focused on the introduction of new grape varieties and a reduction in the variability of output. This has been done in order to produce wines of consistent taste and quality, despite variability in climate conditions, soil characteristics and other local conditions. This new scientific approach has been possible due to increased global knowledge codification and a formal investigative effort across a wide range of disciplines related to the wine industry. From the early 1990s to 2006, scientific publications on wine-related issues – mostly within food science, but increasingly involving biology and biotechnology – recorded a growth rate five times larger than the average across the spectrum of scientific disciplines.

This new scientific research required changes in the capabilities of wine producers. Production techniques that were previously driven by farmers' experience and practical problem-solving now required management by highly skilled professionals, as well as inputs of external knowledge. This led to the appearance of the so-called 'flying winemakers'; consultants who advise the most dynamic wine producers across the world, and in this way contribute to the rapid transfer of scientific knowledge to new areas.

The interplay between the two key elements of the wine industry's sectoral system of innovation – demand and the knowledge base – has also altered the nature of the actors in the system; with the new competitive environment, based on technological modernisation, global marketing and large-scale retail chains, leading to a change in the structure of the industry. Since the late 1990s, national and transnational mergers, acquisitions and strategic alliances have led to a rapid process of consolidation, as the branding and volume capabilities of the leading global wine firms – as well as their ability to produce wines of a consistent quality – have made them attractive to large supermarket chains, which prefer to have a few large suppliers in order to reduce procurement costs. The process of concentration and rationalisation has affected the New World most, with the largest wine companies coming from the United States. In 2008, the world's largest wine producers were Fosters of Australia and Constellation Brands of the US; followed by Distell of South Africa and the Chilean company Concha Y Toro.

Finally, institutions have played an important role in the catch-up trajectories of New World producers. Here, Australia has led the way, with successful centralisation and co-ordination of industry organisations and research institutions; and a long-term vision for the industry and its export-related objectives. The two main actors are the Australian Wine and Brandy Corporation (the national sectoral organisation); and the Australian Wine Research Institute (the national research body), which is strongly linked to the Grape and Wine Research and Development Corporation, a government body devoted to the financing of R&D projects.

The initial response of Old World producers was to strengthen their long-established, producer-driven approach, based on local and traditional learning processes, grape varieties, and winemaking techniques. The strict regulatory framework in their countries, however, has restricted their ability to respond as flexibly as New World producers to the changing demand for wine. More recently, Old World producers have sought to respond by differentiating their products and seeking to upgrade them. From this perspective, it can be argued that the highly centralised R&D policies of the New World countries are a hindrance, and that the endowments of traditional wine culture, local knowledge and dense institutional infrastructure of the Old World are a valuable asset. While the wine industry illustrates the opportunities for sectoral catching up at times of significant industry transformation, it may also illustrate how, in world markets, highly diverse innovation strategies and institutional models can coexist.

*

These three case studies, the Taiwanese electronics industry, DRAMs in South Korea, and the world wine industry, show clearly, I believe, that in each case the sector concerned was driven by a capability/market-opportunity dynamic. They also show that in each sector demand, firms, knowledge and institutions played a role.

Finally, in no case did governments pick winning products or companies, or take entrepreneurial decisions, though they did target industries where they thought there was a 'window of opportunity'. Instead the role of governments in countries which have caught up has been one of joining with the private sector to assist firms develop new capabilities with which to create competitive advantages. The evidence, then, supports the view that as well as describing the period when Britain, Germany and the US forged ahead, the dynamic capability theory can account for more recent episodes when other economies have caught up with the world's technological leaders.

7

Falling behind

In the last 150 years, one country – Great Britain – having been a world technological leader, has fallen back. Now, the United States, having also been a world technological leader, appears to be in danger of doing so as well. In Chapters 5 and 6, I tested the dynamic capability theory of economic growth to see if it could be used to explain the performance of countries forging ahead and catching up, and found that it could. In this chapter, I will test whether it can be used to explain the performance of countries falling behind.

The economic growth rate of a country is driven by increases in its labour-productivity growth. However, in recent years, the US, the UK and other G7 countries have seen a diminishing rate of labour-productivity growth, leaving economists, policy-makers and business leaders baffled. This is an issue of great concern to governments, as labour-productivity growth is the key to raising per capita wages and living standards.

A number of economists have put forward explanations for why labour-productivity growth has been slowing in the US and UK. They fall into three camps. The first camp argues that labour productivity is increasingly difficult to measure, and as a result we have failed to capture all the productivity growth that has been taking place. The second 'secular stagnation' camp argues that a shortage of demand and investment opportunities, even in a low-interest-rate environment, leads to lower productivity growth. Finally, the third camp believes the low growth of labour productivity can be attributed to the impact of technology; with some economists arguing that today's innovations are not as transformational as those in the past, and others arguing that the slowdown is due to a lag in the realisation of productivity benefits following the arrival of new waves of technology.

For an explanation to be satisfactory, it would be necessary to show that it applied to all G7 countries; and that it came into effect around 1990 when the growth rates of all the G7 countries started to decline. None of the explanations above, however, pass these two simple tests, and as a result the slowing growth rates of the G7 countries have come to be described as a 'productivity puzzle'. This has left policy-makers without a clear theory to help them chart a path forward. I believe the dynamic capability theory of economic growth does provide an explanation of what has been happening, but before setting this out it is important to understand exactly what it is economists mean when they talk about 'labour productivity'.

When most people talk about labour productivity, they are talking about production efficiency, that is the number of labour hours used to produce a standard product or service. However, in the context of national statistics, economists calculate the labour productivity of a country by making use of value-added per hour figures taken from the national accounts adjusted for price inflation. This is important, as it means the labour-productivity figures of sectors reflect not only their production efficiency and capital intensity, but also changes in their competitive advantage.

As a result, we see significant and relatively rapid movements up and down in the labour-productivity figures per hour of sectors, which seem more likely to relate to changes in the competitive advantages of sectors than to changes in their production efficiency or capital intensity. It also explains why, when we do look at the labour-productivity per hour of an economy, we find that different sectors have very different levels of labour-productivity per hour, and that they are increasing and decreasing at different rates. We have, therefore, to abandon the neoclassical view of the economy as a monolithic entity, and view it instead as made up of different sectors with different levels of labour-productivity per hour changing at different rates. For example, when we look at labour-productivity per hour across UK sectors in 2016, we find it varied from £375.37 per hour in the oil and gas sector, down to just £8.95 per hour for buildings and landscape activities. The median value for all sectors was £31.46 per hour.

It also means that when there is a shift of employment in an economy from a high labour-productivity-per-hour sector to a low labour-productivity-per-hour sector it will lead to a decrease in labour-productivity growth. Conversely, a shift of employment from a low labour-productivity-per-hour sector to a high labour-productivity-per-hour sector will lead to an increase in labour-productivity growth.

Both the UK and the US have seen a slowing down in the labour-productivity-per-hour growth in their economies, and we now need to look at how movement in labour-productivity-per-hour growth rates in different sectors and the shift in employment between sectors have contributed to this trend.

The slow rate of labour-productivity growth in the UK

At this point in the argument we also need to be clear what we mean when we say that a country is 'falling behind'. A country is best described as 'falling behind' when it has a declining level of labour productivity in key high-productivity sectors of its economy and is not managing to replace them with new high labour-productivity sectors, and as a result shows a slow or negative rate of labour-productivity growth. Or, alternatively, employment is shifting from high-productivity sectors to low-productivity sectors.

If we look at labour productivity for the UK's total market sector during the period 1999–2015 (see Table 7.1 overleaf), we see a very clear pattern. Labour productivity grew up until the Financial Crisis. At the onset of the Financial Crisis it declined sharply, before recovering gradually. In 2015, though, it was still below the pre-crisis level.

Also, over this period in the UK there were significant labour-productivity growth differences between sectors of the economy, and also shifts of employment between sectors. Therefore, to understand what happened in the economy, we need also to look at the decomposition of the growth figures in Table 7.1 into the portion caused by changes in the labour productivity of sectors (the 'within effect'), and the portion caused by the shift of employment between sectors (the 'between effect'). Once this is done, it becomes clear that the changes in annual labour-productivity growth were due both to changes in the labour productivity of sectors and to shifts in the employment of sectors.

Table 7.1: **Annual labour-productivity growth (in %), total UK market sector, 1999–2015**

	Total market sector	Within industry effect	Between industry effect
1999–2001	2.9	3.2	−0.3
2002–2004	2.9	3.0	−0.1
2005–2007	2.5	2.5	−0.1
2008–2010	−0.5	−0.6	0.1
2011–2015	0.3	0.4	−0.1

Based on Rebecca Riley, Ana Rincon-Aznar and Lea Samek, 'Below the Aggregate: A Sectoral Account of the UK Productivity Puzzle', ESCoE Discussion Paper No. 2018–06, Economic Statistics Centre of Excellence, National Institute of Economic and Social Research, May 2018

We can further extend the analysis by looking at the total UK market sector, and decomposing overall labour-productivity growth according to the type of economic activity. In order to compute the contribution of each type of economic activity, we look at the labour-productivity growth in each economic activity (within economic activity effect), as well as the change in its relative size in terms of employment (between economic activity effect). Table 7.2 shows

both figures for each economic activity, and the total contribution of
each economic activity to aggregate labour-productivity growth.

Table 7.2: **Contributions to labour-productivity growth (in %)
by broad industry grouping, UK total market sector, percentage
points per annum, 1999–2015**

	1999–2001	2002–2004	2005–2007	2008–2010	2011–2015
Agriculture, forestry, fishing; Mining and quarrying	0.3	0.0	0.1	0.0	−0.3
Within industry term	0.3	−0.1	−0.2	−0.4	0.0
Between industry term	0.0	0.0	0.3	0.5	−0.2
Manufacturing	−0.5	−0.5	−0.3	−0.1	0.1
Within industry term	1.1	0.9	0.7	0.2	0.0
Between industry term	−1.7	−1.5	−1.0	−0.2	0.1
Other production	0.5	0.6	0.7	−0.6	0.3
Within industry term	0.1	0.4	−0.3	0.1	0.0
Between industry term	0.4	0.2	0.9	−0.7	0.3
Market services	2.7	2.9	2.0	0.1	0.2
Within industry term	1.7	1.7	2.3	−0.4	0.4
Between industry term	1.0	1.2	−0.3	0.5	−0.2
Total market sector	2.9	2.9	2.5	−0.5	0.3

Note: UK market sector excluding real estate. Labour productivity refers to a chain volume measure of output per
hour worked. Within and between industry terms are derived using the decomposition proposed by Tang & Wang
(2004). Industry groupings may not sum to market sector totals due to rounding.
Based on Rebecca Riley, Ana Rincon-Aznar and Lea Samek, 'Below the Aggregate: A Sectoral Account of the
UK Productivity Puzzle', ESCoE Discussion Paper No. 2018–06, Economic Statistics Centre of Excellence,
National Institute of Economic and Social Research, May 2018

Table 7.2 shows that the 'within economic activity effect' in manufacturing made a positive contribution to overall labour-productivity
growth during the period of analysis, although it was considerably

stronger in the years prior to the economic crisis. However, because the 'between economic activity effect' was negative throughout the period, except during 2011–15, reflecting an ongoing shift to other, lower-productivity parts of the economy, the manufacturing sector made a negative net contribution to overall growth of labour productivity except for the period 2011–15 when it was marginally positive.

Market services made in total a positive contribution to labour-productivity growth, though it was much stronger in the period prior to the financial crisis. The robust growth in the UK economy in the years leading up to the financial crisis was thus due to the strong growth in market services.

This is in line with growth data from other countries. In fact, the UK did relatively well in labour-productivity growth terms during the late 1990s and early 2000s compared with many other large European economies, due to the market service sector's strong performance compensating for the negative impact of the manufacturing sector. Elsewhere, market services contributed strongly to aggregate labour-productivity growth in Ireland, the Netherlands, Sweden and other Anglo-Saxon countries such as Australia and Canada. By contrast, in countries such as Austria, Germany, Italy and Spain, market services provided almost no contribution to aggregate labour-productivity growth.

Total labour-productivity growth in 'other production' (largely the construction and utilities sectors) was significant except in the period 2008–10 when it fell. Finally, the total contribution of agriculture, forestry, fishing, and mining and quarrying has been marginally positive except for the period 2011–15 when it was marginally negative.

Also, if we use a labour-productivity figure per hour of £30 as the cut-off to define whether a sector is a high labour-productivity service such as financial and legal services or a low labour-productivity service such as restaurants and hotels, we find that in the UK in 2016 the following sectors of the economy produced the following very different labour-productivity figures per hour.

	Current prices £ per hour	% of total GVA excluding real estate
High value services (excluding real estate)	60.85	25
Production	91.27	7
Manufacturing	48.67	10
Low value services	23.41	43
Agriculture	13.15	1

Source: Office for National Statistics

These figures are very important because they confirm the theory put forward in this book about the sectors where it is easiest to create competitive advantage and achieve high labour-productivity figures, and because they explain why successful developing countries have focused on increasing the share of manufacturing in their economies.

They also show why countries which have sectors with such levels of labour productivity should be deeply concerned about a decline in manufacturing unless they are confident that the employment released will go into high labour-productivity services rather than into low labour-productivity services, as seems largely to be the case in the UK today. We should also understand that a significant shift in a country from high labour-productivity manufacturing into low labour-productivity services will have implications for inequality.

As well as showing why labour productivity in the UK market sector grew as it did during the period 1999–2015, looking at the performance of sectors also provides an explanation of why, between 2007 and 2016, the UK underperformed all G7 countries (with the exception of Italy) in terms of labour-productivity growth. Over this period, labour productivity in the UK rose only 1.6 per cent, compared with an average labour-productivity increase in Canada, Germany, Japan and the US of 7.75 per cent. The reason for the low comparative labour-productivity growth of the UK economy during this period is that it was particularly hit by the fall in labour productivity of two major sectors: oil and gas; and financial services. Prior to 2007, these had been significant contributors to labour-productivity growth.

The labour-productivity per hour for the extraction of crude petro-leum and national gas sector fell 56 per cent between 2007 and 2016, to £375.37. Not only this, its share of the economy slumped from 1.85 per cent of GVA in 2007 to 0.73 per cent in 2016. One of the main drivers behind value-added in the oil sector is the price of oil itself. Brent crude oil was around $73 per barrel in 2007, falling to $46 per barrel in 2016. In addition, North Sea extraction activity fell from 77 million tonnes of crude oil in 2007 to 48 million tonnes in 2016.

In the case of the financial services sector (excluding insurance), and the insurance sector, labour-productivity per hour has increased 5 per cent for the former and 13 per cent for the latter between 2007 and 2016, generating £81.48 and £147.79 of labour-productivity per hour respectively. However, both sectors saw a fall in their share of GVA, with financial services declining from 5.48 per cent to 4.35 per cent, and insurance declining from 1.97 per cent to 1.68 per cent. The constant price GVA data fell for both sectors, indicating that overall output since 2007 has fallen.

The reason for falling output is likely to be related to the fall in demand for financial services products following the Financial Crisis. In the run-up to the Financial Crisis, there was clearly a huge demand for financial products in the UK, which could not then be sustained afterwards. However, the trade balance did grow 7 per cent between 2007 and 2016, offsetting some of the lower domestic demand.

The oil and gas industry, and the financial services industry, there-fore, accounted for a decline of 1.5 per cent in labour productivity between 2007 and 2016. If they are excluded from the figures, it can be estimated that labour-productivity growth would have been 3.2 per cent, rather than 1.6 per cent, between 2007 and 2016, putting the UK at almost the same level as France, which grew at 3.4 per cent. However, even using this increased rate of growth, the UK still grew at less than half the rate experienced by Canada, Germany, Japan and the US, who experienced an average growth rate of 7.75 per cent.

Therefore, it is possible to explain, in terms of the performance of sectors and the structure of sectors, both why labour-productivity growth has been slow in the UK between 2007 and 2016; and why it has been slower than all G7 countries, with the exception of Italy. To give a more in-depth account, we would need to look in detail at why labour productivity in particular sectors has risen or fallen, and why there has been a structural shift of sectors. However, given the fairly rapid changes that have taken place and the dramatic success of the I6 countries during this period, it seems safe to conclude that the UK manufacturing sector's negative impact during this period was due to a loss of competitive advantage in world markets by its firms.

Why has the UK lost competitive advantage?

Why did this loss of competitive advantage in world markets, which has been going on for a long time, take place? It was not due to the appearance of new market failures or a lack of resource mobility between old and new industries, as neoclassical economists would like to believe; though the overstaffing of some industries due to union pressure clearly played a part at some moments in time. On the contrary, history shows it was due to a lack of technological and organisational innovation by British firms, which in turn was due largely to the failure of three key British economic institutions: firms' governance and financing; the national system of education and training; and the national system of innovation.[1]

In the third quarter of the nineteenth century, Britain experienced a lengthy economic boom that represented the culmination of the world's first industrial revolution. After three centuries of international competition for control of world markets, and after seven decades of massive capital investment, Britain emerged unchallenged in world markets.

The structure of British industry at this time was much as one finds in today's microeconomic textbooks. Britain's major nineteenth-century staple industries – such as textiles, iron and steel, coal mining, shipbuilding and engineering – were composed of numerous firms with small market shares. Distribution of intermediate and final products relied upon well-developed market mechanisms, often involving specialised merchant firms. As they relied on market mechanisms to co-ordinate economic activity, nineteenth-century British firms were comparatively simple in their internal organisation. Typically, they were run by owner–proprietors or close family associates; managerial staffs were small; and, unlike their German counterparts, there was no in-house research and little role for professional management teams.

One consequence of nineteenth-century competitive capitalism was the consolidation of job control by many groups of workers in the major British industries. During the long mid-Victorian boom, Britain's firms opportunistically opted for collective accommodation with unions of skilled and strategically positioned workers, rather than jeopardising their individual fortunes through industrial conflict.

The late nineteenth century also saw the emergence of what has been called 'corporate capitalism' as the dominant mode of economic organisation in other national economies, most notably in Japan, Germany and the United States. Corporate capitalism was characterised by industrial oligopoly; hierarchical managerial bureaucracy; vertical integration of production and distribution; managerial control over job content and production standards; the integration of financial and industrial capital; and systematic technological research.

To meet the international challenge, British firms needed to transform their structures of industrial relations, industrial organisation and enterprise management. However, vested interests in the old structures made the transition from competitive to corporate modes of organisation extremely difficult. British industrialists clung to family control of their firms, and when horizontal amalgamations did take place, the directors of the participating firms insisted on retaining operational control. As a result of this capability failure, British growth in output per head not only slowed in the last quarter of the nineteenth century, it also began to lag relative to late-developing industrialising countries who benefited from the support of the institutions of corporate capitalism. British growth rates first fell behind those of other countries in the 1870s and 1880s.

There was a further serious loss of competitive advantage between 1899 and 1913. This was linked to the failure of British industry to match the productivity advances of firms abroad, which were reaping the benefits of mass-production methods. With the exception of wartime intervals, the gap in relative productivity growth performance between Britain and most of its competitors has been significant ever since.

The capability failure of British firms can be partly attributed to the shortcomings of two key British economic institutions: the country's educational and training system, and the national system of innovation. If we look first at the education and training system, we find that in the early nineteenth century everyone agreed that artisans, who owed little of their skill and knowledge to formal schooling, were the people who should provide firms with technical knowledge.[2]

The artisans' skills were transmitted through apprenticeships and practical experience, as the educational system was extremely weak. The British government did not establish the framework for a national system of elementary schools until 1870, and even then the schools were neither free nor compulsory. It was not until 1891 that most elementary schools became free. Secondary education lagged still more, with almost no schools outside the private sector, an uneven distribution of schools in different areas of the country, and although only a few of the students went on to universities, classics predominated in the curriculum to the virtual exclusion of science. Only in 1902 did the British government finally begin to organise a coherent system of elementary and secondary education, and to this day, the country does not have a high-quality, high-prestige system of technical education, as I will describe in Chapter 8.

The economic decline of Britain during the twentieth century was also due to a poor record of innovation, caused in part by low levels of industrial research. Analyses – measured either as the share of research employees in total firm employment in the 1930s, or the share of R&D expenditure in total firm sales from the 1950s – suggest that the level of research intensity in British firms was, on average, about one-third of that in US manufacturing firms.

In addition, the organisation of British research was inefficient.[3] Up until the end of the Second World War, British industry relied heavily on research organisations funded by the British government and made use of consulting engineers rather than employing their own staff. Engineers, as opposed to scientists, were also in short supply.

The reorganisation of the structure of the firm carried out in the United States as part of their managerial revolution was also less complete in Great Britain, and this led to a poor integration of research activity and production activity. The low levels of R&D investment and ineffective organisation of research inevitably had an impact on the development of alternative export industries, as well as on the innovation performance of current ones.

As a result of these three institutional failures, and the resulting poor innovation performance of British firms in the first half of the twentieth century, the post-Second World War British economy inherited a set of major industries that were in no condition to survive the renewed onslaught of international competition beginning in the 1950s. In addition, the two major initiatives taken by the state to address these issues failed to produce the internationally competitive industries that were needed.

The first of these initiatives was nationalisation. As competitive pressures mounted, the state began to nationalise industries – such as coal, steel and motor vehicles – that were deemed of strategic importance to the nation, and which were in most cases in danger of collapse. This, though, was not a sufficient response to Britain's long-term economic decline, and, while public ownership overcame the problem of horizontally fragmented private ownership, it did little to overcome the inherited issues of industry structure, managerial organisation and union job control. Nationalised enterprises had to deal with all these obstacles, while attempting to overcome the technological leadership already established by foreign competitors.

The second initiative was the monetarist policies of the Thatcher government. Her adherence to a free-market ideology and attack on the power of the unions sought to achieve an economic revival through severe market discipline. But the belief that there were capabilities latent in the economy, which would create new competitive advantages once these barriers to efficient resource allocation had been removed, proved to be another neoclassical mirage.

People should perhaps not be too puzzled by the slow growth of British labour productivity in recent years. The failure of the government and industry in the twentieth century to modernise the country's staple industries and move strongly into new hi-tech, high value-added per capita industries, combined with competitive advances in the developing world, is the reason why the UK's labour-productivity growth has slowed so dramatically. Furthermore, it won't increase until a new set of high value-added per capita industries is produced that can compete successfully in world markets.

The slow rate of labour-productivity growth in the US

In the US, as in the UK, there has been a decline in labour-productivity growth; with it having fallen to 0.6 per cent in 2014 (see Figure 7.1 overleaf). Again, as in the UK, this has been described as a 'productivity puzzle'. The explanation for this can be found, once more, in the declining competitiveness of the high value-added per capita tradeable sector of the economy, and in the major shift of employment into the lower value-added per capita non-tradeable sector.

To understand what happened over this period, it is most useful to divide the US economy into tradeable and non-tradeable sectors. In the global economy, the tradeable sector consists of the goods and services produced in one country and consumed in another, or, as in tourism or education, consumed by people from another country. The

Figure 7.1 **Labour-productivity[a] growth in the US total economy, 1988–2014 (year-on-year growth, %)**

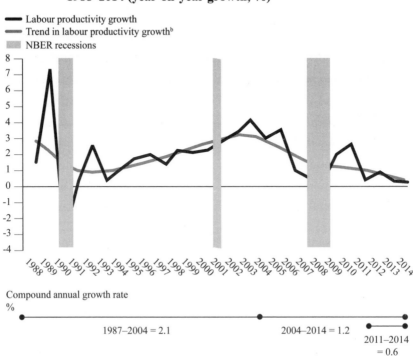

a Productivity is defined as value added per hour worked. Based on BLS total economy measure of real value-added output. Data is only available through 2014.
b Trend line constructed using a Hodrick Prescott filter.
Source: James Manyika *et al.*, 'The Productivity Puzzle: A Closer Look at the United States', Discussion Paper, McKinsey Global Institute, March 2017

non-tradeable sector consists of the goods and services produced and consumed in the same country.

The boundary between the tradeable and non-tradeable sector is not, however, fixed. Twenty-five years ago, business services such as information technology maintenance and support were not traded internationally. Now, Internet connectivity and innovative software allows many of these services to be performed remotely in another country at a lower cost.

If we now look at the number of jobs in the US economy between

1990 and 2008, we find there has been a net increase of 27.3 million on a base of 121.9 million in 1990. Almost all of these new jobs (26.7 million out of the 27.3 million) were created in the non-tradeable sector, including 6.3 million jobs in health care and 4.1 million in the government service. Meanwhile, aggregate employment growth in the tradeable sector was essentially flat: some industries grew and other declined.[4]

This last point about the differing employment growth rates of the tradeable and non-tradeable sectors is significant, because if we now look at value-added per capita employed, we find that, in 1990, it was very similar in both sectors – the tradeable sector, at almost $80,000, was roughly $10,000 above the non-tradeable figure. However, the value-added per capita in the two sectors diverged slowly during the 1990s, then rapidly after 2000. Value-added per capita in the tradeable sector grew at an average of 2.3 per cent per annum; and in the non-tradeable sector at 0.7 per cent per annum. By 2008, value-added per capita in the tradeable sector was just over 50 per cent above that of the non-tradeable sector.

It is very important, though, to understand the story behind these figures for the tradeable sector, as two very different things were going on. In the case of many manufacturing supply chains, the lower value-added components were moved offshore. These areas saw declines in employment and rising value-added per capita. But in other areas, such as high value-added services in which the US economy continued to enjoy a competitive position, employment and value-added per capita increased together. This story is confirmed if we look at the US trade balances for advanced technology goods and all goods over the period 1992–2018 (see Figure 7.2 overleaf).

The figure shows clearly the long-term declining trade balance of the US, even for the advanced technology goods portion of the domestic manufacturing sector. The balance of trade for advanced technology goods was in surplus from 1992 until 2002, when it turned negative. This trend continued even in the face of an approximately 25 per cent decline in the effective exchange rate of the US dollar

Figure 7.2 **US trade balances for advanced technology goods and all goods, 1992–2016 ($, millions)**

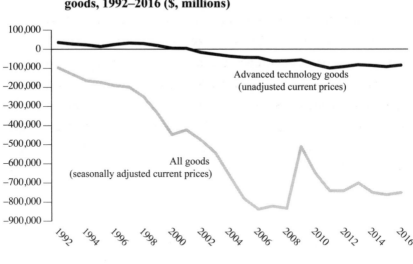

Source: Census Bureau, Bureau of Economic Analysis

between 2002 and 2008. At the same time, a huge negative trade balance opened up for all goods.

Despite a minor improvement in the trade balance during the depth of the recession due to the financial crisis, the negative trend has broadly continued through to 2016. This is clearly one reason for the decline in labour-productivity growth seen in the whole US economy since 2008.

These figures also make clear that in the US economy today, as in the UK, there is no 'productivity puzzle'. Rather, there has been a failure to remain competitive over the entire technology life cycle of some of the country's key industries, as well as a failure to create new high value-added per capita industries to compensate for an inevitable loss of competitive advantage (and, therefore, value-added per capita) in other industries. As a result, the US economy has had a slow rate of productivity growth. These figures also show the US today meets our definition of a country that is falling behind.

Why has the US lost competitive advantage?

We now need to ask why this loss of competitive advantage has taken place, and why the capability/market-opportunity dynamic, which creates new sources of competitive advantage, has not been operating effectively. As in the case of the UK, there has been a poor innovation performance by US firms, and three institutional failures. The US became a world economic leader by making mass-production with interchangeable parts its mainstream method of production, and for more than a century continuously developed new high-productivity technologies.

In the last half of the nineteenth century, the first technologies were textiles and raw material processing. Prior to the First World War, these were followed by machinery making, as well as chemical and steel production, and then consumer durables throughout the twentieth century. Finally, in the last part of the twentieth century, American technological leadership continued with digital technology, and most recently biotechnology. Along with this series of technological life cycles came a number of organisational changes, including corporate capitalism; the multi-divisional company; as well as innovation infrastructures such as intellectual property rules; government research; standardisation; and, more recently, regional technology development clusters.

The capabilities developed by United States firms enabled the country to maintain its economic leadership unchallenged for over a century, but in recent decades US manufacturing's competitive status has come under increasing pressure from foreign competitors. Successful industrialised nations, such as Japan, Germany, South Korea and Taiwan, have developed capabilities that range across all areas of manufacturing, from electronics to discrete parts. As a result, products based on technologies originating in the US economy, such as semiconductors and robotics, are increasingly being both developed and produced elsewhere. Emerging economies, such as China, have also been rapidly acquiring manufacturing capability.

At the same time, the US has seen its ability to innovate and move into new higher value-added technological sectors eroded by three major changes in its economy. These have taken place in the education and training system; its national system of innovation; and its financial system; and the government, for political and ideological reasons, has not been able to respond effectively to them. To fully understand why US industry has been losing competitive advantage, we need to examine these areas in more detail.

Looking first at the US education and training system, we find that its skill levels are being equalled or exceeded by those in other countries. At all levels, the educational system appears to be performing badly. The US school system also looks very out-of-date, having remained largely unchanged from its origins in an agricultural economy, through the manufacturing era to the current information and service-based economy. A vestige of the former agricultural society is the length of the school year, with American students in primary and secondary education averaging 180 days compared with 190–210 days in Europe, and 240 days in Japan. Performance is also poor compared with other countries. The programme of International Student Assessment ranks the United States twenty-fourth out of twenty-nine industrial nations in maths literacy and problem-solving. In fact, the study shows that a large number of high-school students can barely do maths at all.

Turning to the university sector, we find that in just one generation the United States fell from first to ninth in terms of the proportion of its young people with graduate degrees, and now ranks twelfth among all nations. The United States also ranks just twenty-seventh among developed nations in terms of the proportion of college students receiving undergraduate degrees in science or engineering.

In the past, the US was able to make up for its shortage of science and engineering degrees by attracting students from Europe and Asia, the so-called 'brain drain' that began after the Second World War. Many more opportunities abounded in the dynamic US economy, as well as its outstanding university system. Many scientists and engineers emigrated to the United States, and once educated at universities there stayed permanently to work in domestic industries. The contribution of the scientists and engineers who entered the US and then stayed has been immense, with many becoming leaders of innovative companies. Well-known examples include Andy Grove, co-founder and Chairman of Intel; Vinod Khosla, co-founder of Sun Microsystems; Jerry Yang, co-founder of Yahoo!; and Sergey Brin, co-founder and President of Google.

Today, however, globalisation and the associated technological convergence is reducing the US' ability to supply the manpower needs of its high-tech industry in this way. National Science Foundation data shows both lower enrolment by foreign students in US universities, and higher repatriation rates after students complete their education. The rise in the number of research universities in other countries is substantially reducing the number of foreign students coming to the United States to study, while degrees awarded to US citizens are certainly not taking up the slack.

Looking now at the total funding of US R&D, it still appears enviable, accounting for slightly less than one-third of the world total of $1 trillion. However, the best measure of R&D is R&D intensity (the ratio of R&D to GDP). This is because the current output of goods and services is driven by past R&D and, therefore, current R&D spending relative to the size of the economy is a predictor of future economic growth.

If we look at the R&D intensity of the US economy over recent decades, a clear pattern emerges (see Figure 7.3 overleaf). Following President Kennedy's famous 1961 speech calling for greater investment in science and technology in response to the Russian launch of Sputnik in 1957, and the flight of the first man in space in 1961, R&D intensity reached a peak of 2.83 per cent during 1963–67. However, this increased emphasis on science and technology petered out in the 1970s, and national R&D intensity declined steadily to an average of 2.15 per cent for the period 1975–79.

The 1980s brought a more pervasive and market-oriented threat

Figure 7.3 **R&D intensity: Funding as a share of US GDP, 1953–2005**

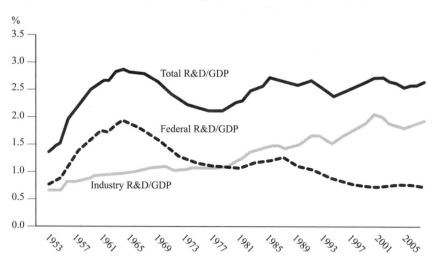

Source: National Science Foundation; reproduced in Gregory Tassey, 'Rationales and Mechanisms for
Revitalizing US Manufacturing R&D Strategies', *Journal of Technology Transfer*, vol. 35(3), 2010, pp. 283–333

from Japan in the form of electronics, optoelectronics, advance
materials (ceramics), and advanced manufacturing (robotics). This
second shock led to sustained higher growth rates in R&D spending by industry, and raised national R&D intensity close to its 1960s
peak. However, due to continued slow growth in government R&D
spending, this critical ratio is today still below the peak average of
the mid-1960s.

The current decade is witnessing an acceleration of global R&D
capability, and if we compare US R&D intensity with that of other
countries, it certainly does not reflect an adaptation to the growing
global R&D capability. Instead, four countries now have significantly
higher R&D intensities (see Figure 7.4).

There is one other aspect of US investment in R&D that should
be noted. As a result of the rising technological capabilities of other
economies, a steadily increasing amount of US firms' R&D has been
offshored. R&D spending by majority-owned foreign affiliates of US

Figure 7.4 **National R&D intensities: Gross R&D expenditures as a percentage of GDP, 2003**

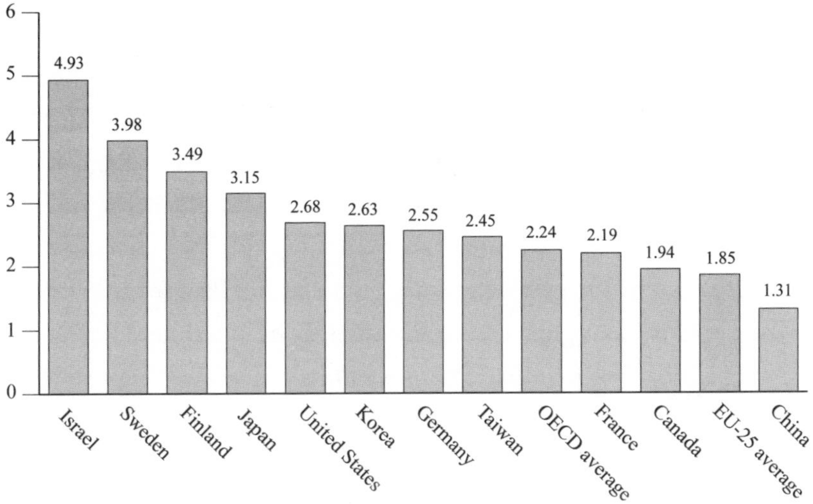

Source: Gregory Tassey, *The Technology Imperative*, Edward Elgar Publishing, Cheltenham, 2007.
Reproduced with the permission of the Licensor through PLS clear

multinational companies grew 50 per cent faster (9.8 per cent average annual rate) than that of their US parents (6.3 per cent).

There are two reasons for investing in R&D overseas. The first is to support local market strategies, and the second is to acquire technical knowledge. These two strategies have been described as 'market seeking' and 'asset seeking', and there is evidence it is the second strategy that has motivated American firms. This is something which should be of great concern to US policy-makers, as it suggests that the country's firms are faced by an increasingly attractive environment for conducting research abroad, as well as difficulty in recruiting qualified staff in the US. Also, if American companies outsource not only manufacturing but also R&D to foreign countries, there is a real danger that future life cycles of new products will be designed and developed in those countries.

A third factor leading to an erosion of the ability of the US to innovate and move into new higher value-added technological sectors, is the financialisation of its economy. The short-term horizons of America's financial institutions has forced firms to concentrate on short-term profits and financial engineering, rather than investing for the long-term. In a 2004 survey of more than four hundred US executives, 80 per cent said that they would decrease discretionary spending on areas such as R&D, advertising, maintenance and hiring, in order to meet short-term earnings targets; while more than 50 per cent said they would delay new projects even if it meant sacrificing value creation.

As a result of the pressures from financial markets for immediate returns, profits have gone disproportionately into dividend payments and share buy-backs, rather than investment. This has happened in the case of US manufacturers, with the ratio of dividends paid to the amount invested in capital equipment increasing from 20 per cent in the late 1970s and early 1980s, to around 40–50 per cent in the early 1990s, to above 60 per cent in the 2000s. Significantly, exactly as predicted by financial experts, dividend payments increased substantially after 2003, when Congress slashed the tax rate individuals paid on corporate dividends. The market-efficiency view of economics – that high rates of hostile takeovers and short-term financial pressures should lead to superior performance – is also not supported by the evidence.

As a result of the failure by its government to reform its institutions in order to provide the best conditions for industry to create new competitive advantages, the US has seen an erosion of its competitive advantages in world markets. This is what lies behind its slow growth rate.

The US continues to lead the world in many strategic areas, notably software, biosciences, social media, and most computer chip technology. In some others, such as aerospace and satellites, America now shares the lead with Europe and Asia. In many other areas, however, including robotics, flat-panel displays, lithium-ion batteries, nuclear power, high-speed trains and memory chips, the US has given up the chase. In the case of clean energy, which was probably the country's best chance of getting a slice of the biggest twenty-first century, high-tech manufacturing growth area, it has thrown away a huge first-mover advantage.

In the mid-1990s, the US accounted for the bulk of global solar-panel production, as well as for most of the world demand (principally from California). But the US share of both global photovoltaic production and capacity has plummeted to below 10 per cent. The United States has gone from being the big fish in a small pond to a small fish in a growing lake.

Any prospect that the United States might shift decisively from fossil fuels to clean energy was thrown away when the Waxman–Markey cap and trade bill failed in the Senate due to lobbying by the big fossil-fuel suppliers, notably oil and gas. It signalled that the United States had abandoned its last opportunity to capitalise on its first-mover advantage in the creation of the solar energy industry.

According to a November 2009 report by the Breakthrough Institute and the Information Technology and Innovation Foundation, the United States would be outspent three to one by East Asia in clean energy between 2010 and 2015. This included spending on high-speed rail, batteries and nuclear power as well as other renewable technologies. By giving up its initial advantage, the US has enabled the clean energy Silicon Valley-style clusters of the future to emerge in places such as 'Electricity Valley' in Baoding, China, and around Seoul as part of South Korea's 'Green New Deal', rather than in California.

The United States' failure to capitalise on its first-mover advantages in clean energy also illustrates a fundamental fact about the country's growth rate in recent years, which is that it has not been slow because there are no opportunities for it to create new competitive advantages, but because it has failed to fully develop its capabilities to take advantage of them.

A faster rate of innovation

A serious weakness of neoclassical economic growth theory is that it does not attach great importance to the international competitiveness of a country's firms, and, therefore, does not draw attention to the falling or rising international competitiveness of other countries, and the impact this has on a country's rate of economic growth. But as we have seen in this chapter, the failure of the UK and the US to innovate as fast as some other countries has led to their economic growth rates falling back.

In 2009, at the height of the Great Recession, the ITIF published a report entitled 'The Atlantic Century',[5] which assessed the global innovation-based competitiveness of thirty-six countries, both as they stood at around 2007, and in terms of their progress since the early 2000s. The report relied on sixteen indicators from six broad categories: (1) human capital; (2) innovation capacity; (3) entrepreneurship; (4) IT infrastructure; (5) economic policy; and (6) economic performance. Two years later, the exercise was repeated and a second report produced, entitled 'The Atlantic Century II'.[6] The report produced some extremely interesting figures and confirmed the findings of the earlier report. In terms of innovation-based competitiveness, the top six countries (in order) were: Singapore, Finland, Sweden, the US, South Korea and the UK. China ranked thirtieth. In addition, the report confirms the slow improvement in the global innovation-based competitiveness of the UK and the US compared with other countries, as well as making it clear how difficult it will be for G7 countries to increase their rates of economic growth when faced with the rising rates of innovation in countries elsewhere in the world.[7]

The figures on the rate of change produced by the report were also extremely interesting. In terms of improved performance, the top six countries (in order) were: China, South Korea, Cyprus, Slovenia, Estonia and the Czech Republic. The UK came twenty-third of the forty countries, and the US came second-to-last, ahead only of Italy.

Interestingly, the report also compared individual US states using

seven indicators and found that the nine most competitive states –
Massachusetts, California, Connecticut, New Jersey, Washington,
Delaware, Maryland, Colorado and New Hampshire – would lead the
world if they were countries. Even the least competitive, Mississippi,
would still fall towards the middle of the pack. Furthermore, were
Massachusetts to be its own nation, it would be the most innovative
economy in the world.

It is possible to argue about the details of these calculations, but
what they show seems broadly to reflect what is known to be happening in different countries and different states of the US, and they
should, therefore, be taken seriously by policy-makers. They show
why the growth rates of countries such as the US and UK have been
slow in recent years in the face of increased competition from other
countries. They also make it clear that if countries such as the US and
UK want to raise their rate of growth in the years ahead, they will
need to raise their rate of innovation. Finally, they show that, contrary
to the neoclassical market-efficiency model, the failure to maintain
competitive advantage through innovation feeds directly through to
the value-added per capita of the whole economy, with potentially
dangerous consequences for overall living standards.

It is not easy, however, for countries to raise their level of innovation and competitive advantage, and so in the next three chapters
I will look at what governments need to do to raise the innovation
performance and competitive advantage of their firms by reforming
their countries institutions.

8

National systems of
education and training

An effective national system of education and training

A national system of education and training has a number of objectives. In this chapter, however, I will focus on just one of these: giving young people the knowledge and skills necessary to get fulfilling and productive jobs. The reason for focusing on this aspect is that it is one of the most relevant to enabling firms to build up their capabilities and create well-paying jobs. It is also my personal view that this is one of the most important objectives of any national system of education and training, as it is difficult for young people to acquire such knowledge and skills any other way, and because having a challenging and productive job is a key feature of a happy and fulfilling life.

While politicians everywhere will acknowledge that a high-quality national system of education and training is essential to a country having a rapid rate of growth in today's competitive world, too many countries have failed to reform substandard national systems. This can be either for political reasons or because of poor policy analysis.

Parents, teachers and policy-makers tend to focus on the performance of the main elements making up a national system of education and training: schools; technical and vocational colleges; universities; the apprenticeship systems of firms; the national system of qualifications; and the funding of students while they are learning. While policy-makers must look at the performance of these entities, they must also look at the relationships between them, rather than tinkering endlessly with the individual parts. This is because the elements making up a national system of education and training will not spontaneously come together to best perform their function of enabling people to acquire the knowledge and practical skills they need in order to have fulfilling and productive lives. The design of education and training systems is something for which governments have to take responsibility.

If a country is to have a successful and effective national system of education and training, there are five issues a government has to tackle: designing a national system of qualifications; designing an educational system that has both a high-quality technical pathway and a high-quality academic pathway; funding the system; designing a good system of careers advice; and manpower planning.

Designing a national system of qualifications

A national system of qualifications that is well understood and works in the marketplace is important, as students will only work hard to get a qualification if they know which qualification is relevant to the job they want to do. Also, they need to know that, should they get the qualification, an employer with a relevant vacancy will give it to them rather than to someone who hasn't got the qualification, all other things being equal. If there is a vast range of qualifications, and the acquisition of them is not valued by employers – either because they don't know what skills the people with these qualifications have, or because they don't value the ones they do acquire – then people will not be motivated to do the hard work necessary to get the qualifications.

Also, the design of a national system of qualifications cannot be left to employers, as individual firms have very different interests, and so will tend to design very narrow qualifications to meet their own needs. The qualifications will, therefore, reflect the needs of particular jobs rather than occupations, and consequently have limited transferability. Such an approach is also likely to lead to a vast proliferation of qualifications that no one understands, and the value of which is unclear to both individuals and employers.

Governments, therefore, have to take responsibility for the design of national systems of qualifications. However, when it comes to specifying the skills each qualification needs to cover, then industry experts need to be employed to ensure that these skills are the ones the relevant industry needs its employees to have. Such experts need to be consulted on the basis that they are representatives of their area of expertise, rather than their firms.

Designing a system of academic and technical pathways

The second key issue for policy-makers is tackling the system of academic and technical pathways that most developed countries have adopted, though in widely differing forms. This covers a number of key decisions. The first is deciding at what age students are assigned to one of the two pathways, and on what basis the assignment is made. Is it on the basis of an exam, the student's school record, or is it a decision made by the student's parents and teachers? A second key decision is whether the technical and vocational pathway is college-based or takes the form of apprenticeships in industry, or is a mixture of the two. A third decision concerns the different programmes covered by each pathway; and a fourth is whether students are able to move between the two pathways if they feel they have made the wrong choice.

Designing a funding system

The third issue facing policy-makers is how the different parts of the education system are funded. This can be done by the state funding them; by giving students loans that have to be paid back from future earnings; or, in the case of apprenticeships, by either relying on employers to fund them, the state funding them, or by means of a training levy. In all these cases, the government has to balance issues of equity and cost.

In the UK, the recent introduction of a system giving loans to students to fund their university education has proved to be a failure. The logic of the state having an interest in seeing that young people have a good education up to the age of eighteen but not thereafter, seems, at least to me, to be faulty. In addition, the idea that charging fees to university students would result in a market system making students more demanding and universities more competitive has not proved to be the case.

It is clearly not socially just to burden poorer students with debt for a large part of their lives. Countries have to decide whether a high-quality education system is an essential part of a fast-growth country or not, and if it is, they need largely to fund it. This would not, however, preclude requiring wealthy parents to pay the costs of their children's university education.

In the UK, we have, without rigorous policy analysis, created an appalling system of university funding, which will, in due course, mean that at least a quarter of our society will have to carry a burden of debt for most of their working lives. This was done in order that my generation – which had a free university education – does not have to pay the costs of university education today, and the sooner the whole system is dismantled the better.

Turning to the funding of apprenticeships, it is clear that such a system does not work unless a way is found to deal with the problem of firms poaching apprentices trained by other firms. Firms will not take on the cost of training apprentices if they know that, as soon as they have trained them, they will be poached by other companies who do no training and who can, therefore, afford to offer them higher wages.

The German system of apprenticeship training, which is widely and rightly admired, works because their institutions operate in such a way as to discourage poaching. Firstly, almost all firms in Germany are members of their local Chambers of Commerce and Industry, and firms know that to be a respected member they need to do their share of training. Secondly, wage bargaining at an industry level between firms and trade unions makes it, in many cases, much more difficult for firms to poach qualified employees by offering inflated salaries. Thirdly, there is a much wider gap in Germany than in the UK between the wages paid to apprentices and the wages of qualified staff, and, therefore, the cost to the employer is seen as much lower. The Japanese are similarly able to prevent poaching undermining their in-firm system of technical education due to their system of lifetime employment.

The funding of apprenticeship training by governments, or by means of a training levy, is also problematic if they are not based on a national system of qualifications, and if the training of apprentices is not properly and independently assessed. If these two conditions are not met, it is very difficult to ensure firms make good use of the funds available to them.

This is an issue that policy-makers in the United States, for example, ought to be thinking about, as companies there are investing half as much in training as a share of GDP as they did a decade ago. In part, this is because the payoffs increasingly flow to other firms due to workers switching jobs more frequently; and in part because companies are operating under increasing pressures to make short-term profits. For example, to incentivise greater workforce training, Congress could institute a tax credit for the expenses associated with such training.[1]

Finally, the point needs to be made that, whatever the basis of funding, governments need to make available the necessary resources to both the academic pathway and the technical pathway. Only then can they provide the inspiring, properly qualified teachers and modern facilities necessary to teach the students in each of the pathways that industry and society needs.

Designing a system of careers advice

The fourth issue policy-makers need to tackle is that of ensuring a good careers advice service in schools. Without this, it is not possible for students to know, in a dynamic economy, what well-paid and fulfilling jobs are likely to be available to them over their careers, and what knowledge and skills they will need to get specific technical jobs. A good system of careers advice is also extremely helpful to firms seeking to build up their capabilities in new areas.

To provide students with the information and advice they need, it is not necessary to have a large, government-funded, national careers advisory service. However, governments should lay down the standards for the career advice given in schools. This is not difficult to do, as Sir John Holman showed in his study (which my charitable trust funded) of careers advice in independent schools in the UK, and in other European countries known for having good advisory services.[2] I am delighted that the guidelines he set out have now been accepted by the UK government as a national standard.

Manpower planning

A final issue for governments to tackle is manpower planning. In the US and the UK in recent decades, it has generally and erroneously been agreed that governments should not do anything that might remotely be seen as manpower planning. No one wants to see governments making detailed projections of the number of chefs or electrical engineers their economies will require in the future.

A skilled workforce is, however, so important for innovation and growth in a modern economy that governments cannot ignore the fact that, for example, their education and training systems are not producing enough scientists and engineers, or enough technicians. There is an unavoidable planning problem at the level of the whole economy, and the belief that everything can be solved by the individual choices of workers and firms through the market mechanism is a neoliberal dogma long since falsified by experience.

To remedy such institutional failures, governments need to do two things. Firstly, in areas where there are shortages, make certain that there are courses taught by well-qualified teachers in well-equipped facilities, and that they are part of a well-understood system of qualifications that works in the marketplace. This is the only way courses can acquire high prestige and become attractive to students.

Secondly, governments, as far as possible, need to align the education and training places available to the needs of industry and society. Otherwise, a country is likely to stumble into the situation we face in the UK today, whereby too many university students are produced who find it difficult to get a university-level job when they leave higher education, while at the same time we are not producing enough technicians for the needs of industry and society. Governments need to do this in the interests of both students and firms.

These are simple policies, however, which UK governments have consistently failed to develop and implement. Left-wing governments, for example, have usually sought to solve the shortage of technicians by trying to give them 'parity of esteem', claiming that a specific technical qualification is equivalent to some academic qualification. Nobody believes them, though, and so the situation is not improved. The same line of thinking also recently led a Conservative government to create 'degree apprenticeships', to be taught by high-prestige universities. However, it is doubtful this will achieve anything, as high-prestige universities are not particularly good places to teach young people industrial skills, and the introduction of degree apprenticeships simply reinforces the message that a university degree is the only qualification that really counts.

Equally, right-wing governments have sought to solve the mismatch between knowledge and skills and the needs of industry and society by leaving everything to the market. This has involved handing the design of qualifications over to employers and allowing awarding bodies to compete in designing and assessing qualifications.

Both initiatives have led to chaotic qualification systems, which are not well understood, do not work in the marketplace, and produce variable and usually poor standards of education and training.

Hopefully, the new system of technical qualifications the present Conservative government is introducing, described at the end of this chapter, will produce a set of high-quality qualifications for technicians that will gain high prestige, prove attractive to young people, and significantly reduce the disastrous shortage of technicians from which industry in the UK suffers.

The five issues outlined above provide a framework against which to judge the policies shaping a national system of education and training. The importance of the design and resource decisions that policymakers have to make regarding their country's national system of education and training, and the impact these decisions can have on the supply of people with the necessary qualifications countries need to fuel their economic growth, can be very clearly seen by looking at the national education and training system in England and Wales.

The performance of the national system of education and training in England and Wales

At present, the academic pathway in England and Wales performs extremely well in world university league tables, attracts outstanding students from around the world, and in most subject areas university degrees are highly valued by employers. Also, the number of students who, as a percentage of their student cohort, get a science degree – an important measure of a university system's effectiveness from an industrial competitiveness point of view – is reasonably high in comparison with other countries. However, a lower percentage of students than is desirable from a competitiveness point of view take an engineering degree and go into industry. This is due both to the history of engineering in the UK, and to poor policy-making in the past.

The reasons behind the good performance of English and Welsh universities are not difficult to understand. In the first place, students are largely chosen on the basis of the results they achieve in their A-level exams – a single, subject-based exam system for the whole country, which is well understood, and which appears to be an effective way of choosing which students go to university. Students also know that their A-level results will determine both whether they are able to go to university at all, and whether or not they are able to go to one of the top universities. Getting a good university degree is also seen as a way of getting an interesting and well-paid job post-university. Students are, therefore, motivated to work hard to achieve good results both in their A-level and university exams. Finally, as a result of the academic prestige they have built up in the last 150 years, British universities are able to attract many outstanding academic staff and are reasonably well funded (though not in comparison with top American universities).

The performance of the technical education pathway in England and Wales is, however, very poor. It is extremely complex, with over 13,000 qualifications currently available for those aged between sixteen and eighteen. These often provide little value for either individuals or employers. The pathway is also poorly funded, with the result that it is not able to provide the capable and inspiring teachers or modern facilities required. As a result, the pathway fails to provide the skills most needed for the twenty-first century, and by 2020 the UK is set to fall to twenty-eighth out of the thirty-three OECD countries in terms of developing intermediate skills. The size of the post-secondary technical education sector in England and Wales is also extremely small by international standards.

The poor quality of the English and Welsh technical education pathway also means that there is currently a serious shortage of technicians in industry at a time when over 400,000 young people aged between sixteen and twenty-four are unemployed. It is hard to believe that none of these young people have the ability or motivation to train as technicians if given good opportunities to do so, and the shortage of technicians in industry must be seen as a major failure of the system of technical education.

This failure to design and resource a high-quality technical education pathway has clearly had a very serious impact on the country's economic performance. In the 1980s, as part of a broad investigation into why there were large international differences in productivity, a study was made by Professor Sig Prais[3] and his team at the National Institute of Economic and Social Research, of a series of matched manufacturing plants in industrial sectors as varied as clothing, furniture and biscuits. These comparisons showed clearly how the lack of people with intermediate-level skills led to lower productivity in British manufacturing plants.

Also in the 1980s, David Finegold and David Soskice argued that UK companies were trapped in a 'low-skilled equilibrium', in which, unable to get skilled technicians, British industrialists settled for producing low-quality goods and services.[4] At a time when many developing countries with lower wages were rapidly developing their organisational and technological skills, it is difficult to think of a more disastrous strategy for British firms to adopt.

It has been suggested on many occasions that the reason for this 'low-skilled equilibrium' is a cultural one. But if we examine the history of the UK's technical education pathway in light of the design and resource decisions highlighted at the beginning of this chapter, it becomes clear that its low quality is the result of a long period of neglect going back to the nineteenth century; and in more recent times deficient policy-making, as well as an endless stream of initiatives, few of which were in place long enough to produce useful results, even if they had been intelligently designed.

A long history of low-quality policy-making

The neglect of technically trained managers and workers goes back a long way. In 1868, Bradford dye manufacturer William Henry Ripley told a commission investigating science education that, knowing as he did the great want of scientific knowledge in Britain, he was astonished the country held the industrial position it did.[5]

Britain's industrial supremacy did not last, however, and the emergence of new science-based industries in the second half of the nineteenth century threw Britain's undersupply of scientifically educated managers and technically trained workers into sharp relief. The British educational system was not geared to the production of such managers or technicians, but rather to the socialisation of gentlemen into the cultural life of an elite, and the merger of a rising group of manufacturers' sons into the aristocracy. However, this emphasis on traditional values does not explain why Britain failed to change its educational system as her economic competitors gained ground in the latter part of the nineteenth century. The problem of explaining this puzzle becomes all the greater when one compares Britain's performance with that of Germany.

Germany had a more traditional social structure than Britain in the nineteenth century, but her rulers built an educational system far more directed to the economic needs of their country than that created by Britain's rulers. Here, Britain's highly competitive form of capitalism may provide an explanation.

British capitalism evolved in a comparatively undirected fashion, without government playing a strong interventionist role. This meant that traditional values about classical subjects being suited for upper-class students, and practical subjects being suited for working-class students, were not challenged by any powerful industrialising ideology backed up by state action.

In Germany, on the other hand, the state was in the hands of a modernising elite, who created the polytechnics and scientific facilities enabling Germany to become a world leader in the chemical industries and other science-related fields. To do this, Germany's political leaders had to overcome some of the same kinds of cultural resistance that appeared in Britain, but they had the concentrated political and social power to override objections, as well as the industrialising ideology to motivate action.

In Britain, in the early nineteenth century, members of all social classes considered artisans to be the appropriate bearers of technical skills. However, British artisans owed little of their skill and knowledge to formal schooling. Historically, their skills had been transmitted through apprenticeships and practical experience. This lack of formal schooling stemmed in part from the weakness of the educational system, with, as outlined in Chapter 7, the British government failing to establish the framework for a national system of elementary schools until 1870, and secondary education lagging behind still more. Only in 1902 did the British government begin to organise a coherent system of elementary and secondary education.

Fast-forwarding to the end of the Second World War, the state of secondary education at the time is best described by the 1938 Spens Report on secondary education, which noted that little had been done since 1900 to 'foster the development of secondary schools of quasi-vocational type designed to meet the needs of boys and girls who desired to enter industry and commerce at the age of 16'. Even more damagingly, 'although 85 per cent of pupils did not remain at school beyond 16' the curriculum was 'still largely planned in the interests of pupils who intended to go to a university'. Thus, the vast majority of children left school with a meagre knowledge of Latin, English, religious knowledge and science. Only in recent years has our education system begun to be transformed from one in which each stage is designed for those who go onto the next stage, regardless of whether they actually progress or not.

The next educational landmark was the Butler Act of 1944. This established free, compulsory schooling for children between the ages of five and fifteen, with the state sector coming under Local Education Authorities. The Ministry clearly intended that there should be three types of state schools – grammar, secondary modern and technical – and that there would be at least part-time compulsory education up until the age of eighteen. Before the Act was passed, Education Minister R. A. Butler had written that the main need 'was for industrial and technical training and the linking up of schools with employment'.

However, the Act led to little progress in that area. The Norwood Committee, tasked with studying curriculum issues, reported in 1943, before the Butler Act was passed. Its chairman was a classical scholar, and the Committee argued that a traditional academic education was best for everyone.

As a result, the new technical schools never got built and the country lost many of those it had. Secondary modern schools, with spending on each pupil about a third of that in grammar schools, did nothing to 'link schools with employment', and, for twenty years, the few technical schools there were catered to just 2 per cent or less of the school population.

The Butler Act did nothing to improve technical education in Britain, and in the seventy or so years since it was passed, successive governments have produced an endless stream of reports, legislation and organisation changes in an attempt to improve the situation. Since 1981, the amount of change in technical education has been absurd, and ultimately self-defeating.[6] During this period, there have been twenty-eight major Acts of Parliament relating to vocational and further education and skills training in the UK, and over the last few decades there has been an endless stream of agencies responsible for this area, including the Manpower Services Commission; the Training Commission; the Training Agency; Training and Enterprise Councils; the Further Education Funding Council; the Learning and Skills Council; the Young People's Learning Agency; the Skills Funding Agency; and most recently the Education and Skills Funding Agency.

There have also been a wide range of programmes and initiatives, many of which have now been abolished altogether. Key initiatives include the Training Opportunities Scheme; the Youth Training Scheme; Youth Training; Entry to Employment; and the Technician and Vocational Education Initiative. Worst of all, there has been a constant churn and change in qualifications: in 1986, National Vocational Qualifications were introduced, to be followed just six years later by General National Vocational Qualifications. When the latter was abandoned, the Advanced General National Qualification was replaced by an Advanced Certificate of Education, which then became Applied GCEs. In the case of apprenticeships, the government finally handed the whole problem over to employers, allowing virtually any small group of employers to devise their own apprenticeship qualification. This predictably led, in a short space of time, to a vast proliferation of narrow qualifications of varying and uncertain quality.

This constant process of change has created an unstable and complex landscape for both users and providers. As some commentators have joked about the resultant landscape of post-compulsory education and training provision: if you are not confused by it, then you have not understood it. Above all, successive governments have failed to provide clear and effective answers to the key design and resource decisions highlighted at the start of this chapter.

Despite all the policy changes that have been made, the country still does not have a national system of qualifications that is well understood and works in the marketplace, even though this is essential if the level of technical education in the country is to be raised. The one major attempt to produce one – National Vocational Qualifications – was so badly conceived that it failed completely. The qualifications were not valued by employers and, therefore, delivered no benefits to those that acquired them.

In addition, as part of the technical education pathway, no attempt has been made to lay out clear routes linking the education and training that students receive with specific occupations; while no provision has been made for students to change from the technical pathway to the academic pathway, or vice versa, should they decide they have made a mistake.

The policy-makers who failed to create a highly valued technical education pathway at the secondary level also failed to do so at the higher-education level, but for different reasons. In the 1950s, there was a major debate in the UK over the expansion of technical education. Should it find a place within the universities, or remain as a separate pathway? The Conservative White Paper of 1956 finally led to action. Twenty or so 'regional' technical colleges were identified and given support, becoming the nucleus of the polytechnics of the 1960s; and eight colleges (later ten) were designated as Colleges of Advanced Technology (CATs). However, the new Labour government, at the urging of the Robbins Committee, gave the CATs university status; while under a new binary policy, thirty polytechnics were created in England and Wales, in most cases by merging smaller colleges.

Finally, in 1992, the polytechnics – in one of the worst educational decisions of recent years – were given full university status. Thus, the opportunity to create a strong technical sector, with a strong technological stream in secondary schools leading on to high-prestige, advanced colleges of technology, was lost. The result is that today the UK is producing more university graduates than industry and society needs, and too few people with high-level technological skills.

As far as the funding of the education and training system is concerned, the policy of charging fees and giving loans adopted for the university sector can be regarded as a clear failure. Elsewhere, while the funding of apprenticeships has resumed in recent years, and very recently an industrial training levy has again been introduced, such schemes will not do much to improve technical education unless they are based on a national system of qualifications that produces the skills industry and society needs; with the skills of apprentices being assessed by experts before they are awarded qualifications.

The system of careers advice is another area where the policies of successive governments have been of poor quality. The Thatcher administration privatised the national careers advisory service, which was not a success; while the Labour government that came to power in 1997 introduced a new scheme called Connexions, which focused on NEETs (those not in education, employment or training). This, again, was not a success, as the most able students received little advice, and using the advisory service became associated with failure. However, nothing was done to reform the system until 2017, when the government launched a new careers guidance strategy, explicitly based on the benchmarks for good careers advice developed by Sir John Holman for my charitable trust.

Finally, the further education colleges, which should be the backbone of the technical education system, have not been well funded. Despite endless changes to the funding system, standards of education and training have remained low, and attempts to link the courses delivered to the needs of local business have failed.

In the light of this long history of low-quality policy-making, it is not surprising that the technical education system in the UK is not held in high esteem. This is not due to some ingrained cultural attitude towards technical education, but to a long history of neglect and low-quality policy-making. Therefore, there remains at this time both a huge need and an important opportunity to reform the technical education pathway, thereby increasing its contribution to the UK's economic performance.

A technical education pathway for the twenty-first century

Given the circumstances outlined above, I was delighted to be asked in November 2015 by the Minister for Skills, Nick Boles, to chair an Independent Panel on Technical Education.[7] This was tasked with advising on actions to improve the quality of technical education in England; with simplifying the over-complex system; and with ensuring the new system provided the skills most needed for the twenty-first century.

I was particularly pleased to take on this task as it gave the panel an opportunity to examine and redesign the whole system, using our knowledge of best practice in countries renowned for their world-class systems of technical education. We reported in April 2016, proposing a major redesign of the whole system. Our report, which had three main recommendations, was accepted in its entirety by the government in May 2017.

Firstly, we recommended that the government develop a coherent technical education system, based on a well-understood national system of qualifications that works in the marketplace. Young people will only work hard to get a qualification, and value it highly when they get it, if employers when recruiting give priority to individuals who possess it.

This technical education system should have two modes of learning: employment-based (typically an apprenticeship), and college-based. While it is necessary for government to design the overall national system of technical education, employer-designed standards must be put at its heart in order to ensure it works in the market-place. A single, common framework of standards should cover both apprenticeships and college-based provision. These standards should be designed to deliver the knowledge, skills and behaviours required to successfully perform in specific occupations, rather than the narrower job role-focused needs of individual employers.

The technical option, pursued through either mode of learning, should be clearly delineated from the academic option. At the same time, movement between the two must be possible. The technical education option should not cut off movement to undergraduate study at university, while young people who follow A-levels should be able to move into the technical education route. We therefore recommended that the government incentivise the development of a short, flexible, bridging provision, enabling individuals to move in either direction, as well as supporting adults returning to study.

Secondly, we recommended that a common framework of fifteen routes be established, encompassing all employment-based and college-based technical education at levels two to five. The proposed routes were defined through an analysis of labour-market information regarding the size and nature of occupations, grouped together to reflect shared requirements for skills and knowledge.

Thirdly, we recommended that the government introduce a new efficient and effective mechanism for developing and awarding qualifications. In England, there is currently a market-based approach to qualifications, which allows anyone to produce qualification systems. This had led to a huge number of competing qualifications of variable quality.

As of September 2015, there were over 21,000 qualifications on Ofqual's Register of Regulated Qualifications, offered by 158 different awarding organisations. Individuals wanting to take up a career in plumbing, for example, have to choose between thirty-three qualifications. This proliferation is very confusing for both individuals and employers, and results in the whole system performing badly. It is a classic example of the foolishness of thinking that everything in life is improved if it is turned into a market.

We therefore recommended that the government move away from the awarding organisation model, where qualifications that deliver similar but different outcomes compete with one another, and instead adopt a licensing approach. Any technical education qualification at levels two and three should be offered and awarded by a single body or consortium, under a licence covering a fixed period of time following an open competition.

As a result of this systematic process of simplification, we were able to produce a simple diagram showing progression pathways through the English education system, which would previously have been impossible (see Figure 8.1 overleaf). Given the importance of the choices young people have to make about their careers, one would have thought that this is something that would have been produced long ago.

Additionally, in January 2017, the government announced the creation of a network of ten to fifteen Institutes of Technology, tasked with delivering high-quality technical education to meet the needs of employers in local areas; an idea which had been developed by the staff of my charitable trust.

It is clearly inefficient for all 200-plus further education colleges to attempt to teach science, technology, education and mathematics (STEM) courses at higher levels, given the high cost of equipment and significant teacher expertise and employer engagement required to deliver quality provision. It is, therefore, better to concentrate provision on a smaller number of centres of excellence.

These initiatives launched by the Conservative government do

Figure 8.1 **Progression pathways through education**

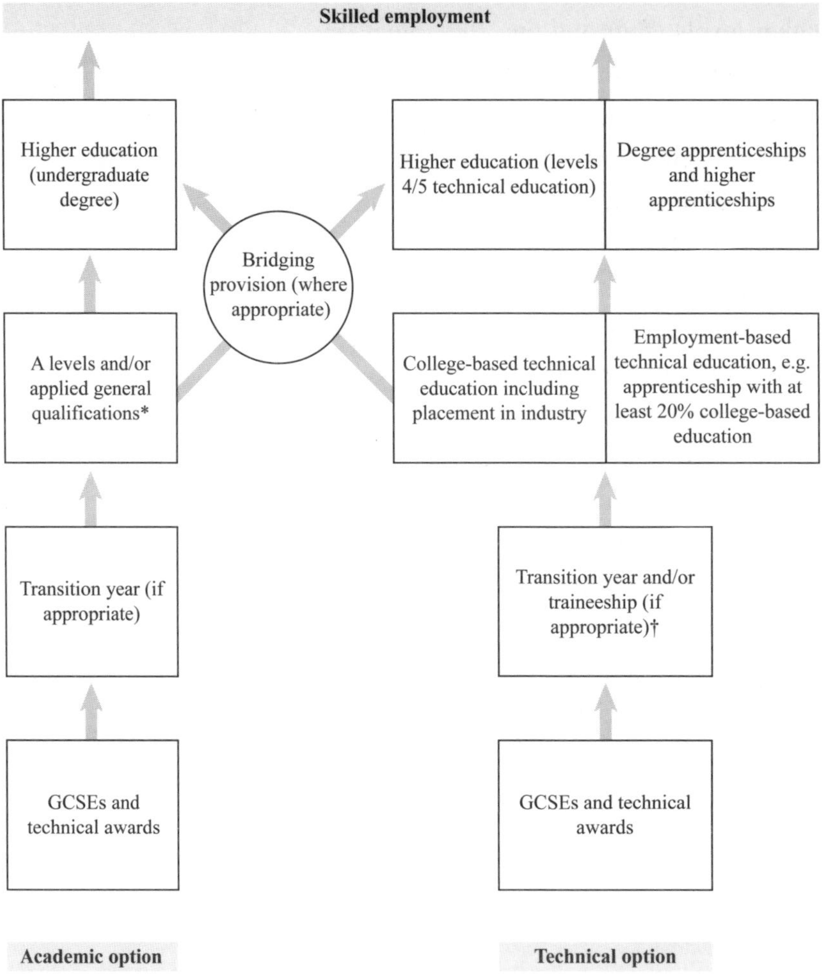

Skilled employment

Academic option		Technical option	

Higher education (undergraduate degree)

Higher education (levels 4/5 technical education)

Degree apprenticeships and higher apprenticeships

Bridging provision (where appropriate)

A levels and/or applied general qualifications*

College-based technical education including placement in industry

Employment-based technical education, e.g. apprenticeship with at least 20% college-based education

Transition year (if appropriate)

Transition year and/or traineeship (if appropriate)†

GCSEs and technical awards

GCSEs and technical awards

Academic option   **Technical option**

*Some students will move directly from A levels and/or applied general qualifications to degree and higher apprenticeships.

†Where a student does both, the traineeship will follow the transition year. Students doing both the transition year and a traineeship may progress directly to employment.

Source: Report of the Independent Panel on Technical Education, April 2016, p. 28

not, however, complete the reforms that need to be made. There is still a need to design a set of technical education qualifications at higher levels (four and five) that meet the needs of employers, and this is something that should now be done.

If countries want to have a high rate of economic growth, and create fulfilling and well-paid jobs for their citizens, they need to develop high-quality education and training systems, aligning them with the needs of industry and society. It is a political outrage that, as a result of a long history of neglect and low-quality policy-making, this has not happened in the area of technical education in the UK. An opportunity has been created by the government's latest reforms to create these high-quality education and training systems, but it will require consistent leadership and a national commitment, as well as significant resources over many years, to produce a technical work-force with the skills to tackle the challenges the country faces.

It also makes no sense to produce a new generation of young people with the skills necessary for the 'race to the top', if industry does not innovate and create new competitive advantages. The next chapter will, therefore, look at what the government needs to do to create a national system of innovation to aid entry into new, high value-added per capita industries.

9

National systems of innovation

If innovation is the engine of economic growth, governments need to make raising their country's rate of innovation a major target. That is why, in recent years, many countries have sought to improve their country's 'national system of innovation'. The concept of a national system of innovation was first used in published form by Christopher Freeman in 1987,who defined it as 'the network of institutions in the public and private sectors whose activities and interactions initiate, import, and diffuse new technologies'.[1] As a concept, the national system of innovation has proved useful as a way of thinking coherently about a country's innovation policies, which cover such areas as its funding of scientific research and new technologies; its systems of intellectual property rights and standards; its universities, research institutes and company laboratories; and its use of tax incentives and procurement policies to encourage innovation.

Before looking at how countries can build up effective national systems of innovation, it is necessary to say something about the nature of science and technology. If policy-makers are going to create the best conditions for economic growth, they need to understand the relationship between science and technology, as well as the difference between generic technologies, proprietary technologies and infratechnologies.

The nature of science and technology

In order to characterise science and the distinct elements of technology, it is necessary to introduce a piece of microeconomic theory. This states that goods and services are 'rival' if one buyer's consumption reduces the amount available to others. Goods and services are also considered 'excludable' if the owners can prevent consumption by others. Pure public goods are those that are neither rival nor excludable, with the result that private markets will underinvest in such assets as they cannot appropriate the full value created by any investment. Using these two criteria we can categorise science and the distinct elements of an industrial technology as public or private goods; and also by the different roles they play in the process of innovation and the economic growth performance of countries, though they interact synergistically in that process.

Scientific research is seen almost everywhere as a pure public good that should be funded by government, and that is usually funded separately from technological research. This is because it almost always involves the discovery of new laws of nature, which cannot be patented. In most countries, universities are the most important public organisations performing R&D, and governments fund university R&D activities in a number of ways. In the past, they have provided general support via block grants from their ministries of education, part of which is used by university staff to carry out R&D. Such funding is still very important in small, highly R&D intensive countries such as the Netherlands, Sweden and Switzerland.

Governments may also provide grants to encourage research 'for the advancement of knowledge' or grants to obtain the knowledge needed for government missions, such as defence and health. In the UK, most of this type of support is provided by United Kingdom Research and Innovation (UKRI) which has under it seven Research Councils and Innovate UK, and gives grants to individual projects selected on a competitive basis, while in the US this is done by the National Institutes of Health and the National Science Foundation.

The research record of these organisations would suggest that this is the ideal way to get a high level of scientific excellence.

In many countries, the funding system for science also includes public research institutes or national laboratories that carry out the same type of R&D activities as universities, as well as more applied research and technology development work. Although the relative importance of universities in terms of performing R&D has increased in most countries, public research organisations remain important.

Public research organisations may be linked to universities and included in the higher-education sector, or may be independent of them. The largest in the OECD area is the Centre National de la Recherche Scientifique (CNRS) in France, which receives the largest share of direct funding of R&D in the higher-education sector and provides support for projects normally carried out in collaboration with university researchers. In the United States, the higher-education sector also contains a large number of public research laboratories. This is different from the Max Planck Gesellschaft in Germany, the Consiglio Nazionale delle Ricerche in Italy (CNR), and the Consejo Superior de Investigaciones Cientificas (CSIC) in Spain, which are all independent national research institutes.

After the basic scientific research stage, the next critical phase in the R&D cycle is the demonstration of the commercial feasibility of new technology. The end point of this phase is described as 'generic technology'. The concept of 'generic technology' was adopted by research agencies and innovation policy-makers in the United States in the late 1980s, at a time when US industry was losing industrial leadership to Japan in the key semiconductor and electronics industries. These were technology domains that had largely been created by the 'strategic technology' programmes of the US Department of Defence, but were under intense pressure from Japanese firms receiving government support for co-operation on precompetitive semiconductor R&D.

A generic technology can be defined as one that has the potential to be applied to a wide variety of applications across many industries, and that requires subsequent research and development by the private sector before it can be deployed in commercial applications. Examples of generic technologies can be found in areas such as advanced materials, biotechnology, additive manufacturing, information technologies, semiconductors, robotics and artificial intelligence. The importance of the research that produces generic technologies stems from the fact that it acts as the bridge between basic science and the considerable private-sector investment in applied R&D necessary to spawn innovative products. It is also a major investment barrier to the emergence of radical new technologies and has been characterised as the 'valley of death' because of the high risk faced by the private sector in this phase of the R&D cycle.

Generic research is partially excludable because property rights are partially attainable. It elicits some industry funding and should therefore be called a 'quasi-public good'. This attribute, along with the long lines of commercialisation, explains the complicated funding pattern, involving both industry and government, that characterise this phase of technology research.

The next phase of the R&D cycle is proprietary research, which is excludable and hence fundable by industry. By this stage, sufficient risk reduction has generally been achieved, so that – given appropriate risk-taking, financing and an intellectual property rights infrastructure – the necessary large amounts of production-and-process-specific applied R&D will be forthcoming.

A final, critical, if often unrecognised, element of an industrial technology should be mentioned at this point. This is the set of 'infra-technologies' that make up an industry's technical infrastructure. They are needed to provide measurement and test methods; to provide the basis for the technical and functional interfaces that make-up a system; and to provide product-acceptance testing protocols and standards.

Such infratechnologies have economic utility only if they are uniformly and widely used as an industry standard. This characteristic inevitably leads to systematic underinvestment by the private sector due to 'free-rider' problems, and is, therefore, another area where government has a role to play. If we take the Internet, for example, its efficient operation depends on a large number of standards, some of which – the Internet protocol for data transmissions, for example – are very complex and based on a large number of infratechnologies. These are very important for the IT service industries as they help define output, interoperability, security protocols and intellectual property.

All the technologies driving a modern economy are supported by such infratechnologies, and economic studies of individual infratechnologies have shown they deliver substantial net economic benefits and lower entry barriers.

A final point to be made about technology is that it is becoming increasingly based on new scientific discoveries. In the past, technology was less science-based and less complex, and individuals could make inventions without necessarily advancing the underlying science. Today, while examples can be found of specific inventions appearing before a major science base and subsequent generic technology platforms have been established, no major technology has advanced on a broad front in such a way for the past fifty years. The following figures, for example, show the increasing dependency of US patents on scientific publications (see Figure 9.1).

What this means is that, unless it has an excellent science base, a country will struggle to create competitive new industries once it has reached the world's technological frontier. This, for example, may be one of the reasons why Japan – which has a surprisingly weak academic science base given its high level of technological development – has not forged ahead in any new industries in recent years.

Innovation policy

Having looked at the differences between science and the distinct elements of technology, and how countries fund scientific research, we now need to look at how they develop and implement innovation

Figure 9.1 **References to scientific publications in US patents**

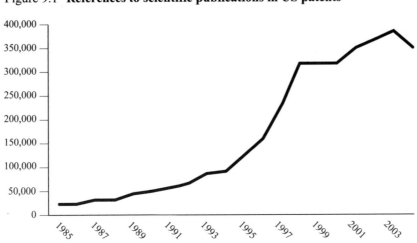

Source: Francis Narin, 'Research and Equity Markets'; McMillan et al. (2000). Reproduced in Gregory Tassey, *The Technology Imperative*, Edward Elgar Publishing, Cheltenham, 2007, p. 139

policies to improve their rates of economic growth. Innovation policy involves bringing together two policy areas, and then focusing them on improving the country's rate of innovation.

Firstly, there is the set of policies that countries deal with all the time. For example, countries can operate their government procurement policies in the same way they have always done, or they can redesign them in such a way as to promote innovation. Equally, countries can operate their corporate tax systems simply to raise revenues, or to raise revenues in ways that drive innovation and increase the competitive advantage of their firms.

Secondly, governments need to understand that generic technologies and infratechnologies play a key role in the innovation performance of their countries, and will not necessarily be produced if the government fails to provide some of the funds, and put in place the organisation, to ensure the necessary technology development takes place.

Why are such policies necessary? Innovation policy is a

recognition of the fact that businesses innovate with the help of many other institutions, and that innovation failures can occur if public policy does not play an active role. It also recognises that technological progress depends on certain tangible and intangible infrastructure investments, and on specific innovations that are too risky, complex or interdependent with other breakthroughs, for private firms to risk the large investments needed.

There are three areas where innovation failures are likely to occur if government does not play an active role.[2] Firstly, in the observable world – as opposed to the world of microeconomic textbooks – the 'rational' company will not invest in next-generation technologies, however great the rewards, if they involve high levels of risk and exceedingly lengthy R&D time frames. This is why it was the US government's Defense Advanced Research Projects Agency (DARPA) that supported the initial development of the Internet (then the ARPANET), rather than private-sector communications or computer companies. This made the Internet a reality decades before the free market would have done, assuming that firms would ever have had the motivation to do so.

Secondly, because of the complexity of today's innovation process, firms cannot maximise innovation by working in isolation. To maximise their rate of innovation, they need to work with organisations such as suppliers, customers, competitors, universities, research institutes and government entities, in order to gain the required knowledge and information, and achieve the co-ordination necessary to make breakthroughs. Such interactions take time, commitment and resources, and the pattern of co-operation between the parties involved will not necessarily be as fast or smooth as it could be. This is why government agencies such as DARPA have played such a useful role.

As well as its role in funding research, DARPA orchestrates the involvement of established companies with start-ups and industry experts; supports knowledge sharing between industry competitors through invitation-only workshops; provides third-party validation of new technology directions; and supports technology platform development. For example, DARPA played an important role in identifying emerging directions in the research community, co-ordinating star scientists, and seed-funding initial research into materials technology for silicon-germanium (Si-Ge) semiconductors, which was crucial for improving the innovation performance and competitive advantage of the US semiconductor industry in the late 1980s.

Thirdly, an innovation failure is likely to occur where multiple parties need to act synergistically to build new technology platforms in areas such as near-field communications (NFC), which includes enabled contactless mobile payments; intelligent transportation systems (ITS); health IT platforms; digital signatures and electronic IDs; and the smart electric grid. In these markets, where there are chicken-or-egg challenges, government can play a useful role by facilitating the development of systems and funding infrastructure, so that once the platform is deployed the private sector can innovate on top of it.

To deal with such potential innovation failures, governments have designed a number of policies. Firstly, in many cases they have identified a range of core industries where they believe they can develop the necessary capabilities to innovate, and where they need to develop new technology in order to achieve a competitive position in the global economy. For example, Germany's High-Tech Strategy, released in 2006, identified seventeen advanced cross-cutting technologies judged to be critical to enabling the country's firms to compete. These ranged from biotechnology, nanotechnology and microsystems technology to optical materials, production, and information and communication technologies. The aim of the strategy was to identify gaps and co-ordinate the limited resources of Germany's government, firms and universities in producing technology roadmaps, and making the necessary investment to ensure German leadership in these technologies.

Secondly, many governments have reshaped how they buy goods and services in order to drive innovation through 'intelligent demand'.

All too often, government departments procure the goods and services they need on the basis of out-of-date specifications and the lowest cost tenders. In this way, government cannot be accused of favouring one supplier over another. However, by being an intelligent customer; engaging suppliers early in the procurement process; combining this early involvement with contracts based on well-defined outcomes; being less risk-averse; and making use of grand challenge competitions, government can use its procurement to drive innovation in the economy.

Thirdly, having recognised that incentives are an important driver of innovative behaviour, a number of countries have begun to offer generous and stable R&D tax credits, both to encourage existing companies to expand R&D activity and to attract globally mobile R&D activity.

Fourthly, many governments also support the innovation capabilities of their SMEs, especially in manufacturing. This can take the form of extension services, as operated by Japan's Kohsetsushi centres; or the United States' Manufacturing Extension Partnerships (MEP), which teach SMEs such manufacturing techniques as lean manufacturing and quality control, as well as new product-development skills and technology adoption. Several countries have also used Innovation Vouchers to encourage SMEs to buy expertise from universities, national laboratories or private research institutes.

Finally, because IT plays an increasingly vital role in driving productivity and facilitating the innovation process, many countries have implemented specific IT policies. For example, in 2004, South Korea launched its IT 8.3.9 Information Technology Development Strategy, which identified eight key service areas; three telecommunications infrastructures (ubiquitous next-generation wired and wireless broadband networks, and implementation of the IPV6 next-generation Internet protocol); and nine IT product areas, where South Korea sought world leadership. Many countries also leverage IT to drive innovation in specific segments of their economies, as Denmark has done in its national health service.

This range of policies, when effectively implemented and combined with a high level of funding for scientific and technological research, can help a country's firms innovate and create competitive advantage, and we now need to look systematically at how countries organise themselves to deliver such innovation policies, and what impact they have on the level of innovation and economic growth of their countries.

National policies and agencies

While neoclassical economists interested in economic growth continue to focus on market failures and the allocation of scarce resources, many countries have come to realise that innovation is the engine of economic growth and have implemented a range of policies to improve the innovation performance of their firms. By 2012, as reported by economists Robert D. Atkinson and Stephen J. Ezell, some three-dozen countries had created formal national innovation strategies, and over two dozen had created national innovation agencies.[3]

As part of these strategies, many countries have set themselves ambitious goals to lead the world in certain industries, technologies or application areas, in the belief that the private, non-profit and government sectors need ambitious goals to guide and motivate them in taking the necessary steps.

A good example of a country setting ambitious goals is Singapore. In the late 1990s, it decided to drive its economy through innovation, openly stating that it sought world leadership in the life sciences, digital media, and water/environment industries. Ten years later, Singapore had succeeded. As we have already seen in the ITIF's 'The Atlantic Century' report, in 2009 Singapore ranked first of thirty-six countries in terms of innovation-based competitiveness, beaten only by China in terms of the speed of its progress between 1999 and 2009. Singapore was also placed first when ITIF released its 'Atlantic Century II' report in 2011.[4]

As an example of how it implemented its ambitious goals, in 2003 Singapore launched Biopolis, a two-million-square-foot biomedical research centre, to support its goal of becoming a world leader in the life sciences. The centre houses some seven thousand PhD graduates in the life sciences, including some of the world's most distinguished biomedical researchers. To put this into context the total number of life sciences PhDs in the United States is about ten thousand.

It should also be noted that, in terms of GDP per capita in international dollars, Singapore in 2017 (according to World Bank figures) ranked fourth in the world – behind only Qatar, Macau and Luxembourg – with a GDP per capita figure of 94,000 Int $. On the same basis, the United States came eleventh, with a GDP per capita of 60,000 Int $, and the United Kingdom came twenty-fourth, with a GDP per capita of 44,000 Int $.

China has also made clear it wants to win the race for global innovation advantage. In January 2006, it launched a fifteen-year 'Medium to Long-term Plan for the Development of Science and Technology'. The plan made clear that, by 2020, China was aiming to become an 'innovation-oriented society'; increase R&D expenditure to 2.5 per cent of GDP; limit dependence on imported technology; and become one of the top five countries in the world in the number of patents granted. Furthermore, in 2011, China announced its 'China Innovation 2020 goals'; and in 2015 it launched its 'Made in China 2025' plan.[5] In it, China makes clear its view of economic history:

Manufacturing is the main pillar of the national economy, the foundation of the country, tool of transformation and basis of prosperity. Since the beginning of industrial civilisation in the middle of the 18th Century, it has been proven repeatedly by the rise and fall of world powers that without strong manufacturing there is no national prosperity. Building internationally competitive manufacturing is the only way China can enhance its strength, protect state security and become a world power.

The plan also stated that one of its guiding principles would be 'innovation-driven development', and that China will:

- Make innovation the guiding theme of manufacturing with breakthroughs in key technologies
- Adapt institutions for innovation
- Promote trans-industrial and interdisciplinary collaborative innovation, digitalisation, network technologies, and smart technologies in manufacturing
- Follow the innovation-driven path

It also announced that China would be promoting breakthroughs in ten key sectors: information technology; numerical control tools and robotics; aerospace equipment; ocean engineering equipment and high-tech ships; railway equipment; energy saving and new-energy vehicles; power equipment; new materials; medicine and medical devices; and agricultural devices.

In case anyone was in doubt, China made clear that by 2049, the centennial of the founding of the New China, it aimed to become the leader among the world's manufacturing powers.

Because neoclassical economists believe that governments can do little to improve the growth rates of their countries, they fail to pay much attention to what governments say they are doing to stimulate economic growth; what they do; and what happens as a result to the rate of growth in their economies. However, in the case of countries such as Singapore and China, one gets as good a proof of innovation and learning being the engine of economic growth as can ever be gleaned from any theory in economics.

As well as formulating national innovation strategies, at least two dozen countries – recognising that neither traditional science support agencies nor economic ministries have the knowledge and skills to support innovation strategies – had created innovation agencies by 2012.[6] A few countries have had innovation agencies for some time: Taiwan's Industrial Technology Research Institute (ITRI) was set up in 1973; Finland's National Agency for Technology and Innovation, Tekes, in 1983; and Ireland's Forjas in 1994. But it was the first decade of this century that saw a multitude of nations setting up institutions to support their innovation policies. In 2000, India launched its National Innovation Foundation; in 2001, Sweden created VINNOVA; in 2003, Portugal introduced its Agência de Inovação; in 2004 Norway created Innovasjon Norge, the Netherlands launched Senter Novem, and the UK set up its Technology Strategy Board (which later became Innovate UK); in 2006, Denmark created the Danish Agency for Science, Technology and Innovation; and, in 2008, Uruguay launched its National Research and Innovation Agency.

In addition, Australia, Austria, Chile, France, Germany, Iceland, Italy, Malaysia, New Zealand, Spain and Switzerland also have dedicated innovation-promotion agencies. Not only do all these countries have agencies that fund research at universities and national laboratories, they have also realised that if they want to grow economically in today's highly competitive, technology-driven global economy, they need an institution tasked specifically with promoting technological innovation.

Innovation policy in the US

The position of the countries above should be contrasted with that of the United States, where no innovation strategy has been adopted and no innovation agency set up. The government has, however, taken steps, in spite of a national belief in market fundamentalism, to improve its national rate of innovation. But, because of the failure of its government to understand the scale of the competitive challenge it faces in world markets, and because of its failure – for political economy reasons – to adopt a national innovation strategy, such efforts have not been enough to prevent a fall in the country's national innovation-based competitiveness.

It was concern about the ability of US firms to compete successfully in the global economy that forced the subject of support for innovation onto the political agenda in the first place. Furthermore, it was concern about the worsening trade deficit and the economic success of Japan that led the US government to introduce eleven major initiatives supporting innovation between the end of the Carter Administration and the start of Bill Clinton's Presidential term in 1993. In other words, the vast majority of these initiatives took place during the free-market administrations of Ronald Reagan and George W. Bush, a time during which proponents of an explicit industrial policy were decisively defeated.

It is worth mentioning four of these initiatives to illustrate the range of initiatives taken to aid American firms in building up their competitive advantage. Firstly, there was the Small Business Innovation Development Act of 1982. This Legislation created the Small Business Innovation Research Program (SBIR), which was a joint project of the Small Business Administration and government agencies with large research budgets, such as the Departments of Defence, Energy, and Environmental Protection. The agencies were required to devote a fraction, initially 1.35 per cent, of their research funding, to support initiatives that came from small, independent, for-profit firms. Small Phase One awards of $50,000 could be followed by larger Phase Two awards of $500,000.

Secondly, the National Science Foundation in 1985 established a programme of Engineering Research Centers. These were designed to create a decentralised network of researchers, working on concrete problems of translating scientific breakthroughs into usable technologies.

Thirdly, the Bayh-Dole Act of 1986 provided blanket permission for performers of federally funded research to file for patents on the results of such research, and to grant licences for these patents, including exclusive licences to other parties.

Finally, the Manufacturing Extension program was set up in 1988, authorised by the Omnibus Trade and Competitiveness Act of that year. It established a network of manufacturing extension projects, modelled on agricultural extension programs, providing locally available expertise to help manufacturers make use of advance technologies.

At the same time as it was delivering these programmes the United States government also funded a massive programme of generic technology research, though in recent years it has declined. It has done this while maintaining its tradition of laissez-faire and reliance on the market by carrying out technological research within the framework of national defence.

In the years after the Second World War, innovation policies in the US were carried out by the Pentagon, which worked closely with other national security agencies, such as the Atomic Energy Commission and the National Aeronautics and Space Administration (NASA). As a result, government funding and infrastructure played a key role in developing such new technologies as computers, jet planes, civilian nuclear energy and lasers. This method of supporting the development of generic technologies was pioneered by the Advanced Research Projects Agency (ARPA) in the Pentagon. ARPA was created in February 1958 by President Dwight Eisenhower in response to the Soviet launching of Sputnik I in 1957, and aimed to push the technological frontier of Pentagon procurement efforts. Its name was changed to Defense Advanced Research Projects Agency (DARPA) in May 1972, though it was changed back to ARPA briefly between February 1993 and March 1996.

ARPA's objective was to provide funding for 'beyond the horizon' technologies, as the rest of the Pentagon's budget for R&D was focused on the short-term procurement of weapons for the various military services. Its initiatives covered a range of technologies, but it was those that supported technological advances in the field of computers that established a new type of technology policy. While bodies such as the National Science Foundation relied heavily on proposals being peer reviewed – which left most of the initiative in the hands of the research community – ARPA made a practice of hiring visionary technologists and giving them a high degree of autonomy to give out research funds. The organisational structure was also extremely lean, with a minimum of paperwork.

ARPA's Information Processing Technique Office (IPTO) was initially set up in 1962 and played a key role in the advance of computer technology in the 1960s and 1970s. It provided the resources to create computer science departments at major universities, as well as funding a series of research projects that pushed forward advances in the human-computer interface. Many of the technologies that were ultimately incorporated into personal computers were developed by ARPA-funded researchers.

The Internet also began as an ARPA project in the late 1960s, designed to encourage communication among computer researchers funded by the agency. While responsibility for the early Internet eventually shifted from ARPA to the National Science Foundation, it was in the ARPA period that the technological barriers to networked communication among computers was overcome.

A parallel and independent development of generic technologies was started in the 1970s by the National Institutes of Health (NIH). The NIH officials did not set technological goals in the way that ARPA routinely did, instead relying heavily on the peer-review model in which funds are distributed to the research projects deemed best by other scientists. However, the NIH's funding mandate rested on progress in fighting human disease, and as their officials grasped the disease-fighting possibility of genetic engineering, they aggressively supported the advance of the technology, as well as the science.

The American Association for the Advancement of Science's R&D funding data show that in the fiscal year of 2004, the NIH funded $14.8 billion in basic research, but also $12.1 billion in applied research, including a $600 million small-firm grants programme consisting largely of early-phase technology research. In this way, it could be said that the NIH invented the biotechnology industry.

As a result of NIH funding over the years, the growth in biotechnology firms was dramatic, 32 in 1978, 42 in 1974, 52 in 1980, and 100 in 1981. Some of these start-ups failed, and the industry's performance has not lived up to the expectations of investors looking for quick results. However, it is important to remember that in recent years most of the successful new pharmaceuticals are products of these new technologies.

As a result of the successful initiatives of ARPA and the NIH, the American government became a major funder of generic technologies. The scale and importance of this funding for the success of American industry can be demonstrated by looking at one product: the iPhone.

The economist Mariana Mazzucato, in analysing the iPhone, found that behind the cool design and hardware there were twelve key technologies that enable it to work. First of all, there is the hardware: (1) tiny microprocessors; (2) memory chips; (3) solid-state hard drives; (4) liquid crystal displays; and (5) lithium-based batteries. Then there are the networks and the software: (6) fast Fourier transform algorithms; (7) the Internet; (8) HTTP and HTML, the languages and protocols that turn the hard-to-use Internet into the easy-to-access World Wide Web; (9) cellular networks; (10) Global Positioning Systems; (11) the touchscreen; and (12) Siri, the voice-activated artificial intelligence agent.

All these technologies are important components of what makes an iPhone work. What Mazzucato discovered when she assembled this list of technologies and reviewed their history, was that the development of every one of them had been supported in significant ways by governments, often the American government.

Take, for example, the last of these, the girl with the silicon voice, Siri. In 2000, seven years before the first iPhone, DARPA commissioned the Stanford Research Institute to develop a sort of proto-Siri, a virtual office assistant that might help military personnel do their jobs. Twenty universities were brought into the project, all working furiously on the different technologies necessary to make a voice-activated virtual assistant a reality. Seven years later, the research was commercialised as a start-up, Siri Incorporated, and it was only in 2010 that Apple bought the company for an undisclosed sum.

While the United States government has initiated and operated a number of innovation programmes, and funded generic technology development through the Department of Defence and the NIH, it has not made raising its rate of innovation a major target for government policy. As a result, it has not funded these initiatives at the scale necessary to maintain America's world technological leadership. The federal government, primarily through DARPA, was throughout most of the post-Second World War era the major source of funding for generic technology research in the physical and information areas. However, DARPA funding has been flat in constant dollars for over two decades, while over the same period total Department of Defence R&D funding has increased substantially. As a result, the generic research of the Department of Defence has become a smaller proportion of the GDP growth it supports.[7]

It is also a mistake to think that venture capital can fill this gap. In the world of venture capital, the funding that is the nearest to generic research is called 'seed capital', and in 2005, for example, only $55 million was allocated by venture capitalists to this phase of technology. Also, in 2007, less than 1 per cent of private venture capital went to this phase of technology research.

At the same time, NIST's Advanced Technology Program (ATP), which was set up in 1991 under the administration of President George H. W. Bush to stimulate early-stage advanced technology development that would otherwise not be funded, has been shut down for political reasons. The case for the program was not based on systematic policy analysis by either its opponents or supporters, but was based only on a general perception of market failure at an early stage of research. Opponents argued that all stages of technology research are private goods and offer private rates of return to bring about desirable levels of industry funding. They therefore labelled the program as 'corporate welfare'. As economist Gregory Tassey has said, 'Into a policy void, incorrect decisions will rush', and the ATP, which when it was first conceived was seen as potentially a $1 billion-per-year program, was gradually closed down.[8]

The world technological leadership of the United States has, therefore, not only been undermined by a fall in federal funds for scientific research as a share of GDP, but also by the failure of the government to adequately fund generic research. Additionally, its innovation performance has been further weakened by failures of its system of corporate governance and finance, and its national system of education and training.

Innovation policy in the UK

Finally, I want to look at innovation policy in the UK over the last twenty years, as during this period I and a number of other politicians have sought to put innovation policy at the centre of government attempts to raise the country's economic growth rate. It is, I believe, valuable to make an appraisal of what has been done, because while it has been successful to a certain degree, it could have been much more effective and consistent had it been informed by a generally-accepted, production-capability theory of economic growth such as I have set out in this book.

The New Labour government, which came to power in May 1997 under Prime Minister Tony Blair, had few new industrial policies, its main economic goals being to show that it had ceased to be a political party that supported state ownership of industry, and that it had intelligent macroeconomic policies. The government also had few ideas about science policy and innovation policy other than a commitment to raise the level of science funding, which had been allowed to languish under Margaret Thatcher, who believed that government funding of scientific R&D drove out private funding by industry. By the time Thatcher left government in 1990, however, she had conclusively proved that this was not the case.

At that time, the Department of Trade and Industry (DTI) was responsible for science and innovation policy, but the department inherited by the Labour Party had little idea of what its role should be, other than a firm belief that government should not attempt to 'pick winners', and that it should not take any action unless it could be shown that there was a 'market failure'.

When I joined the government as Minister of Science in 1998, after thirty-five years in industry in the family business, the first task I set myself was increasing government funding of scientific R&D. This I was able to do with the enthusiastic support of the Chancellor of the Exchequer, Gordon Brown. When the government came to power, the science budget was £1.3 billion. As a result of substantial increases in a number of spending reviews, the science budget more than doubled in real terms by 2007/8, including £500 million a year for the renewal of scientific facilities in universities. A fifteen-year roadmap for large facilities was also produced, so as to provide the UK's world-class scientists with world-class scientific infrastructure.

At the time, there were a number of programmes designed to stimulate innovation that had been introduced by previous ministers, but they were not considered of any importance, and were not the responsibility of the Minister of Science. It was only after the General Election of 2001, when the Labour government was returned to power, that I was given responsibility for innovation policy. This was due, I suspect, to my being the only junior minister interested in being responsible for it. It also needs to be said that at that time the DTI had very little policy-making capability, very little information on the performance of British industry, and almost no knowledge of what was going on in the rest of the world. Therefore, it quickly became clear to me that if I was going to get anything done I would have to do the policy analysis myself.

As a result of enthusiastic support by the Enterprise and Growth Unit – which Gordon Brown had set up in the Treasury, and which under the leadership of a couple of brilliant civil servants took a pragmatic approach to solving the problems faced by British industry – I was able to make substantial progress in four areas.

The first area where the government sought to support innovation was knowledge transfer from universities. A lack of university knowledge transfer had been a great weakness of the UK innovation system in the past, and the government introduced a number of schemes to improve the UK's performance. These appear to have produced a major cultural change within our universities; building capability, increasing professionalism and making higher-education institutions (HEIs) more valuable partners for business.

The schemes that the government introduced included the 'The University Challenge Fund', which provided seed funds to universities, 'Science Enterprise Funds', to teach entrepreneurial skills to science and engineering undergraduates, and, in 2001, the 'Higher Education Innovation Fund', to incentivise universities to transfer knowledge into industry and society. The former two schemes were fairly quickly merged into this latter scheme in order to simplify things for the universities.

These schemes have led to a large increase in recent years in knowledge transfer from British universities, with the private sector putting a value of £3 billion on its collaborative and contract research with UK universities in 2009/10 (see Figure 9.2).

These schemes also led to a dramatic increase in the number of spin-off companies. In 2009/10, for example, 273 spin-off companies were created (see Table 9.1 on page 222). While limited data is available before 2000/01, as many HEIs did not monitor or record knowledge transfer performance until then, between 1994 and 1999, an average of seventy spin-off companies per annum were recorded, so clearly a substantial increase took place.

Early in its life, the government also sought to encourage spin-offs from universities by allocating £50 million to setting up high-tech incubators attached to universities. The Sheffield Advanced Manufacturing Park, which has attracted international companies such as Boeing to start up manufacturing operations there, was also set up at this time.

A second major initiative of the government was the setting up of the Technology Strategy Board in October 2004, now known as Innovate UK. When the Labour government came to power in 1997,

Figure 9.2 **Universities working with business**

A period of growing government funding for universities has also seen universities do increasingly well at business interaction and attracting external income. Last year universities secured over £3 billion from external sources.

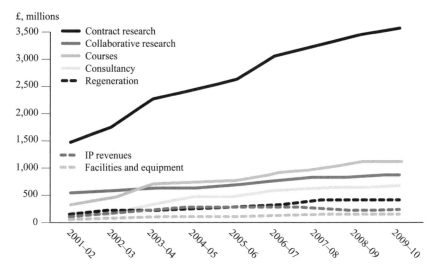

£, millions

Source: Department for Business, Innovation and Skills, 'Innovation and Research Strategy for Growth', December 2011

it found that a few collaborative, applied R&D programmes – introduced by successive governments over the years – lingered on in the DTI, administered by civil servants with little industrial or technological knowledge or experience.

There was also no knowledge of what was happening in this policy space in the US or elsewhere in the world, and innovation was low down on the agenda of the department. It was to improve this situation that I set up the Technology Strategy Board. As a result of its early success, the Technology Strategy Board was turned into an executive non-departmental public body in 2007. This gave it greater independence, the potential to make a consistent and greater difference to the UK's innovation performance, and the ability to staff itself with people with industrial and technological experience.

One of the Technology Strategy Board's major programmes was focused on collaborative, applied R&D. This was achieved through

Table 9.1: **Academic spin-off firms in the UK**

	Number established	*Number surviving after 3 years*
2005–6	186	746
2006–7	226	844
2007–8	219	923
2008–9	215	976
2009–10	273	969

Source: HESA (2009/10); Department for Business, Innovation and Skills, 'Academic Spin-off Firms in the UK', Economics Paper No. 15, December 2011

an open competition for funding, held every six months. The projects supported were part-funded by government, and brought together business and research partners to carry out research with a future commercial goal. By 2007, this programme had already proved to be highly successful, with over 600 user-driven collaborative R&D projects having already been approved for funding at levels varying from £3,000 to £95 million. There was an average of five partner organisations per funded project, with small companies making up a third of the organisations involved. The 600 projects approved for funding represented over £900 million of R&D investment by government and business, with £465 million having been committed by business, and the same amount committed by government.

In time, the Technology Strategy Board effectively became the innovation agency of the government; looking after, for example, the work of the DTI on emerging technologies, which was initiated following a recommendation in 'The Race to the Top', the report I did for Gordon Brown after I left government.[9] It is a measure of how little the DTI knew about what was happening in the rest of the world that I thought I was doing something new and radical in setting up the Technology Strategy Board, when, as we have already seen, a number of other countries had already set up innovation agencies.

A third initiative of the government was the launch in 2001 of the Small Business Research Initiative (SBRI), modelled on the Small Business Innovation Research (SBIR) scheme in the US. At first, the Small Business Research Initiative in the UK was not a success. A target of 2.5 per cent of external government R&D to be spent on SMEs was set, but government departments largely spent this on pieces of research relating to the development of policy. Then, in April 2009, the Technology Strategy Board having taken over its administration, the programme began to perform the function it was originally intended to perform – that is, issue challenges, articulated by government, to industry about meeting its needs, and invite companies to respond with solutions, in the process, becoming 'lead customers'. In the period up until 2014, 158 SBRI competitions had been run in partnership with fifty-nine public-sector organisations, resulting in contracts worth over £189m.

A fourth initiative was the Manufacturing Advisory Service, which was launched in 2001 to provide help to small businesses with new manufacturing technology. This was also based on an American scheme – the highly successful Manufacturing Extension Partnership – and was a great success.

The Coalition government, formed by the Conservative and Liberal Democrat parties in May 2010, successfully built on the innovation policies initiated by the Labour government. However, the Conservative government that came into power in May 2015 reverted to a more market-efficiency view of its role, and the Manufacturing Advisory Service was closed down by Sajid Javid, the then Secretary of State of the Department of Business, Innovation and Skills. In doing so, he presumably invoked the well-worn neoclassical argument that all businessmen know what technical knowledge they need to import into their businesses and must pay the full price for doing so.

Finally, in July 2016 there was another lurch in policy, as Theresa May became Prime Minister and launched her government's

'Industrial Strategy'. Observing this endless changing of policy, I have become convinced that the only way to lay the basis for more effective policies is to develop a new and realistic production-capability theory of economic growth, one that better represents the observable world, and to which more politicians can sign up. It was this thought that inspired the writing of this book.

10

The role of governments in creating wealth

The role of government

In the history of economic growth theory no issue has been so fiercely debated as the role of governments in the creation of wealth. This is partly due to the differing political visions people hold, but is also due to the different theories they have of economic growth. If one holds a neoclassical view of economic growth, and believes in the 'rational harmony' of the economic system, one will see a limited role for government, largely restricted to classic market failures such as public goods. But if one holds a production-capability view of economic growth, and believe that innovation is the engine of economic growth, then one needs to look very carefully at the evidence concerning whether governments can assist firms in developing the capabilities they need to take advantage of market opportunities.

All too often, debates on economic growth theory fall into two extreme camps: the advocates of interventionist government policies who have little trust in markets; and advocates of laissez-faire government policies who strongly distrust government. However, as we have seen, the history of economic growth shows that market-based theories and government involvement are not incompatible, with government policies having played a critical role in the early stages of most countries' economic development. As Alice Amsden, the great expert on the economic growth of South Korea, wrote in an

editorial in the journal *World Development*, entitled 'Bringing Production Back In: Understanding Government's Economic Role in
Late Industrialisation':

> As the North Atlantic economies and Japan demonstrate,
> moving closer to the world technological frontier and becoming
> internationally competitive have involved a deliberate
> creation of 'distortions' in the form of firm specific skills,
> knowledge-based monopolies and other types of entry barriers.
> Government's role has been one of joining with the private
> sector to socially construct competitive assets (resources,
> capabilities and organisations) rather to create perfect markets.[1]

The key challenge is, of course, defining precisely what sort of
role the government should play. In making this choice, it is useful to
think in terms of the continuum put forward by Robert D. Atkinson
and Stephen J. Ezell in their book *Innovation Economics*.[2] The continuum runs from the political right to the political left, in the form of: (1)
leave it principally to the market; to (2) support factor conditions (e.g.
science and skills); to (3) support key broad industries/technologies;
to (4) pick specific firms/technologies/products. This last category is
equivalent to most people's conception of an industrial strategy.

As we have seen, none of the countries that have gone from
poverty to wealth have adopted a policy of leaving it to the market
(1). Equally, I think most economists who have studied the economic
growth policies of countries would agree that countries who have
tried to pick specific firms, technologies or products (4), have not
been successful. There is a long history of such attempts in the United
States, Europe and Japan, and they have almost all been unsuccess-
ful. In Europe, for example, governments tried for decades, without
success, to build a strong semiconductor industry by offering targeted
subsidies to designated national champions; while French President
Jacques Chirac's attempt to make the French-backed search engine
Quaero into a 'Google-killer' was a clear failure.

Meanwhile, the United States in the 1960s heavily subsidised the development of a commercial supersonic transport jetliner, largely in response to similar efforts by European governments. None of these programmes were a commercial success. Additionally, the American government's funding, in the late 1970s and 1980s, of a corporation to develop commercial plants for making alternatives to imported fossil fuels was another example of failed targeting.

Governments should not attempt to play the role of banker or venture capitalist. Picking products that are likely to be commercially success-ful, or picking companies that are going to be profitable, requires deep insights into market dynamics, competitive conditions and customer needs. These are capabilities that even the best civil servants do not have. Also, once such decisions are in the hands of government, they become subject to the distortions of the political process, including pressures from special interest groups and political constituencies.

When, however, governments have engaged at points (2) and (3) on the continuum – supporting factor conditions or key broad industries/technologies – they have generally been successful. The US government, which has over the years publicly adopted a strong laissez-faire policy, has, for example, a long and successful history of bringing technologies to the market. These include: interchangeable parts; the microwave; the calculator; the transistor and semiconduc-tor; the relational database; the laser; jet propulsion; nuclear energy; the Internet; the graphical user-interface; and the global positioning system (GPS) among many others.

The National Institutes of Health, by supporting research, also played a key role in creating the US biotechnology industry. And even Google's web research engine is not a pure creation of the free market, as the search algorithm it uses was developed as part of the National Science Foundation-funded Digital Library Initiative.

Effective government policies to increase economic growth start from a recognition that innovation is the engine of economic growth; that firms innovate with the help of many other institutions, such as universities; and that public policies can either help or hinder firms' innovation activities. They further recognise that technological progress depends on certain tangible and intangible infrastructure investments; and that specific innovations – such as the Internet – are too risky, complex or interdependent with other breakthroughs, for private firms to risk the substantial investments needed.

As the Obama administration's September 2009 'Strategy for American Innovation' sensibly argued: 'The true choice in innovation is not between government and no government, but about the right type of government involvement in support of innovations'.[3] The private sector should lead on innovation, but in an era of fierce global competition, governments can and should play an important enabling role in supporting private-sector innovation initiatives, both at the firm and industry level.

Finally, it is interesting to note that when America has in the past wanted, for geopolitical reasons, to develop the economies of other countries, it has helped them with policies that clearly fall within categories (2) and (3) of the continuum. In the 1950s, for example, the US Agency for International Development (USAID) assisted Taiwan in launching the China Productivity Center, which helped its manufacturers become more productive, and in time compete better with US manufacturers. Furthermore, the USAID report 'Expanding Exports: A Case Study of the Korean Experience' documents how, in 1969, the agency assisted South Korea in launching the Korean Productivity Center and the Korean Industrial Research Initiative.[4] At this point in time, of course, the United States was not concerned with the finer points of political economy, but solely with effective ways of stopping South Korea and Taiwan going over to communism.

Competing for the future

If governments are to play a valuable role in creating the wealth of their countries, they need both to create a vision of how their country can compete in world markets and develop policies in the key areas enabling their firms to do so. In the final analysis, it is firms that create wealth, and a government can only, therefore, increase its country's rate of economic growth if it develops a shared vision with industry, and policies that industry can support, and then industry adopts strategies and management practices that transforms the government's vision into a reality.

The vision developed by government must be built on an understanding of the three forces currently shaping the world economy, which I have described in this book: the competitive advantage of nations; the race to the top; and innovation as the engine of growth.

The competitive advantage of nations

Neoclassical economists have argued that 'countries don't compete, only companies do', and that therefore the competitiveness of a country's firms in world markets is not an issue.[5] As a result, I have never heard neoclassical economists make the argument that the slow growth of the G7 countries in recent years is due to the rapidly growing competitiveness of countries such as China, South Korea and Taiwan. Their argument has, however, three major flaws, which need to be exposed.

Firstly, it has been argued that 80 per cent of the US economy consists of non-traded goods and services intended for domestic use, and that therefore the growth rate of US living standards depends largely on the growth rate of domestic productivity, rather than the competitiveness of its goods and services in world markets. And because it is the non-traded sectors of an economy that really drive their productivity and growth, countries are not competing against one another for economic growth. However, this argument is flawed, as it underestimates the preponderance of high value-added per capita jobs in the traded sectors of the economy, and the impact that a loss of jobs or a loss of competitiveness in these sectors has on the economy's growth rate (as we saw in Chapter 7).

Secondly, it has been argued that, while firms in different countries do sell products that compete with each other, firms and consumers in these nations are simultaneously each other's main export markets and suppliers of imports. International trade is not, therefore, a zero-sum game, and if European and Asian countries gain a larger share of export markets, America is compensated by having access to larger export markets, as well as better goods at lower prices. It is, however, difficult to envisage the circumstances where America would, in such a situation, be fully compensated for a loss of high value-added jobs.

Finally, it has been argued that if America loses an industry to foreign competitors, the workers in it will simply be redeployed to other high value-added sectors. In practice, though, they are more likely to end up working in lower-paying sectors. Among US workers laid off between 2007 and 2009, about 75 per cent were employed after three years. Of those, approximately 17 per cent reported earnings that were at least 20 per cent higher than their previous wages, while approximately 30 per cent reported earnings that were at least 20 per cent lower than their previous wages.[6]

It should be kept in mind that a likely explanation for slow growth in a particular country is that its firms in high value-added per capita sectors have lost competitiveness in world markets. As Nobel Laureate Paul Samuelson has written:

> Invention abroad that gives to [other countries] some of the
> comparative advantage that had belonged to the United States
> can induce for the United States permanent lost per-capita real
> income.[7]

Meanwhile, Gregory Tassey, senior economist at NIST, has said:

> Technological change cannot only shift comparative advantage
> through trade but also lower real incomes in the economies that
> do not develop and use technologies in a sufficient degree.[8]

The race to the top

The second force which should underpin a country's vision of its economic future is the 'race to the top' referred to in Chapter 2. It is vitally important that when firms and countries develop their strategies and policies, they do not fall into the trap of seeing globalisation in terms of a 'race to the bottom'; with firms competing by seeking ever cheaper labour, land and capital, and countries competing by deregulating and shrinking social benefits. Instead, politicians need to understand that their citizens' standard of living depends significantly on the ability of firms in their country to create products and services that have a competitive advantage in world markets, and that, as a result, produce high value-added per capita jobs.

Innovation as the engine of growth

Finally, when drawing up a vision of how their countries aim to create wealth in the future, governments need to appreciate the central role innovation plays in creating competitive advantage for their firms, and that it should, therefore, be seen as the engine of economic growth. They need also to understand that if they stop innovating their economies are likely to slow down, and that there is no economic law saying a country cannot enter a period when its firms lose competitive advantage and its standard of living falls. As Erik Reinert has said:

> The driving forces of the economic system are innovations
> created by knowledge. Nations who stop innovating do not
> keep their standard of living even though they keep the same
> efficiency.[9]

Governments need also to understand they have a role to play in supporting the diffusion of new technology in the economy, as well as innovation itself. This is not something that plays any part in neoclassical economic growth theory, as it is assumed that, in a world of perfect information, the rational manager will have no difficulty choosing what new technologies he or she needs to use, and in absorbing them into his business. In the observable world, however, business managers are often not aware of new technologies that could improve the performance of their firms, and the absorption of a new technology into a business is often an extremely difficult task. In both cases, government can play a facilitating role, particularly in the case of SMEs, as can be seen by the success of the Manufacturing Extension Partnership in the United States.

This point is very relevant to the current development of new production methods based on the application of digital technologies, a development known as Industry 4.0. Over the last 250 years, we have seen a number of revolutions in production methods, starting with the development of the factory system during the Industrial Revolution in the UK; followed by the development of interchangeable parts and mass-production in the US. These revolutions gave a huge competitive advantage to the firms adopting the new production methods. Now, manufacturing industry across the world faces a new revolution in production methods.

Already, there are government strategies in place in most developed countries, including Germany (Industrie 4.0), China (Made in China 2025), and the US (America Makes). In the UK, meanwhile, the government produced its 'Made Smarter Review' in 2017.[10] This report was produced by an industry group under the leadership of Jürgen Maier, the CEO of Siemens UK, but the government policies necessary for the diffusion of the new production methods and the enabling manpower policies do not yet appear to have been fully developed.

In the light of the vision it draws up, government should develop policies to increase its economy's rates of innovation and learning, and the capability/market-opportunity sectoral dynamics driving them. It should do this in the four main areas of policy previously outlined in this book, that is: the financing and governance of firms

(Chapter 3); regional policy (Chapter 4); the national system of education and training (Chapter 8); and the national system of innovation (Chapter 9). In doing so, government needs to get industry to buy into the vision and policies it develops, as if these are to be successful, firms will usually need to change their strategies and management practices to take advantage of them. Too often, firms see strategy as simply being about the choice of product markets and the firm's position within them, and focus all their efforts on market and competitor analysis. As a result, they fail to ask themselves what unique skills or capabilities are needed to win at their chosen game, and fail to take advantage of the capability/market-opportunity sectoral dynamics that would give them a significant competitive advantage over their rivals.

In order to become capability-advantaged competitors, firms need to take a number of steps. Firstly, they need to include in the strategy process executives who have deep knowledge of the company's technology, operating processes and customers. Secondly, they need to take a dynamic view, as the most strategically valuable capabilities are invariably the ones that take the longest to create. Thirdly, they need to recognise that superior operating capabilities cannot be bought solely by investing in R&D or new factories, as they are usually rooted in a system of interdependent parts that other firms cannot easily copy.

The Toyota Production System, examined in Chapter 3, is a good example of this latter point. Despite Toyota being happy to open its factories to competitors eager to replicate it, few were able to do so due to Toyota's capabilities being rooted in a complex, interdependent set of decisions, including: how it designs its products, processes and assembly lines; how it manages suppliers, quality and inventory; and how it motivates its workers and implements shop-floor improvement. This makes imitation difficult, which is why Toyota's capabilities give it a long-lasting competitive advantage.

Only if firms take the above steps in response to their government's vision and policies, will they be able to create the capabilities needed to excel in world markets. Governments need, therefore, to develop their vision and policies in close co-operation with industry.

The capability of government

To increase the rate of growth in the economy, a government needs not only to have a vision of what it wants to achieve, but also the capability to develop and implement the policies necessary to put it into practice. My experience as Minister of Science and Innovation between 1998 and 2006 taught me that this is not the case in the UK, and I suspect it is also not the case in a number of other Western governments.

In 1998, after seventeen years of Conservative rule, the Department of Trade and Industry (as it was then called) had no clear idea of what its role should be, other than to manage a number of functions – such as oversight of company law and the Patent Office – that couldn't be outsourced. It also had very little capacity to develop and implement policies. This became very clear to me early on when the Secretary of State, Peter Mandelson, decided he wanted to produce a White Paper on the 'knowledge economy'.

The way this White Paper was created was very simple and instructive. A senior civil servant was tasked with producing it and wrote around to his colleagues enquiring whether they had any good ideas to go in it. These were then written up and presented to the Secretary of State, who decided which ones were politically attractive. It was also decided that the White Paper should include some economic statistics, and this job was given to the Economics and Statistics Section of the department, which produced them in parallel with the process of producing the policy ideas. It apparently did not occur to the civil servants that the policies in the White Paper should be based on a detailed analysis of the performance of British industry compared to other countries, and how it needed to change. This is perhaps not surprising, as the department had very little systematic knowledge about the performance of British industry, and apparently did not see any need to have it. Towards the end of my time as a minister, I initiated an annual Innovation Report to monitor the innovation performance of British industry. However, after I left the department this was outsourced to NESTA (the National Endowment for Science, Technology and the Arts), and eventually disappeared.

If the Department for Business, Energy and Industrial Strategy, as it is now called, is to develop the capability it needs to raise the rate of innovation in the economy, four changes need to be made.

The first change relates to the fact that, as we have seen, economic growth policies cover a wide range of government departments in the UK. In addition to the Department for Business, Energy and Industrial Strategy, key departments include: the Department for Education; the Department of Housing, Communities and Local Government; the Department for Transport; the Department for International Trade; and the Department for Environment, Food and Rural Affairs. All of these need to think about how they can help firms build competitive advantage, and in some areas – such as public procurement – they all need to act, even when they don't see it as being in the essential interest of their particular department.

The British government is, however, incredibly bad at implementing cross-government policies, as no one has the authority at the centre of government to make things happen, other than the Prime Minister. There is therefore a need for a committee or council at the centre of the government to take on this role. A good model for this would be the National Economic Council (NEC), which was created by Prime Minister Gordon Brown in response to the economic crisis of 2007/8, but abolished by the Coalition government in 2010.[11] The NEC was generally seen as a success, joining up departments, speeding up decision-making and delivery, and securing collective buy-in to its positions. Through the means of a strong prime minister, an activist secretariat, and collective high-level support, it managed to break down the silos of government.

The second change that needs to be made is an improvement in the capability of government in the area of economic growth policy-making. It is a great myth of British public life that the British government is good at policy-making, even if there are sometimes problems with implementation. The reality is that, if one looks at the record of policy-making in government departments, one sees an endless policy churn with a very low rate of success.

In 2017, I got the Institute of Government to do a review of government policy in three areas very relevant to economic growth policies: technical education, industrial strategy and regional policy.[12] The review demonstrates a disastrous record of policy-making. Since the 1980s, there have been twenty-eight major pieces of legislation related to further education, and no organisation has lasted longer than a decade. And our system of technical education is as bad as ever.

In the industrial strategy space, there have been at least two strategies in the last decade alone, and we are now moving into a third. In a period of just over twenty years the main vehicles for regional governance have included regional assemblies, regional development agencies and, currently, local enterprise partnerships. Even so, we still do not have a regional structure agreed by the political parties to which some powers of central government could be devolved.

It might be thought that this policy churn has been due to ideological differences between the political parties, but in these areas there is a reasonable degree of agreement between parties, with industrial policy being the only obvious area of ideological difference. Instead, the cause of this disastrous record of policy-making lies in the failure of ministers and civil servants to put in place an effective system of policy-making. There are few policy units in government departments, and new policies are usually devised by generalist civil servants who have little knowledge of the specific policy area under consideration.

As a result, there is usually little institutional memory of the successes and failures of past policies, no ongoing programmes of research, and little knowledge of what policies work effectively in other countries. This last point is a very obvious weakness of the system. Virtually none of the policy issues – other than fox-hunting – that UK government policy-makers have to tackle are unique to one country, and almost always a quick search will reveal that one or two countries do a much better job than others. In every case, of course, one has to take account of cultural and institutional differences, but in almost all cases examining the successful policies of other countries yields valuable insights into what the government should do.

In the absence of an effective system of policy-making, ministers and policy-makers tend to do one of three things. The first solution is to resort to a simple political intervention: if the area is in public ownership they will privatise it; and if it is in the private sector they will nationalise it. The second solution is to abolish the organisation responsible for implementing policy in the area concerned, before setting up an organisation with a new name and slightly different terms of reference. The third solution, to which ministers turn in desperation, is outsourcing the policy-making process by appointing some eminent person, who may or may not know anything about the area, to draw up a new policy. Unsurprisingly, none of these methods of policy-making has a good record of success.

What can be done to improve this disastrous record of economic growth policy-making? I believe the answer is to formalise the role the Treasury has acquired in the last twenty years in the area of supply-side economic policy-making and give it the job of providing the secretariat of a reinstated NEC. One of Gordon Brown's first acts on becoming Chancellor of the Exchequer in 1997 was to set up a properly resourced Enterprise and Growth Unit. Today, the unit is still a key part of the Treasury, with about eighty of the Treasury's 1,100 staff working in it, and has had many successes in developing supply-side policies in areas as diverse as competition policy and science and innovation. Two changes, however, should be made to the way it works. Firstly, it should be tasked with adopting the dynamic capability theory of economic growth set out in this book, rather than the neoclassical economic growth policy it has championed in the past. And, secondly, instead of working on its own, it should be tasked to work closely with relevant government departments, in turn insisting these departments have properly staffed policy units with long-term links to independent policy research units or policy research units in universities.

The third change the UK government needs to make to increase its capability, is to agree with the other political parties a regional structure to which they can all sign up. This is not an easy task, as the UK has never had a regional structure, nor does it have clear economic areas that can form the basis of one. It is also not easy to change government structures in which local politicians have a personal stake. Even so, this is something that needs to be done.

There is a tendency among politicians to take an all-or-nothing approach to decentralisation. However, there are at least four functions of government in each policy area that can potentially be devolved, and decisions need to be taken as to which functions in each area should be devolved, and which should not. The policy-making function should not usually be devolved, as governments generally want to see uniform policies across the country. Then there are funding decisions, which should be kept central unless government either gives a sum of money to cities and regions – allowing them to decide what amounts they wish to assign to which policies – or gives them powers to raise money and spend it on what they see as their priorities. Finally, there are operating decisions and the monitoring function. Operating decisions should be devolved to the organisations doing the work, and the monitoring function devolved to the level just above it.

The fourth change the government needs to make to improve its capability relates to the organisation and staffing of the Department for Business, Energy and Industrial Strategy. It is one of the fundamental arguments of this book that the production homogeneity assumption of neoclassical economics – that all production activities are alike – does not fit the data. Innovation, learning and competitive advantage are industry specific and vary from industry to industry. We should, therefore, reject the idea sometimes advanced by neoclassical economists that, if government does have a role to play, it is a 'horizontal one'. That is, it should concentrate on increasing the supply of production factors that all industries use, rather than provide selective support for industries and technologies.

Instead, economic policy-makers should, in addition to key 'horizontal policies', develop sector policies in partnership with industry, which reflect the specific opportunities and capabilities of key sectors. This is precisely what we find happening in rapidly developing countries such as China and Singapore. For example, China's 'Made in China 2025', while describing a number of horizontal policies, also sets out plans for specific sectors, including: integrated circuits and special equipment; high-end digital-control machine tools; robots; energy-efficient and new-energy automobiles; and bio-pharmaceuticals and high-performance medical equipment.

Singapore, meanwhile, has developed a set of Industry Transformation Maps (ITMs). There are twenty-three ITMs grouped into six clusters: manufacturing; built environment; trade and connectivity; essential domestic services; modern services; and lifestyle. Each ITM consists of a 'growth and competitiveness plan', which examines 'the industry landscape, the future trends and needs to set out a suite of initiatives' in order to 'catalyse transformation and achieve the stated vision of each industry'.[13] Furthermore, the ITMs are supported by two 'horizontals', promoting ICT adoption and skills development across the economy.

However, if the Department for Business, Energy and Industrial Strategy is to take on such a role, it needs to have units tasked with working with specific industrial sectors in order to raise the capabilities of their firms, and which are staffed by people knowledgeable about the industries with which they are involved. These units then need to be backed up by units covering such policy areas as manufacturing, and science and innovation. Again, they need to be staffed by people with expert knowledge, who can give help to the sectoral units. Only in this way can officials in the sectoral units have a constructive dialogue with firms in a particular industry and contribute usefully to building their competitive advantages.

Windows of opportunity

We live in a world of opportunity and danger. Many windows of opportunity are being opened up by advances in science and technology, and this means countries with firms that have the capabilities to take advantage of them will be able to innovate, raise their level of competitive advantage, and increase their rate of growth. There are some economists who believe that a cause of the slowing down of economic growth in the G7 countries is a lack of opportunities to innovate. However, this is clearly wrong, as it is difficult to think of any area of human activity today where it is not possible to see opportunities for innovation.

The world of work is going to be transformed by AI and robotics. In the field of transport, we have electric and autonomous vehicles, and drones; in the field of energy, we have solar and wind power, and, in the long-term, potentially fusion energy; and, in the field of agriculture, a huge revolution is starting to take place due to our ability to genetically modify plants. Also, in the field of health, regenerative medicine and treatments modified to take account of individual genomes will have an impact; as well as there being the very real possibility that our understanding of neuroscience will bring about major changes in the treatment of psychiatric disorders. Even in the technologically modest world of retailing, online shopping is bringing about a major revolution. I also believe the ICT revolution will continue to have an impact on communication, education and entertainment for some time to come. And major advances in new materials will have an impact on many industries.

We should also remember that in the past many advances came as complete surprises. The existence of cars, spaceships and robots were widely predicted, but few people foresaw the arrival of genetic modification, nanotechnology, lasers, superconductors, nuclear energy, or solid-state electronics. No one knows what the transistor of the future will be, but we should not base our strategy for the future on our limited imaginations.

In such a world, the global race for innovation advantage is one that all nations can potentially win, with higher per capita incomes, better products and services, and a major reduction in world poverty. It is also a world in which the potentially catastrophic problems of hunger, disease and environmental degradation can be effectively tackled, meaning the risks of wars breaking out due to scarce resources are reduced.

However, if we fail to understand that innovation is the engine of economic growth, then people in the G7 countries face a world of danger, with the very real possibility that, as a result of the growing competition from countries such as China, India, South Korea and Taiwan, they will see their standard of living fall, bringing with it anger, despair and populism.

The theory of economic growth set out in this book does not provide easy answers for Western developed countries, but it does show that if we are prepared to learn new skills, speed up our rate of innovation and produce new high value-added products and services for world markets, we have a chance to continue raising our standard of living. But if we stop innovating and continue to lose competitive advantage in our key industries, we will inevitably see our standard of living decline.

I hope that in this book I have made the choices we face very clear, as they are vitally important ones, and the quality of life enjoyed by our children and future generations will depend on the decisions we make.

Notes

Chapter 1: The Need for a New Theory

1. Danny Quah, 'The Global Economy's Shifting Centre of Gravity', *Global Policy*, vol. 2(1), 2011, pp. 3–9.
2. Adam Smith, *The Theory of Moral Sentiments*, sixth edition, London, Penguin, 2009 [1790].
3. Paul Krugman, *The Self-Organizing Economy*, Cambridge, MA, Blackwell, 1996.
4. Adam Smith, *The Wealth of Nations*, Chicago, IL, University of Chicago Press, 1976 [1776].
5. Erik S. Reinert, *How Rich Countries Got Rich ... and Why Poor Countries Stay Poor*, London, Constable, 2007.
6. Adam Smith, *The Wealth of Nations*, Chicago, IL, University of Chicago Press, 1976 [1776].
7. Erik S. Reinert, *How Rich Countries Got Rich ... and Why Poor Countries Stay Poor*, London, Constable, 2007.
8. Friedrich List, *The National System of Political Economy*, London, Longman, 1904 [1841].
9. Ibid.
10. Friedrich List, *Outlines of American Political Economy in a Series of Letters Addressed by Friedrich List, Esq., to Charles J. Ingersoll, Esq.*, Letter 4, Wiesbaden, Dr Böttiger Verslags-BMbH, 1827.
11. Joseph Schumpeter, *Capitalism, Socialism and Democracy*, New York, Harper, 1975.
12. Joseph Schumpeter, *Business Cycles: A Theoretical, Historical and Statistical Analysis of the Capitalist Process*, New York and London, McGraw-Hill, 1939.

13. Paul A. Samuelson, 'International Trade and the Equalisation of Factor Prices', *The Economic Journal*, vol. 58(230), 1948, pp. 168–84; Paul A. Samuelson, 'International Factor-Price Equalisation Once Again', *The Economic Journal*, vol. 59(234), 1949, pp.181–97.

14. Ha-Joon Chang, *Kicking Away the Ladder: Development Strategy in Historical Perspective*, London, Anthem Press, 2003.

15. Friedrich List, *The National System of Political Economy*, London, Longman, 1904 [1841].

16. Richard R. Nelson, 'Economic Development from the Perspective of Evolutionary Economic Theory', The Other Canon Foundation and Tallin University of Technology Working Papers in Technology Governance and Economic Dynamics, No. 2, 2006.

17. Lionel Robbins, *An Essay on the Nature and Significance of Economic Science*. London, Macmillan, 1932.

18. R. M. Solow, 'A Contribution to the Theory of Economic Growth', *Quarterly Journal of Economics*, vol. 70(1), 1956, pp. 612–613.

19. Moses Abramovitz, 'Resource and Output Trends in the United States since 1870', *American Economic Review*, vol. 46, 1956, pp. 5–23.

20. Herbert A. Simon, 'Organizations and Markets', *Journal of Economic Perspectives*, vol. 5, 1991, pp. 25–44.

21. Moses Abramovitz, 'Catching up, Forging Ahead, and Falling Behind', *Journal of Economic History*, vol. 46(2), 1986, pp. 385–406.

22. Joseph Schumpeter, *Capitalism, Socialism and Democracy*, New York, Harper, 1975.

23. Daron Acemoglu and James A. Robinson, *Why Nations Fail: The Origins of Power, Prosperity and Poverty*, London, Profile Books, 2012.

24. Colin Clark, *The Conditions of Economic Progress*, London, Macmillan, 1940.

Chapter 2: A Dynamic Capability Theory of Economic Growth

1. Willy Shih, 'Why High-Tech Commoditization is Accelerating', *MIT Sloan Management Review*, Summer 2018.

2. Erik S. Reinert, *How Rich Countries Got Rich ... and Why Poor Countries Stay Poor*, London, Constable & Robinson, 2007.

3. Ibid.

4. Ibid.

5. Ibid.

6. Ibid.

7. Jagdish Bhagwati, 'Cash Machines', *The Economist*, 31 March 2011.

8. Christina D. Romer, 'Do Manufacturers Need Special Treatment?', *The New York Times*, 4 February 2012.

9. Paul Krugman, 'What Do Undergrads Need to Know About Trade?' *American Economic Review*, vol. 83(2), 1993, pp. 23–6.

10. Erik R. Reinert, 'Competitiveness and Its Predecessors – A 500-year Cross-national Perspective', *Structural Change and Economic Dynamics*, vol. 6(1), 1995, pp. 23–42.

11. Ira C. Magaziner and Thomas M. Hout, 'Japanese Industrial Policy', Policy Studies Institute, 1980.

12. Michael E. Porter, *The Competitive Advantage of Nations*, New York, The Free Press, 1990.

13. Sanjaya Lall, 'Technological Change and Industrialisation in the Asian Newly Industrialising Economies', Achievements and Challenges in Linsu Kim and Richard R. Nelson (eds), *Technology, Learning and Innovation: Experiences of Newly Industrializing Economies*, Cambridge, Cambridge University Press, 2000.

14. César Hidalgo, *Why Information Grows: The Evolution of Order, from Atoms to Economies*, London, Allen Lane, 2015.

15. Ibid.

16. Erik S. Reinert, *How Rich Countries Got Rich ... and Why Poor Countries Stay Poor*, London, Constable & Robinson, 2007.

17. César Hidalgo, *Why Information Grows: The Evolution of Order, from Atoms to Economies*, London, Allen Lane, 2015.

Chapter 3: Sectoral Systems of Innovation

1. Erik S. Reinert, 'Catching-Up From Way Behind: A Third World Perspective on First World History' in Jan Fagerberg, Bart Verspagen and Nick von Tunzelmann (eds) *The Dynamics of Technology, Trade and Growth*, Cheltenham, Edward Elgar Publishing, 1994.

2. Michael E. Porter, *The Competitive Advantage of Nations*, New York, The Free Press, 1990.

3. Steven Casper and David Soskice, 'Sectoral Systems of Innovation and Varieties of Capitalism: Explaining the Development of High-technology

Entrepreneurship in Europe', in Franco Malerba (ed.), *Sectoral Systems of Innovation: Concepts, Issues and Analyses of Six Major Sectors in Europe*, Cambridge, Cambridge University Press, 2004. Table reproduced with the permission of the Licensor through PLS clear.

4. David J. Teece 'Profiting from Technological Innovation', *Research Policy*, vol. 15(6), 1986, pp. 285–305.

5. David J. Teece, 'Towards a Capability Theory of (Innovating) Firms: Implications for Management and Policy', *Cambridge Journal of Economics*, 2017, vol. 41(3), 693–720.

6. Joseph Schumpeter, *The Theory of Economic Development*, New Brunswick and London, Transaction Publishers, 2012.

7. David J. Teece, 'Dynamic Capabilities and Entrepreneurial Management in Large Organisations: Toward a Theory of the (Entrepreneurial) Firm', *European Economic Review*, vol. 86(C), 2016, pp. 202–16.

8. William Lazonick, 'Profits without Prosperity', *Harvard Business Review*, September 2014.

9. Steven Casper and David Soskice, 'Sectoral Systems of Innovation and Varieties of Capitalism: Explaining the Development of High-technology Entrepreneurship in Europe', in Franco Malerba (ed.), *Sectoral Systems of Innovation: Concepts, Issues and Analyses of Six Major Sectors in Europe*, Cambridge, Cambridge University Press, 2004. Table reproduced with the permission of the Licensor through PLS clear.

10. Peter A. Hall and David Soskice (eds), *Varieties of Capitalism: The Institutional Foundations of Comparative Advantage*, Oxford, Oxford University Press, 2001.

11. James P. Womack, Daniel T. Jones and Daniel Roos, *The Machine that Changed the World*, New York, Rawson Associates, 1990.

12. Dong Sung Cho and Michael E. Porter, 'Changing Global Industry Leadership: The Case of Shipbuilding', in Michael E. Porter (ed.), *Competition in Global Industries*, Boston, MA, Harvard Business School Press, 1986.

Chapter 4: City and Regional Systems of Innovation

1. Robert D. Atkinson and Stephen J. Ezell, *Innovation Economics: The Race for Global Advantage*, New Haven, CT, and London, Yale University Press, 2012.

2. Robert D. Atkinson and Scott Andes, 'The Atlantic Century II: Benchmarking EU and US Innovation and Competitiveness', Washington, DC, Information Technology and Innovation Foundation, July 2011.

3. Michael E. Porter, *On Competition*, Boston, MA, Harvard Business School Press, 1988.

4. Alfred Marshall, *Principles of Economics*, Macmillan, 1920.

5. Richard Florida, *The Rise of the Creative Class*, New York, Basic Books, 2013.

6. Ibid.

7. Lynne G. Zucker, Michael R. Darby and Marilynn B. Brewer, 'Intellectual Human Capital and the Birth of US Biotechnology Enterprises', *American Economic Review* vol. 88(1), 1998, pp. 290–306.

8. Allen Scott, 'Origins and Growth of the Hollywood Motion-Picture Industry: The First Decade', in Pontus Braunerhjelm and Maryann P Feldman (eds), *Cluster Genesis: Technology-Based Industrial Development*, Oxford, Oxford University Press, 2006.

9. Timothy Bresnahan and Alfonso Gambardella (eds), *Building High-Tech Clusters: Silicon Valley and Beyond*, Cambridge, Cambridge University Press, 2004.

10. Dennis P. Leyden and Albert N. Link, 'Collective Entrepreneurship: The Strategic Management of Research Triangle Park', in David B. Audretsch and Mary Linderstein Walshok (eds), *Creating Competitiveness: Entrepreneurship and Innovation Policies for Growth?* Cheltenham, Edward Elgar, 2013.

11. Centre for Cities, 'Industrial Revolutions: Capturing the Growth Potential', Centre for Cities and McKinsey & Company, 2014.

Chapter 5: Forging Ahead

1. Chris Freeman and Luc Soete, *The Economics of Industrial Innovation*, Third Edition, Cambridge, MA, The MIT Press, 1997.

2. Chris Freeman, 'Continental, National and Sub-national Innovation Systems: Complementarity and Economic Growth', *Research Policy*, vol. 31(2), 2002, pp. 191–211.

3. Joshua B. Freeman, *Behemoth: A History of the Factory and the Making of the Modern World*, New York, W. W. Norton & Co., 2018.

4. William Mass and William Lazonick, 'The British Cotton Industry and International Competitive Advantage: The State of the Debates', Working Paper 90–06, Department of Economics, Columbia University, New York, 1990.

5. Ashish Arora, Ralph Landau and Nathan Rosenberg, 'Dynamics of Comparative Advantage in the Chemical Industry' in David C. Mowery and Richard R. Nelson (eds), *Sources of Industrial Leadership: Studies of Seven Industries*, Cambridge, Cambridge University Press, 1999.

6. James P. Womack, Daniel T. Jones and Daniel Roos, *The Machine that Changed the World*, New York, Rawson Associates, 1990.

7. Timothy F. Bresnahan and Franco Malerba , 'Industrial Dynamics and the Evolution of Firms' and Nations' Competitive Capabilities in the World Computer Industry', in David C. Mowery and Richard R. Nelson (eds), *Sources of Industrial Leadership: Studies of Seven Industries*, Cambridge, Cambridge University Press, 1999.

Chapter 6: Catching Up

1. Annalee Saxenian, 'The Silicon Valley Connection', in Anthony P. D'Costa and E. Sridhavan (eds), *India in the Global Software Industry: Innovation, Firm Strategies and Development*, Basingstoke, Palgrave Macmillan, 2004.

2. John A. Mathews, 'National Systems of Economic Learning: The Case of Technology Diffusion Management in East Asia', *International Journal of Technology Management*, vol. 22(5/6), 2001, pp. 455–79.

3. C. Perez and Luc Soete, 'Catching Up in Technology: Entry Barriers and Windows of Opportunity' in G. Dosi et al. (eds), *Technical Change and Economic Theory*, London and New York, Pinter Publishers, 1988.

4. Ibid.

5. Keun Lee and Franco Malerba, 'Catch-up Cycles and Changes in Industrial Leadership: Windows of Opportunity and Responses by Firms and Countries in the Evolution of Sectoral Systems', *Research Policy*, vol. 46(2), 2017, pp. 338–51.

6. Keun Lee and Chaisung Lim, 'Technological Regimes, Catching-up and Leapfrogging: Findings from the Korean Industries', *Research Policy*, vol. 30(1), 2001, pp. 459–83.

7. John A. Matthews, 'Electronics in Taiwan: A Case of Technological Learning, in Vanda Chandra (ed.) *Technology, Adaptation, and Exports: How Some Developing Countries Got It Right*, Washington, DC, The World Bank, 2006.

8. John A. Matthews, 'The Origins and Dynamics of Taiwan's R&D Consortia', *Research Policy*, vol. 31(4), 2002, pp. 633–51.

9. Jang-Sup Shin, 'Dynamic Catch-Up Strategy, Capability Expansion and Changing Windows of Opportunity in the Memory Industry', *Research Policy*, vol. 46(2), 2017, pp. 404–16.

10. Lucia Cusmano, Andrew Morrison and Roberta Rabellotti. 'Catching-up Trajectories in the Wine Sector', in Elisa Giuliani, Andrew Morrison and Roberta Rabellotti (eds), *Innovation and Technological Catch-Up: The Changing Geography of Wine Production*, Cheltenham, Edward Elgar Publishing, 2011.

Chapter 7: Falling Behind

1. Bernard Elbaum and William Lazonick, 'An Institutional Perspective on British Decline', in Bernard Elbaum and Lazonick William (eds), *The Decline of the British Economy*, Oxford, Clarendon Press, 1986.

2. Julia Wrigley, 'Technical Education and Industry in the Nineteenth Century', in Bernard Elbaum and Lazonick William (eds), *The Decline of the British Economy*, Oxford, Clarendon Press, 1986.

3. David C. Mowery, 'Industrial Research, 1900–1950', in Bernard Elbaum and Lazonick William (eds), *The Decline of the British Economy*, Oxford, Clarendon Press, 1986.

4. Michael Spence and Sandile Hlatshwayo, 'The Evolving Structure of the American Economy and the Employment Challenge', Working Paper, Council on Foreign Relations, March 2011.

5. Robert D. Atkinson and Scott Andes, 'The Atlantic Century: Benchmarking EU and US Innovation and Competitiveness', Washington, DC, Information Technology and Innovation Foundation, September 2009.

6. Robert D. Atkinson and Scott Andes, 'The Atlantic Century II: Benchmarking EU and US Innovation and Competitiveness', Washington, DC, Information Technology and Innovation Foundation, July 2011.
7. Ibid.

Chapter 8: National Systems of Education and Training

1. Robert D. Atkinson and Stephen J. Ezell, *Innovation Economics: The Race for Global Advantage*, New Haven, CT, and London, Yale University Press, 2012.
2. John Holman, 'Good Career Guidance', The Gatsby Charitable Foundation, 2014.
3. Sigbert I. Prais, *Productivity, Education and Training: An International Perspective*, Cambridge, Cambridge University Press, 1995.
4. David Finegold and David Soskice, 'The Failure of Training in Britain: Analysis and Prescription', *Oxford Review of Economic Policy*, vol. 4(3), 1998, pp. 21–53.
5. Julia Wrigley, 'Technical Education and Industry in the Nineteenth Century', in Bernard Elbaum and Lazonick William (eds), *The Decline of the British Economy*, Oxford, Clarendon Press, 1986.
6. Emma Norris and Robert Adam, 'All Change: Why Britain is So Prone to Policy Reinvention, and What Can Be Done About It', The Institute for Government, March 2017.
7. 'Report of the Independent Panel on Technical Education', April 2016.

Chapter 9: National Systems of Innovation

1. C. Freeman, *Technology Policy and Economic Performance: Lessons from Japan*, London, Pinter, 1987.
2. Robert D. Atkinson and Stephen J. Ezell, *Innovation Economics: The Race for Global Advantage*, New Haven, CT, and London, Yale University Press, 2012.
3. Ibid.
4. Robert D. Atkinson and Scott Andes, 'The Atlantic Century II: Benchmarking EU and US Innovation and Competitiveness', Washington, DC, Information Technology and Innovation Foundation, July 2011.

5. 'Made in China 2025', State Council, 7 July 2015.
6. Robert D. Atkinson and Stephen J. Ezell, *Innovation Economics: The Race for Global Advantage*, New Haven, CT, and London, Yale University Press, 2012.
7. Mariana Mazzucato, *The Entrepreneurial State*, London, Anthem Press, 2013.
8. Gregory Tassey, *The Technology Imperative*, Cheltenham, Edward Elgar Publishing, 2007.
9. Lord Sainsbury, 'The Race to the Top: A Review of Government's Science and Innovation Policies', October 2007.

Chapter 10: The Role of Governments in Creating Wealth

1. Alice Amsden, 'Bringing Production Back In: Understanding Government's Economic Role in Late Industrialisation', *World Development*, vol. 25(4), 1997, pp. 469–80.
2. Robert D. Atkinson and Stephen J. Ezell, *Innovation Economics: The Race for Global Advantage*, New Haven, CT, and London, Yale University Press, 2012.
3. National Economic Council, 'A Strategy for American Innovation: Driving Towards Sustainable Growth and Quality Jobs', Washington, DC, Executive Office of the President, September 2009.
4. Amicus Most, *Expanding Exports: A Case Study of the Korean Experience*, Washington, DC, USAID, 1969.
5. Paul Krugman, 'Competitiveness: A Dangerous Obsession', *Foreign Affairs*, vol. 73(2), 1994, pp. 28–44.
6. Robert D. Atkinson and Stephen J. Ezell, *Innovation Economics: The Race for Global Advantage*, New Haven, CT, and London, Yale University Press, 2012.
7. Paul Samuelson, 'Where Ricardo and Mill Rebut and Confirm Arguments of Mainstream Economists Supporting Globalisation', *Journal of Economic Perspectives*, vol. 18(3), 2004, pp. 135–46.
8. Gregory Tassey, 'Rationales and Mechanisms for Revitalising US Manufacturing R&D Strategies', *Journal of Technology Transfer* 35(3), 2010, pp. 283–333.
9. Erik S. Reinert, 'The Role of the State in Economic Growth', *Journal of Economic Studies*, vol. 26(4/5), 1999, pp. 268–326.

10. Department for Business, Energy and Industrial Strategy, 'Made Smarter Review', October 2017.
11. Dan Corry, 'Power at the Centre: Is the National Economic Council a Model for a New Way of Organising Things?' *The Political Quarterly*, vol. 82(3), 2011, pp. 459–68.
12. Emma Norris and Robert Adam, 'All Change: Why Britain is so Prone to Policy Reinvention, and What Can be Done About It', Institute for Government, March 2017.
13. Singapore Ministry of Trade and Industry, 'Media Factsheet: Industry Transformation Maps', 2016.

Index

Abramovitz, Moses 27, 31
absolute poverty 129
academic pathways 182, 184, 187, 192, 193, 196, 198
academic spin-off firms 220, 222
academic stars 93
activity-specific technology 19, 29, 63–6
Advanced Certificate of Education 193
Advanced National Vocational Qualifications 192
Advanced Research Projects Agency (ARPA) 214–15, 216
Advanced Technology Program (ATP) 217
aerospace industry 48, 104, 176, 227
Africa 6–7, 8, 130
agency theory 70
AGFA 114
agglomeration 86–7, 90, 94–5, 102, 110–11
Agnelli, Giovanni 120
agriculture 14–16, 25, 42–3, 128, 141, 160–61, 172, 240
AI (artificial intelligence) 240
air freight 132
Akamatsu, Kaname 54
Allen, Paul 88
America Makes strategy 232
American Association for the Advancement of Science 215

American School of economic philosophy 16
American System of Manufacturing 117
Amsden, Alice 225–6
Anglo-Saxon liberal market economies 73
Apple 28, 36, 38, 56, 67, 125–6, 135, 216
application-specific integrated circuits (ASICs) 146
Applied GCEs 193
apprenticeships 165, 180, 182–4, 191, 193, 194, 196
appropriability of innovations 63, 64, 65
Argentina 25, 150
Arkwright, Richard 33, 109, 110
armouries 117–18
ARPA (Advanced Research Projects Agency) 214–15, 216
ARPANET 206
artificial intelligence (AI) 240
artisans 165, 191
Asia 6–7, 8, 230
Asian Miracle 1, 10, 130
ASICs (application-specific integrated circuits) 146
assembly lines 75–6, 119, 120–21
asset-seeking strategies 175
Atkinson, Robert D. 209, 226
'The Atlantic Century' reports 178, 209

Atomic Energy Commission 214
ATP *see* Advanced Technology
    Program
Austin, Herbert 120, 121
Austin, Texas 87
Australia 150, 152–3, 160, 212
Australian Wine and Brandy
    Corporation 153
Austria 160, 212
automobile industry
    city and regional systems 83, 104
    dynamic capability theory 37, 55
    Japan 37, 59, 73–8, 121–2, 233
    sectoral innovation 59, 61, 67,
        73–8, 142
    United Kingdom 104, 120–21, 166
    United States 83, 107, 117–22

Bacon, Francis, 'An Essay on
    Innovations' 14
Baldwin, Richard 5
Bangalore 89, 90
barter 11, 13
baseball production 39–40
BASF 114
Bayer 114
Bayh-Dole Act (1986) 213
Bell Laboratories 91
Bhagwati, Jagdish 42
bilateral investment treaties (BITs)
    134
Biopolis, Singapore 210
biotechnology
    city and regional systems 84, 86,
        92–3, 96, 99
    sectoral innovation 64, 65
    United States 84, 86, 92–4, 96, 99,
        171, 215–16, 227
    wine industry 152
Birth of a Nation (film) 95
BITs *see* bilateral investment treaties
Blair, Tony 218
Boeing 103, 220
Boles, Nick 195

Boston, USA 84, 86, 93, 96
bounties 22, 23
Boyer, Herbert 92
brain drain 101, 137, 172
Breakthrough Institute 177
Bresnahan, Timothy 97, 98
Brin, Sergey 173
Britain *see* United Kingdom
British Classical School 18
Brown, Gordon 3, 219, 222, 235, 237
Brownsville, Texas 81
Brunel, Isambard Kingdom 33
Buffalo, New York 81
Bush, George H. W. 217
Bush, George W. 213
business cycle 20
Butler, R. A. 191
Butler Act (1944) 191–2
buy-backs 70–71, 176

California 94–6, 151, 177, 179
call centres 89
Cambridge, England 89
Cambridge, USA 93, 96
Canada 160, 161, 162
capabilities of firms
    'catching-up' countries 134–40
    neoclassical theory 2, 28, 29
    production-capability theory 19
    sectoral innovation 66–70, 73
capability/market-opportunity
    dynamic
    'catching-up' countries 130, 149,
        150, 153
    dynamic capability theory 29, 30,
        31, 35
    'falling-behind' countries 171
    'forging-ahead' countries 108, 112,
        115, 116, 127
    government role in creating wealth
        233
    high-tech clusters 88–97
    sectoral innovation 59, 72, 77,
        78, 80

capability of government 234–9
capitalism 18–19, 20, 32, 66, 71, 73, 164, 190
careers advice 185, 194
car industry *see* automobile industry
'catching-up' countries 128–54
    capabilities of firms 134–40
    economic reform 128–31
    overview 153–4
    sectoral dynamics 43, 140–43
    South Korea DRAM industry 146–9
    Taiwan electronics industry 144–6
    windows of opportunity 131–4
    worldwide wine industry 150–53
CATs (Colleges of Advanced Technology) 194
cell phones 36, 38, 89, 142–3, 216
Central Manchester Development Corporation 105
Centre for Cities 103
Centre National de la Recherche Scientifique (CNRS) 202
centre of gravity of global economy 8–9
chaebols 147, 148
Chambers of Commerce and Industry 184
Chandler Jr, Alfred D. 113
Chaplin, Charlie 94
chemical industry 104, 107, 112–16, 190
Chile 150, 152, 212
China
    capabilities of firms 135, 137, 138
    competitiveness 1, 171, 177, 178
    dynamic capability theory 38, 52, 57
    economic reform 128–9, 130
    'Electricity Valley' 177
    government role in creating wealth 228–9, 232, 239, 241
    growth rates 7, 129

Made in China 2025 plan 210, 232, 239
    national system of innovation 209, 210–11
    wage differences 133
China Productivity Center 228
Chirac, Jacques 226
cinema *see* movie industry
Citroën, André 120
city and regional systems of innovation 81–106
    capability/market-opportunity theory of high-tech clusters 88–97
    creative class 85–8
    local economic development 84–8
    overview 81–4
    reinvention of cities 102–6
    strategic management of place 97–102
    uneven cities and regions 43
Clark, Colin 34
clean energy 176–7
clothing industry 55, 57, 61, 82; *see also* textiles industry
clusters
    capability/market-opportunity theory of high-tech clusters 88–97
    dynamic capability theory 43
    local economic development 85, 86, 87, 88
    loss of US competitive advantage 171, 177
    reinvention of cities 103–4
    sector policies 239
    strategic management of place 97–8, 99, 101, 102
CNR *see* Consiglio Nazionale delle Ricerche
CNRS *see* Centre National de la Recherche Scientifique
coal industry 113, 166
Coalition government 223, 235

Cohen, Stanley 92
Colbert, Jean Baptiste 16
Cold War 19, 20, 84
college-based learning 196
Colleges of Advanced Technology (CATs) 194
colonialism 22
Colt Armory 118
commodities 35–6
Commodore 125
communication technologies 89, 111, 113, 132–3, 135, 138, 240
communism 19, 228
Compaq 126
competitive advantage
  Asia growth rate 7
  'catching-up' countries 130, 151, 154
  dynamic capability theory 30, 35–7, 42–9, 57–8
  'forging-ahead' countries 112, 115, 116, 119, 126, 127
  German chemical industry 115, 116
  government role in creating wealth 229–33, 235, 240–41
  high-tech clusters 89, 96
  international competition 57–8
  international trade 43–6, 130, 230
  labour-productivity growth 156, 161, 163, 170
  ladder of economic development 47–9
  of nations 229–30
  neoclassical theory 2
  sectoral innovation 42–3, 62
  United Kingdom 112, 161, 163–7
  United States 119, 126, 170, 171–7
competitiveness 45–6, 57–8, 80, 178, 229, 230
computer industry
  'catching-up' countries 133, 137, 146

'forging-ahead' countries 107, 122–7
  high-tech clusters 96
  innovation policy 214, 215
  knowledge and knowhow 55–6
  neoclassical theory 28–9
  sectoral innovation 67
  United States 84, 90–92, 122–7, 214–15
Connexions 194
Consejo Superior de Investigaciones Cientificas (CSIC) 202
Conservative government 193, 197, 223–4, 234
Consiglio Nazionale delle Ricerche (CNR) 202
containerisation 131–2
co-ordinated market economies 73
Corn Laws 23
corporate capitalism 164–5, 171
corporate control 69, 70, 71, 72
corporate welfare 217
cosmopolitan economics 16
cotton industry 59, 61, 105, 107, 108–12
creative accumulation 64
creative class 85, 86, 87, 88
creative destruction 33, 64
creative industries 104
Crompton, Samuel 109
crude oil 162
CSIC see Consejo Superior de Investigaciones Cientificas
cumulativeness of technology 63, 64, 65

dairy industry 63
Darby, Michael 93
DARPA (Defense Advanced Research Projects Agency) 206, 207, 214, 216, 217
Data General 84, 125
DEC see Digital Equipment Corporation

decentralisation 238

Defense Advanced Research Projects Agency *see* DARPA

defence industry 84, 91, 123, 202, 206–7, 213–14, 216–17

Defoe, Daniel, *A Plan for English Commerce* 21

degree apprenticeships 186

demand 28–9, 50, 61–3, 152, 153

demand windows of opportunity 142, 149, 150, 151

Deng Xiaoping 128, 129

Denmark 208, 212

Department for Business, Energy and Industrial Strategy 235, 238, 239

Department of Business, Innovation and Skills 223

Department of Defence (US) 123, 202, 213, 217

Department of Trade and Industry (DTI) 3, 218, 219, 221, 222, 234

Derby, England 110

design skills 37–8

Detroit 119, 120, 121, 124

developing countries
  capabilities of firms 135, 136, 139
  dynamic capability theory 31, 46, 48, 57–8
  extreme poverty 8
  global economy shift 9
  government role in creating wealth 239
  growth policies 10
  growth rates 5, 6, 46
  labour-productivity growth 161
  ladder of economic development 3, 30, 46, 48
  race to the top 57, 58
  sectoral dynamics 141
  shipbuilding industry 79–80
  windows of opportunity 131, 132, 133, 134
  wine industry 150

DHL 132

digital entertainment 82

Digital Equipment Corporation (DEC) 84, 125

Digital Library Initiative 227

digital technology 171, 232

diversification 56

dividends 70–71, 176

division of labour 13, 15

DRAMs (dynamic random-access memories) 146–9, 153

DTI *see* Department of Trade and Industry

Duke University 99

dyes 61, 112–13

dynamic capability theory of economic growth 35–58
  'catching-up' countries 154
  dynamic capabilities 67–8
  government role in creating wealth 237
  labour-productivity growth 156
  ladder of economic development 46–57
  new theory of economic growth 29–31
  new theory of international trade 43–6
  overview 1, 35
  race to the top 57–8
  sectoral and regional dimensions of economic growth 39–43
  sectoral systems of innovation 61, 67–9

dynamic catch-up strategy 147

East Asia 8, 10, 24–5, 54, 139, 144, 177

East India Company 108

economic centre of gravity 8–9

economic complexity 50, 51–3

economic development 3, 14; *see also* ladder of economic development

economic growth
  Africa and Asia 6–8
  city and regional systems 82, 87,
    88, 102
  'falling-behind' countries 155, 178
  'forging-ahead' countries 107, 112,
    125, 127
  government role in creating wealth
    225–7, 229, 231–7, 240–41
  history of economic thought 15,
    17–19
  innovation as engine of growth
    231–4
  ladder of economic development
    52–3
  market-efficiency theory 11–12
  national systems of innovation
    209, 211, 218
  need for new theory 1–2, 5–10
  neoclassical growth theory 26–9
  neoclassical schools of thought
    10–20
  new theory of 29–34
  production-capability theory
    11–12, 20
  sectoral and regional dimensions
    39–43
  sectoral systems of innovation 59,
    61, 67, 69
  technical education 199
  technology diffusion 139
  see also dynamic capability theory
    of economic growth; growth
    rates
economic policy see policy-making
economic reform 128–31
economies of scale and scope 22,
  113, 115, 141
economy, as self-organising system
  12
education
  competitive advantage 165, 172
  elementary education 165, 191
  funding 182–4, 188, 194–5

further education 103, 192, 195,
  197, 236
government role in creating wealth
  236
higher education 115, 193, 202,
  220
List on 17
progression pathways 197, 198
secondary education 165, 191–4
vocational education 180, 182, 192
see also national systems of
  education and training; technical
  education
Edward III 21
Eisenhower, Dwight 214
'Electricity Valley', China 177
Electronics Research and Service
  Organization (ERSO) 100, 101,
  145
electronics industry
  'catching-up' countries 135, 137,
    140–42, 144–7, 153
  city and regional systems 90–91,
    100
  'flying geese' model 55
  national system of innovation 202
  South Korea 147
  Taiwan 100–101, 144–6
  United States 90–91, 123, 144, 174
elementary education 165, 191
Elizabeth I 21
employment-based learning 196
employment growth 169
employment training 180, 185, 188,
  191–2
energy industry 176–7, 240
engineering 37, 172–3, 187
Engineering Research Centers 213
England
  automobile industry 120
  economic history 14, 21
  education and training 187–9, 195,
    197
  Industrial Revolution 32–3

reinvention of cities 103, 105–6
  see also United Kingdom
Enterprise and Growth Unit 219, 237
entrepreneurs
  city and regional systems 92, 102,
    104
  dynamic capability theory 33, 36
  history of economic thought 15, 19
  sectoral systems 66, 68
equilibrium 11, 18, 27
ERSO *see* Electronics Research and
  Service Organization
'An Essay on Innovations' (Bacon)
  14
Ethernet 146
Europe 123, 137, 226, 230
exchange 13
exchange rates 169
excludable goods 201, 203
exogenous growth theory 27, 28
experiential learning 49
export-processing zone 144
exports 51–3, 144, 150
extension services 208
externalised technology transfer 135,
  136
extractive institutions 32
extreme poverty 8
Ezell, Stephen J. 209, 226

factor-driven competitive
  development 47
factor-price equalisation 19
factory system 15, 69, 104, 110, 232
Fairchild Semiconductor 91
'falling-behind' countries 155–79
  definition 157
  faster rate of innovation 178–9
  labour-productivity growth in the
    UK 157–63
  labour-productivity growth in the
    US 167–70
  loss of UK competitive advantage
    163–7

loss of US competitive advantage
    171–7
  overview 155–7
FDI *see* foreign direct investment
Federal Express 132
film industry 94–7
Financial Crisis 157, 162, 170, 235
financialisation of economy 176
financial services sector 84, 104, 160,
    161, 162
Finegold, David 189
Finland 178, 212
firms
  dynamic capability theory 35–7,
    41
  governance and financing 163,
    164–5
  neoclassical growth theory 28
  representative firm 12, 41, 45
  value-added per capita 35, 36
  see also capabilities of firms
firm-specific knowledge 65–6
Florida, Richard 85, 87, 88
'flying geese' model 54–5
flying shuttle 109
flying winemakers 152
forces of agglomeration *see*
  agglomeration
Ford (company) 76, 120
Ford, Henry 36, 74, 75, 117, 118–19
foreign direct investment (FDI) 134,
    148, 174–5
'forging-ahead' countries 107–27
  American automobile industry
    117–22
  American computer industry
    122–7
  British cotton industry 108–12
  dynamic capability theory 43
  German chemical industry 112–16
  overview 107
Forjas, Ireland 212
Formula 1 104
fossil fuels 177, 227

France 14–15, 16, 117, 150, 151, 162, 202, 212
Freeman, Christopher 17, 20, 200
free market 167, 213
free riders 133, 203
free trade 15, 16, 19, 23
full employment 27
funding
   decentralisation 238
   education and training 182–4, 188, 194–5
   national system of innovation 201, 202, 209
   research 217, 219
further education 103, 192, 195, 197, 236
fusion energy 240

Gambardella, Alfonso 97, 98
garment industry 55, 57, 61, 82; see also textiles industry
gas industry see oil and gas sector
Gates, Bill 41, 88
GATT see General Agreement on Tariffs and Trade
GDP (gross domestic product) 5–7, 10, 51–3, 129, 173, 210
General Agreement on Tariffs and Trade (GATT) 131
General Motors (GM) 67, 74, 76, 119–20
General National Vocational Qualifications 192
generic technologies 200, 202–3, 204, 205, 214–17
genetic engineering 215, 240
geographic distribution of industries 50, 56
German Historical School 11, 17–18
Germanic/Scandinavian co-ordinated market economies 73
Germany
   automobile industry 117
   chemical industry 112–16
   competitive advantage 164, 171
   education and training 183–4, 190
   as 'forging ahead' country 107
   Industrie 4.0 232
   labour-productivity growth 160, 161, 162
   List's economic thought 16, 17–18
   national system of innovation 202, 207, 212
   sectoral innovation 61, 73, 74
global economy centre of gravity 8–9
globalisation 57, 62, 83, 173, 231
global shipbuilding industry 78–80
global value chains (GVCs) 131, 132–3, 135–6, 138, 139
GM see General Motors
golf ball production 39, 40
Google 173, 226, 227
government role
   capability of government 234–9
   city and regional systems 97–100, 102–4
   competing for the future 228–9
   competitive advantage 166–7, 174, 176, 229–30
   creating wealth 225–8
   education and training 31, 181, 182–5, 191–3, 197
   innovation as engine of growth 231–4
   innovation policy 204–9
   innovation policy in the UK 218–23
   innovation policy in the US 212–14, 216–18
   manpower planning 185–7
   national systems of innovation 200, 201, 203, 204, 211
   race to the top 58, 231
   technology diffusion 139–40
   windows of opportunity 240–41
   see also policy-making
grammar schools 191, 192

Grape and Wine Research and
  Development Corporation, 153
Great Britain *see* United Kingdom
Great Britain, SS (ship) 79
Great Convergence 5
Great Depression 105
Great Divergence 5, 133
Great Recession 178
'Green New Deal', South Korea 177
Griffith, D. W. 94, 95, 96
gross domestic product *see* GDP
gross value added (GVA) data 103,
  162
Grove, Andy 173
growth rates
  China 7, 129
  competitive advantage 164–5,
    176–7
  developing countries 5, 6, 46
  economic reform 129
  education and training 180
  government role in creating wealth
    230, 234, 240
  G7 countries 1, 6
  innovation 178, 179, 211
  labour-productivity growth 6, 10,
    155–7, 160
  ladder of economic development
    46
  need for new theory 1, 3, 5–10
  sectoral systems of innovation
    59, 67
  successful economic policies 25
  United Kingdom 10, 112, 160,
    164–5
  United States 119, 121, 125, 176–7
  see also economic growth
G7 countries
  'Atlantic Century' report 178
  dynamic capability theory 31, 42,
    43
  'falling-behind' countries 155, 156,
    161, 163, 178
  global economy shift 9

global value chains 133
government role in creating wealth
  229, 240, 241
growth rates 1, 6
labour-productivity growth 7, 156,
  161, 163
share of GDP 5, 10
Gulf states 25
GVA *see* gross value added data
GVCs *see* global value chains

Haiti 40
Hamilton, Alexander 11, 15–16, 23
hardware products 37, 137
Hargreaves, James 109
Harpers Ferry armoury 117
Harrod and Domar models 27
Haussman, Ricardo 49, 50, 51
health services 208, 240
HEIs (higher-education institutions)
  220
Henry VII 21–2
Hewlett-Packard Company (HP) 56,
  91, 125
Hidalgo, César 49, 50, 51, 56
higher education 115, 193, 202, 220
Higher Education Innovation Fund
  220
Highland Park, Detroit 119, 120, 121
high-tech sector
  capability/market-opportunity
    theory of high-tech clusters
    88–97, 98, 102
  city and regional systems 82–3,
    86, 103
  ladder of economic development
    48
  sectoral dynamics 141
  strategic management of place
    97–8, 102
High-Tech Strategy, Germany 207
high-voltage distribution (HVDC)
  equipment 62
Hodges, Luther H. 98

Hoechst 114
Hoffman, August 116
Hollywood 94, 95, 96
Holman, Sir John 185, 194
home demand 62
horizontal policies 2, 239
household-responsibility system 128
HP *see* Hewlett-Packard Company
Hsinchu Science Park, Taiwan
    98–102, 138
human nature 13
Hume, David 45
HVDC *see* high-voltage distribution
    equipment
Hynix 149
Hyundai 148

IBM 67, 122, 123–6, 146
IC *see* integrated circuit industry
ICT *see* information and
    communication technologies
immigration 78, 138; *see also*
    migration
Ince, Thomas 94–5, 96
inclusive institutions 32, 33
inclusive market economies 128, 129
incremental innovation 64, 65, 73
Independent Panel on Technical
    Education 3, 195
independent schools 185
India 52, 90, 108–9, 128–30, 137–8,
    142, 212, 241
individual economics 16
Indonesia 129
industrialisation 5, 32–3, 140
industrial policy 148, 213, 236
industrial relations 164
Industrial Revolution 15, 32, 69, 78,
    163, 232
industrial strategy 22, 224, 226, 236
Industrial Technology Research
    Institute (ITRI), Taiwan 100, 140,
    144–5, 146, 211
Industry 4.0 232

industry linkages 56–7
industry location 50, 56
Industry Transformation Maps
    (ITMs) 239
inequality 161
infant industry strategy 16, 23, 24, 58
information and communication
    technologies (ICT) 89, 133, 135,
    240
Information Processing Technique
    Office (IPTO) 215
Information Technology and
    Innovation Foundation (ITIF) 84,
    177, 178, 209
information technology (IT) 84, 90,
    101, 168, 208
infratechnologies 200, 203–4, 205
Innovate UK 201, 212
innovation
    activity-specific technology 63–6
    capability/market-opportunity
        theory of high-tech clusters
        88–97
    city and regional systems 81–106
    clusters 85–9
    competitive advantage 165–6
    competitive development 48
    definitions 38–9
    demand of a sector 61–3
    dynamic capability theory 30–32,
        36, 38, 46, 55
    as engine of growth 231–4
    entrepreneur and firm capabilities
        66–72
    'forging-ahead' countries 108, 115,
        116, 127
    government role in creating wealth
        225, 227–8, 231–4, 235, 240–41
    history of economic thought 14,
        17, 19
    institutions 72–3
    local economic development 84–8
    national policies and agencies
        209–12

national systems of innovation 200–224

need for new theory 2, 3, 4

production-capability theory 11, 19, 20

rate of 178–9

reinvention of cities 102–6

sectoral systems 59–80

shipbuilding industry 78–80

strategic management of place 97–102

successful economic policies 23, 25

Toyota Motor Company 73–8

UK policy 218–24

US policy 212–18

Innovation Report 235

Innovation Vouchers 208

Institute of Government 236

Institutes of Technology 103, 197

institutional windows of opportunity 142, 149

institutions 72–3, 74

insurance sector 162

integrated circuit (IC) industry 89, 101, 102, 124

Intel 126, 173

intellectual property rights 65, 171, 200, 203

intelligent demand 207–8

intelligent transportation systems (ITS) 207

interchangeability of parts 117–18, 119, 171, 227, 232

internalised technology transfer 135, 136

international trade 19, 43–6, 131, 230

Internet 83, 89, 133, 168, 204, 206, 208, 215, 228

Interstate Highway System 83

investment 48, 71–2, 90, 134, 147–9, 174, 203

invisible hand 12

iPhone 36, 38, 216

IPTO see Information Processing Technique Office

Ireland 90, 160, 212

iron industry 78–9, 108

I6 (Industrialising Six) 5, 163

Israel 89, 90

IT see information technology

Italy 14, 150–51, 160–61, 163, 178, 202

ITIF see Information Technology and Innovation Foundation

ITMs see Industry Transformation Maps

ITRI see Industrial Technology Research Institute

ITS see intelligent transportation systems

Japan
apprenticeships 184

automobile industry 37, 59, 73–8, 121–2, 233

competitive advantage 164, 171, 174

computer industry 123

'flying geese' model 55

government role in creating wealth 226

labour-productivity growth 161, 162

ladder of economic development 46, 47, 55

movement of people 137

national system of innovation 202, 204, 208, 213

sectoral innovation 59, 72, 75, 78, 79

South Korea DRAM industry 147, 148, 149

successful economic policies 25

Taiwan electronics industry 144, 145

technology diffusion 139

wage differences 133

Javid, Sajid 223
Jefferson, Thomas 117
Jobs, Steve 28, 36, 56
John Deere 38
just-in-time system 77, 111

Kanban system 77
Kay, John 109
keiretsu 148
Kennedy, John F. 173
Keynes, John Maynard 20
Khosla, Vinod 173
KIBS *see* knowledge-intensive
  business services
knowhow 38, 49–51, 56, 135
knowledge
  activity-specific technology 63–6
  'catching-up' countries 135, 151–2
  dynamic capability theory 39,
    49–51, 54, 56
  history of economic thought 18
  limit to progress 13
  manpower planning 186
knowledge economy 234
knowledge-intensive business
  services (KIBS) 102, 104, 105
knowledge spillovers 86–7
knowledge transfer 63–4, 219–20
Kohsetsushi centres, Japan 208
Korean Industrial Research Initiative
  228
Korean Productivity Center 228
Krugman, Paul 11, 12, 45

labour
  division of 13, 15
  laws 74, 75
  markets 86, 90
Labour government 194, 218–19,
  220–22, 223, 234, 235
labour productivity
  definition 156
  G7 countries 7
  growth rates 6, 10

labour-productivity growth 155–
  63, 167–70
  United Kingdom 157–63, 167
  United States 83, 167–70
ladder of economic development 3,
  30, 46–57, 67
laissez-faire policies 18, 21, 214,
  225, 227
Lall, Sanjaya 48
Lancashire 105, 110, 111
laptop PCs 145–6
latecomer firms 141–3
latent demand 28–9, 61, 75, 88,
  108–9, 112, 117
Lazonick, William 70, 110
lean manufacturing 75, 77, 121, 208
leapfrogging 143
learning 49, 139, 196
Lee, Keun 20
liberal market economies 73
Licence Raj 129
Liebig, Justus von 115
lifetime employment system 78
Lincoln, Abraham 13–14
List, Friedrich 11, 15–17, 23, 24, 25
Liverpool cotton exchange 111
living standards *see* standard of living
loans, student 183, 194
local economic development 84–8
Local Education Authorities 191
local enterprise partnerships 236
Lombe, John 110
Lombe, Thomas 110
Los Angeles 94, 96, 97
low-skilled equilibrium 189
Luxembourg 210

Macau 210
machine tools 55, 64, 65, 118
macroeconomics 33, 218
Made in China 2025 plan 210, 232,
  239
Made Smarter Review 232
Maier, Jürgen 232

mainframe computers 122, 123, 124, 125, 126
Malaysia 7, 55, 212
Malerba, Franco 20
Malthus, Thomas 13
Manchester 104–5, 109, 110, 111, 112
Manchuria 139
Mandelson, Peter 234
manpower planning 173, 185–7, 192
manufacturing
  city and regional systems 82, 102
  decline in 2
  history of economic thought 17
  innovation as engine of growth 232
  labour-productivity growth 159–61, 163, 169
  mercantilism 15
  national system of innovation 208, 210–11
  sectoral dimensions of growth 39, 42, 43
  Taiwan 144, 146
  technical education 189
  United Kingdom 21–2, 108, 161, 163, 189
  United States 82, 169, 171
  world trade patterns 130
Manufacturing Advisory Service 223
Manufacturing Extension Partnership (MEP) 208, 213, 223, 232
market economy 12, 30, 32, 73, 128–30
market-efficiency school of thought 11–14, 19, 21, 25, 29, 176
Marshall, Alfred 11, 85, 87
Massachusetts Institute of Technology 84
mass-production 74–6, 117–21, 165, 171, 232
Mass, William 110
mathematical models 20, 31
maths literacy 172
Max Planck Gesellschaft 202

May, Theresa 223
Mazzucato, Mariana 216
memory market 146, 148–9
MEP see Manufacturing Extension Partnership
mercantilism 15, 22
Mexico 133
microcomputers 122, 125, 126
microeconomic theory 201
Microelectronic Technology 148
microprocessors 125, 146
Microsoft 88, 92, 93, 126
migration 23, 83, 136–9
military research 91, 214, 216
Mill, John Stuart 18
minicomputers 122, 125, 126
MNCs see multinational corporations
mobile PCs 145–6
mobile phones 36, 38, 89, 142–3, 216
Model T Ford 118, 119
modern industrial enterprise 113
monetarist policies 167
monopolies 33, 96
Morris, William 120, 121
Motion Picture Patents Company (the Trust) 95–6
motor industry see automobile industry
Motorola 146
motorsport 104
movement of people 136–9
movie industry 94–7
moving assembly line 119
mules (cotton industry) 109
multinational corporations (MNCs) 139, 140, 147

nanotechnology 82, 103, 207, 240
Naples 14
National Aeronautics and Space Administration (NASA) 214
National Agency for Technology and Innovation, Tekes, Finland 212
National Chiao Tung University 100

National Economic Council (NEC) 235, 237–8
national economics 16
National Endowment for Science, Technology and the Arts (NESTA) 235
National Institute of Economic and Social Research 189
National Institutes of Health (NIH) 201, 215–16, 217, 227
nationalisation 166–7, 237
National Science Council (NSC) 100
National Science Foundation 173, 201, 213, 214, 215, 227
national system of economic learning (NSEL) 139
The National System of Political Economy (List) 17
national systems of education and training 180–99
  academic and technical pathways 182
  careers advice 185
  effective national system 180–81
  England and Wales performance 187–9
  funding system 182–4
  history of low-quality policy-making 189–95
  loss of UK competitive advantage 163, 165
  manpower planning 185–7
  national system of qualifications 181–2
  technical education pathway 195–9
national systems of innovation (NSI) 200–224
  definition 200
  innovation policy 204–9
  innovation policy in the UK 218–24
  innovation policy in the US 212–18

loss of UK competitive advantage 163, 165
loss of US competitive advantage 172
national policies and agencies 209–12
nature of science and technology 201–4
overview 3, 200
technology diffusion 139
National Vocational Qualifications 192, 193
Navigation Acts 22
near-field communications (NFC) 207
NEC *see* National Economic Council
NEETs (not in education, employment or training) 194
Nelson, Richard 20, 26
neoclassical economics
  dynamic capability theory 42, 45–6, 50, 58
  government role in creating wealth 225, 229, 238
  labour-productivity growth 156
  loss of UK competitive advantage 163, 167
  national system of innovation 209, 211
  need for new theory 1–2, 4–10
  rate of innovation 179
  schools of thought 10–20
  sectoral systems of innovation 66, 67, 68–9
  world trade patterns 130
neoclassical growth theory
  dynamic capability theory 36, 39, 41
  failure of 25, 67, 69, 178
  government role in creating wealth 232, 237
  history of 11, 26–9
  need for new theory 5, 10
  sectoral systems of innovation 61, 66, 67, 69

NESTA (National Endowment for Science, Technology and the Arts) 235
Netherlands 24, 160, 201, 212
neuroscience 240
Newcomen, Thomas 78
New World wine producers 150, 151, 152, 153
New York 82, 94, 95, 96
New York Motion Picture Company 94
New Zealand 25, 63, 212
NFC see near-field communications
NIH see National Institutes of Health
Nokia 142–3
nomination committees 71–2
non-tradeable (non-traded) sector 82, 83, 167–8, 169, 229
North Carolina 89, 98
North, Douglass 27
North Sea oil 162
Norway 212
Norwood Committee 192
NSC see National Science Council
NSEL see national system of economic learning
NSI see national systems of innovation
nuclear energy 176, 177, 214, 227, 240

OBM see own brand manufacturing
ODM see own design and manufacturing
OECD see Organization for Economic Co-operation and Development
OEM see Original Equipment Manufacturing
offshoring 133, 135, 174–5
Ofqual 197
Ohno, Taiichi 75, 76, 77, 78
oil and gas sector 104, 157, 161, 162, 177

Okita, Saburo 54
Old World wine producers 150, 153
Omnibus Trade and Competitiveness Act (1988) 213
online shopping 240
ordinary capabilities 67–8
organic chemical industry 112–13, 114, 115
organisational capabilities 68, 69, 108, 109, 112, 127
Organization for Economic Co-operation and Development (OECD) 38, 188, 202
Original Equipment Manufacturing (OEM) 135, 136, 148
own brand manufacturing (OBM) 136
own design and manufacturing (ODM) 135

patents 63, 72, 87, 96, 115, 204, 205, 210, 213
path-creating catching up 143, 150
path-following catching up 143, 144
PCs see personal computers
Pentagon 214
Perez, Carlota 141, 142
perfect competition 18, 30, 36
Perkin, William 112, 116
personal computers (PCs) 28–9, 55–6, 61, 84, 89, 101–2, 125–6, 145–6, 215
pharmaceutical industry 48, 99, 114, 216
photovoltaic production 177
Physiocrats 11, 14, 15, 16
piece rates 121
A Plan for English Commerce (Defoe) 21
planned economies 19, 32
Poland 128, 130
policy-making
    education and training 189–95

government role in creating wealth 225, 236–8, 239
innovation policy 204–9
innovation policy in the UK 218–23
innovation policy in the US 212–18
international trade 46
national innovation policies and agencies 209–12
strategic management of place 97
successful policies 20–25
polytechnics 190, 194
populism 9, 241
Porter, Michael 46, 62, 85
Portugal 212
poverty 8, 9, 129, 241
Power PC microprocessor 146
Prais, Sig 189
price competition 18–19, 57
Prime Computer 125
Principles of Economics (Marshall) 85
privatisation 128, 194, 237
procurement policies 200, 205, 208
production
  efficiency 35, 156
  free trade 15
  methods 232
  neoclassical growth theory 27–8
  tools 37–8
production-capability theory 11–15, 19–21, 24–5, 31–2, 218, 224–5
productivity
  competitive advantage of nations 229
  education and training 189
  labour-productivity growth 155–63, 167–70
  Toyota 77
  United Kingdom 157–63, 165, 189
  United States 83, 118, 121, 167–71
productivity puzzle 10, 156, 167, 170

product space 56
product standards 62–3
progress, limits to 13
property rights 33, 65, 72, 171, 200, 203
proprietary research 200, 203
protectionism 16, 58
public goods 201, 225
public research organisations 202
public-sector agencies 139, 140
public-sector laboratories 145
pure public goods 201

Qatar 210
Quaero 226
Quah, Danny 8, 9
qualifications 103, 180, 181–2, 184, 186–8, 192–7
quality circles 37, 76
Quesnay, François 15

R&D (research and development)
  'catching-up' countries 145, 148, 151–3
  competitive advantage 38, 165–6, 173–5
  golf ball production 40
  innovation policy 200, 206, 208, 215, 217, 219, 221–2
  nature of science and technology 201–3
  R&D consortia 139, 140, 145, 146, 148
  R&D intensity 173–5
race to the bottom 57, 58, 231
race to the top 1, 45, 57–8, 199, 231
'The Race to the Top' report 3, 222
radical innovation 64–5, 73
Radio Shack 125
Rao, Narasimha 129
Raymond, Daniel 16
Reagan, Ronald 213
recession 170, 178
regional clusters 87, 171

regional policies 85–6, 105–6, 236, 238
Register of Regulated Qualifications 197
regulation 62, 72
Reinert, Erik 13, 14, 39–40, 41, 45, 231
Renault, Louis 120
representative firm 12, 41, 45
research *see* R&D
Research Councils 201
Research Triangle Park, North Carolina 98–9, 102
research universities 115, 116, 173
retail 240
Ricardo, David 11, 13, 18, 25, 45
Ripley, William Henry 189–90
rival goods 201
Robbins, Lionel 26
Robbins Committee 194
robotics 79, 171, 174, 240
Romer, Christine 42
Romer, Paul 27
Rover 121
Russia 19, 33

Samsung 148, 149
Samuelson, Paul 11, 19, 230
San Diego 86, 89, 93, 97
San Francisco Bay Area 91, 92, 93, 97
Santa Fe, New Mexico 81
Say, J. B. 16–17
SBIR *see* Small Business Innovation Research Program
SBRI *see* Small Business Research Initiative
Scandinavia 89, 151
Schmoller, Gustav van 18
school system 165, 172, 180, 185, 191
Schumpeter, Joseph 11, 14, 18–19, 25, 32–3, 68
Schumpeter Mark I and II patterns 63

science
    chemical industry 115, 116
    competitive advantage 165, 172–3
    education and training 187, 190
    history of economic thought 17, 34
    innovation policy 218, 219
    national system of innovation 3, 200–205
    nature of science and technology 201–5
    production-capability theory 20
    scientific publications 204, 205
    scientific research 200–202, 219
    wine industry 151–2
Science Enterprise Funds 220
science parks 98, 100–103, 138
Scott, Allen 94
sea freight 132
search engines 226, 227
Seattle 87–8, 89, 92, 93
secondary education 165, 191–4
sectoral systems of innovation 59–80
    activity-specific technology 63–6
    definition of sectors 59
    demand of a sector 61–3
    entrepreneur and firm capabilities 66–72
    government role in creating wealth 239
    institutions 72–3
    overview 59–61
    sectoral dimensions of economic growth 39
    sectoral dynamics 140–43
    shipbuilding industry 78–80
    Toyota Motor Company 73–8
seed capital 217
semiconductor industry
    capabilities of firms 137, 139
    city and regional systems 90, 101
    government role in creating wealth 226
    ladder of economic development 48, 55

national system of innovation 202,
207
sectoral dynamics 141
South Korea DRAM industry
146–9
Taiwan 100–101, 144, 146
United States 119, 125, 171
Semiconductor Trade Agreement
(STA) 149
Seoul 177
Serra, Antonio, *Breve trattato* ('Brief
treatise') 14
services sector 2, 42, 43
share buy-backs 70–71, 176
Sharp 148
Sheffield Advanced Manufacturing
Park 220
Sheffield Advanced Manufacturing
Research Centre 103
shipbuilding industry 78–80
shipping 131–2
Shockley, William 91, 92
shoe production 40–41
Silicon Valley 56, 84, 88–92, 96,
100–102, 137–8, 148, 177
Simon, Herbert 28
Singapore 7, 135, 139, 140, 178,
209–11, 239
Singh, Manmohan 129
Siri 216
Sloan, Alfred 74, 119–20
Small Business Administration 213
Small Business Innovation
Development Act (1982) 213
Small Business Innovation Research
Program (SBIR) 213, 223
Small Business Research Initiative
(SBRI) 223
SMEs (small and medium-sized
enterprises) 145, 208, 223, 232
Smith, Adam
history of economic thought
11–16, 24, 25, 69
Theory of Moral Sentiments 12

The Wealth of Nations 13, 15, 16
social learning 49
Soete, Luc 141, 142
software 64, 65, 137
solar energy 177, 240
Solow, Robert 2, 10, 26–7
Soskice, David 189
South Africa 150, 152
South Carolina 98
South Korea
'Atlantic Century' report 178
'catching-up' countries 129, 135,
139, 141, 145, 153
competitive advantage 171, 177,
229
DRAM industry 146–9
dynamic capability theory 55, 58
government role in creating wealth
225, 228, 229, 241
'Green New Deal' 177
growth rates 7
innovation policy 208
rate of innovation 178
successful economic policies 25
space travel 173
Spain 151, 160, 202, 212
specialised services 86, 87
Spens Report (1938) 191
spinning 105, 109, 110
spin-off companies 220, 222
Springfield Armory 117
Sputnik 173, 214
STA *see* Semiconductor Trade
Agreement
stage-skipping catching up 143, 149
standard of living
corporate governance 72
dynamic capability theory 35, 45,
55, 57, 58
government role in creating wealth
229, 231, 241
ladder of economic development 3
rate of innovation 179
Stanford Research Institute 216

Stanford University 91
stars, academic 93
start-ups 86, 93, 138, 206
state role *see* government role
state schools 191
steam power 55, 78–9, 113
steel industry 79, 166
STEM courses (science, technology,
   education and mathematics) 197
St Louis, Missouri 41
strategic management of place
   97–102
strategic technology programmes 202
Strategy for American Innovation
   228
student loans 183, 194
suborning 23
Sun Microsystems 173
supplier associations 77
supply-side economic policy 237
Sweden 62, 71–2, 160, 178, 201, 212
Switzerland 24, 201, 212
Syracuse, New York 81

Taipei 101, 102
Taiwan
   'catching-up' countries 129, 135,
      137–41, 153
   city and regional systems 89, 98
   competitive advantage 171, 229
   dynamic capability theory 55, 58
   electronics industry 100–101,
      144–6
   government role in creating wealth
      25, 228, 229, 241
   Hsinchu Science Park 98–102, 138
   Industrial Technology Research
      Institute (ITRI) 100, 140, 144–5,
      146, 211
   national system of innovation 211
tariffs 23–4, 58, 131, 132, 134
Tassey, Gregory 217, 230
taxation 184, 200, 205, 208
technical colleges 193–4

technical education
   competitive advantage 165
   government role in creating wealth
      236
   Independent Panel on Technical
      Education 3
   manpower planning 186, 187
   national system of education and
      training 180, 184, 188–91,
      192–5
   reinvention of cities 103
   technical education pathway 182,
      184, 193, 195–9
technical schools 191, 192
technological capabilities 68–9, 108–
   9, 112, 123, 127, 139–40, 145
technological change 26–7, 39, 142,
   230
technological cumulativeness 63,
   64, 65
technological knowledge 39, 135,
   138, 139, 165
technological windows of
   opportunity 142, 149
technology
   activity-specific technology 29,
      63–6
   competitive advantage 23, 37, 171,
      173
   diffusion by governments 139
   dynamic capability theory 37, 40,
      54
   high-tech clusters 89
   innovation as engine of growth
      231, 232
   national system of innovation 3,
      200–204
   nature of science and technology
      201–4
   sectoral dynamics 142
   Smith avoidance of 15
   transfer 135–6
Technology Strategy Board 212,
   220–22, 223

Teece, David 65, 67, 69
telecommunications 89, 111, 113, 208
Terman, Frederick 91, 92
textiles industry 21–2, 55, 61, 83,
  105, 108–12, 163, 171
Thailand 55, 129
Thatcher, Margaret 167, 194, 218
*The Theory of Economic
  Development* (Schumpeter) 68
Theory of Moral Sentiments (Smith)
  12
thick labour markets 86, 87
TNCs *see* transnational corporations
total factor productivity 27
Toyota Motor Company 67, 73–8,
  233
Toyota Production System 75, 233
trade
  balance of trade 162, 169–70, 213
  barriers 133
  competitive advantage 43–6, 130,
    230
  free trade 15, 16, 19, 23
  international trade 19, 43–6,
    130–31, 230
  liberalisation 131
  mercantilism 15, 22
tradeable (traded) sector 82–3, 167–
  8, 169, 229
training 31, 165, 180–85, 188, 191–2,
  194; *see also* national systems of
  education and training
transistors 91, 240
transnational corporations (TNCs)
  135
transnational technical communities
  138
transportation 113, 114, 131–2, 138,
  240
Treasury 237
the Trust (Motion Picture Patents
  Company) 95–6

UK *see* United Kingdom

unemployment 188, 229–30
unions 163, 164, 166, 167, 184
United Kingdom Research and
  Innovation (UKRI) 201
United Kingdom (UK)
  automobile industry 104, 120–21,
    166
  cotton industry 59, 108–12
  economic history 20–23
  education and training 183, 184,
    187–8, 189–99
  as 'falling-behind' country 155
  as 'forging ahead' country 107
  and German chemical industry
    112–13, 114, 115, 116
  government role in creating wealth
    232, 234, 236–8
  growth rate 10, 112, 160, 164–5
  innovation policy 218–24
  labour-productivity growth
    157–63
  loss of competitive advantage
    163–7
  Made Smarter Review 232
  manpower planning 186
  movement of people 136–7
  national system of innovation 201,
    210, 212, 218–24
  rate of innovation 178, 179
  reinvention of cities 103–6
  sectoral systems of innovation 59,
    61, 71–4, 78–9
  shipbuilding industry 78–9
  successful economic policies 21
  wine industry 151
  woollen industry 21–2
United States (US)
  America Makes strategy 232
  automobile industry 83, 107,
    117–22
  biotechnology 84, 86, 92–4, 96,
    99, 171, 215–16, 227
  city and regional systems 81–4,
    89–96, 98, 101

computer industry 84, 90–92,
 122–7, 214–15
education and training 184
electronics industry 90–91, 123,
 144, 174
as 'falling-behind' country 155
as 'forging ahead' country 107
government role in creating wealth
 226–30, 232
growth rate 119, 121, 125, 176–7
high-tech clusters 89–90, 101
history of economic thought
 15–16, 23–4
infant industry strategy 23
innovation policy 212–18
labour-productivity growth 157,
 161, 162, 167–70
loss of competitive advantage 164,
 166, 171–7
movement of people 137, 138
movie industry 94–7
national system of innovation 201,
 202, 207, 208, 210, 212–18
rate of innovation 178, 179
Research Triangle Park 98–9,
 102
sectoral and regional growth
 40–41, 43
sectoral systems of innovation
 60–61, 72, 78
South Korea DRAM industry 147,
 149
successful economic policies
 20–21
wage differences 133
wine industry 150–52
universities
 chemical industry 115, 116
 competitive advantage 165, 172–3
 computer industry 123
 fees 194
 high-tech clusters 91, 93, 98–9,
  104
 manpower planning 186

market-efficiency theory 19
movement of people 137
national system of education and
 training 180, 183, 187–8, 191,
 193, 194, 196
national system of innovation
 200–202, 219–21
reinvention of cities 103, 104
research universities 115, 116,
 173
University Challenge Fund 220
University of North Carolina at
 Chapel Hill 99
UPS 132
Uruguay 212
US see United States
USAID (US Agency for International
 Development) 228

value-added per capita
 competitive advantage 36, 167,
  229–30
 cotton industry 59, 112
 dynamic capability theory 35–6,
  42, 43, 44–5
 government role in creating wealth
  229–31
 international trade 44–5
 labour-productivity growth 169,
  170
 ladder of economic development
  48, 49, 53
 rate of innovation 179
 reinvention of cities 103, 104
 sectoral systems of innovation
  59, 61
Varian Associates 91
Varieties of Capitalism approach 73
Venice 14
venture capital 86, 90, 91, 93, 101,
 217
vertical integration 137
Vietnam 55, 82
virtual assistants 216

vocational education 180, 182, 192

wages
  apprenticeships 184
  dynamic capability theory 40, 43,
    48, 49, 53, 57
  global value chains 133, 135
  wage bargaining 184
Wales 187–9; *see also* United
  Kingdom
Walpole, Robert 22
Wang 84, 125
Washington, George 15
water power 109, 110
Watt, James 33, 78
Waxman–Markey cap and trade bill
  177
wealth creation 225–41
  capability of government 234–9
  competing for the future 228–9
  competitive advantage of nations
    229–30
  competitive development 48
  government role 225–8
  innovation as engine of growth
    231–4
  market-efficiency theory 11, 14
  mercantilism 15
  production-capability theory 11
  race to the top 231
  windows of opportunity 240–41
The Wealth of Nations (Smith) 13,
  15, 16
weapons production 117–18, 214
weaving 109

Weber, Max 18
Wedgwood, Josiah 33
white goods 37
windows of opportunity
  'catching-up' countries 130–35,
    141–4, 147, 149–51, 153
  definition 141
  dynamic capability theory 36, 39,
    41–3, 53
  'forging-ahead' countries 109, 115
  government role in creating wealth
    240–41
  need for new theory 1, 2
  neoclassical growth theory 29
  production-capability theory 12
  sectoral dynamics 67, 141–3
wind power 240
wine industry 141, 150–53
woollen industry 21–2, 108, 112
World Bank 210
world economy 8–9, 131
world trade *see* international trade
worldwide shipbuilding industry
  78–80
worldwide wine industry 141,
  150–53
Wozniak, Steve 56

Xerox 56

Yahoo! 173
Yang, Jerry 173
youth training schemes 192

Zucker, Lynne G. 93